People Making History
BOOK 1

P. Garlake and A. Proctor

Zimbabwe Publishing House

Zimbabwe Publishing House (Pvt) Ltd,
P.O. Box 350
Harare, Zimbabwe

©Garlake Property (Pvt) Ltd 1985

First Published by ZPH 1985
Reprinted 1994

Cover design by David Corbett

ISBN 0 949225 10 X

All rights reserved. No part of this publication may be
reproduced, stored in a retrieval system or transmitted in
any form or by any means, electronic, mechanical, photocopying
recording or otherwise, without the prior permission
of the publishers

Typeset by Colorset
Printed by Penrose Book Printers, Pretoria West

Acknowledgements

The publishers and the authors would like to thank the following for the use of illustrations reproduced in this book. The publishers have made every effort to trace copyright holders, but if they have inadvertently overlooked any they will be pleased to make the necessary arrangements at the first opportunity.

BCC Hulton Picture Library, 5, 12, 13, 19, 54, 60(top), 67, 79, 103, 105, 155, 172, 173, 174, 181; British Museum(Natural History), 17, 23(left), 27, 32; Joel Chikware, 3(right), 4, 14, 18, 61; Tessa Colvin, 87; Collen Crawford-Cousins, 16, 20, 21, 23(right), 24, 25, 26, 28, 30, 31, 34, 37, 53(bottom), 55(right), 64, 68, 93, 95, 96, 98, 99, 102, 179, 180, 182, 183, 184, 185; Peter Garlake, 92, 97, 126, 127; David Lan(from *Guns and Rain*, ZPH, 1985), Mutapa tradition and discussion, 113-14; Barbara Mendelsohn and Marjorie Wallace, 22, 40(left), 53(top), 65, 88, 94, 106, 110(bottom), 115(top), 128, 131, 143, 147, 153, 157, 165, 170, 175; Ministry of Information, 83, 136, 142; National Archives of Zimbabwe, front cover, 6, 9, 10(bottom), 39, 40(right), 48, 49, 59, 60(bottom), 64, 71, 75(right), 108, 110(top), 111, 115, 122, 123, 125, 138, 145, 148, 150, 151,152, 160, 161, 162, 163, 166, 167; D W Phillipson,116(top); Queen Victoria Museum, 113, 132, 159; Mike White and Peter Garlake(from *Early Life in Zimbabwe and Life at Great Zimbabwe*, Mambo Press, 1982), 38, 42, 43, 45–47, 50, 55(left), 82, 84, 85, 86, 89, 116(bottom), 118, 134, 135, 137, 141; Zimbabwe Newspapers, 7, 10(top).

The publishers gratefully acknowledge the Canadian International Development Agency (CIDA) and the Canadian Organisation for Development through Education (CODE) for their assistance in providing paper for this book.

The authors

The authors are both Zimbabweans. Peter Garlake is a prehistorian. He has undertaken research in Somalia, Kenya, Tanzania, Mozambique, Zimbabwe and Nigeria. He has taught at universities in Nigeria, Britain and Zimbabwe. He is the author of several books and papers on the prehistory and early history of Africa. Andre Proctor is a history teacher with experience in Zimbabwe, Tanzania and Botswana.

Contents

To the teacher
1. What is history? — 1
2. Explaining history — 8
3. Evolution — 16
4. The earliest people — 22
5. The development of human society — 30
6. The Late Stone Age — 36
7. Hunter-gatherers — 39
8. Rock paintings — 45
9. The change to farming — 48
10. The first farmers — 52
11. Developments in farming — 58
12. Lineages — 66
13. Ruling classes — 72
14. The state — 78
15. Great Zimbabwe — 81
16. East African city-states — 91
17. Feudalism — 102
18. The Portuguese in Africa — 105
19. Mutapa origins and society — 112
20. Mutapa politics — 120
21. South-western Zimbabwe — 130
22. Torwa or Kame — 136
23. The Rozvi state — 140
24. Nguni societies in the 19th century — 146
25. The Ndebele state — 156
26. Gaza — 164
27. Ancient Egypt — 169
28. Kush — 178
29. Stages of history — 181
Multiple choice questions — 185

To the teacher

This book is the first in a two-book series covering the ZJC syllabus. Book 1 deals with the pre-colonial history of Africa, focusing particularly on Zimbabwe. There are 'theoretical' chapters (in which concepts are explained) and 'content' chapters (in which concepts are applied). Different historical methods and approaches are described and compared in chapters 1 and 2. This book is written from a socialist perspective, the key concepts of which are explained in chapter 2, and elaborated on in chapters 13, 14 and 29. It is up to you, the teacher, to decide whether to teach chapters 1 and 2 at the beginning of the year, or later when your pupils have begun to use historical materialist concepts in the 'content' chapters. Either way, your pupils will benefit from constant cross reference between the 'theoretical' chapters and 'content' chapters.

The summaries at the beginning of each chapter indicate the main points to be covered and the connections between chapters, for example between chapters 3, 4 and 5. The vocabulary lists will assist you in preparing your class. Where time permits or with the co-operation of the English teacher, pupils could be given language exercises to practise the use of essential vocabulary. The text 'boxes' give background information, examples, and issues that historians are not yet agreed on. Words in bold type in the text indicate the themes of particular paragraphs.

Learning through activity and discussion is emphasised throughout the course. Discussion topics appear within the text to consolidate pupils' understanding, to recall information from earlier in the book, to relate the material to the pupils' own experiences, or to allow for consideration of related issues. Many of the discussion topics can also be used for revision later.

The time frieze (explained in chapter 4) will be invaluable for your pupils' understanding of chronology and time. In addition, different groups in the class could be assigned theme projects — for example, a display of drawings to show shelters in different societies through the book. If possible, encourage your pupils to do their own additional research, and to try doing some of the things discussed in the book, such as making pots, smelting metal, or planting the seeds of wild grasses. These could be group or holiday projects.

Initially, most pupils will need guidance in answering essay and source-based questions. The assisted answer questions in chapters 3 to 10 show different models for guiding the selection and organization of information. Until pupils are confident about planning and writing essays, you could continue to prepare and guide them by breaking down th questions and discussing the topics in class. You may want to use the photographs, drawings, maps and tables in the book to set additional source-based questions. Sample multiple choice questions are provided at the end of the book. Together with your own multiple choice questions, these will be useful for tests and revision.

1. What is history?

In this chapter:
We will ask: How did farming first develop?
We will learn how historians study history.
We will look at how historians find out about the past.

You will need to know the meanings of these words:
society — people living together with others.
development — gradual growth into something more complex.
invent — create something new.
develop — grow, or make growth more complete, or make progress.
culture — a society's beliefs and customs.
opinion — what one believes, usually without proof.
fact — something that has really happened or is certainly true.
event — something that happens in a short space of time.
prove — show that something is true.
disprove — show that something is not true.
interpret — show the meaning or importance of something.
select — choose.
account — report or description.
affect — influence.
evidence — information, facts, proof of something.
pattern — design, or regular and repeated shape or order.
biased — prejudiced, tending to see things a certain way.
critical — careful to look for faults, not believing things without proof.
judge — decide what is true or best after looking at all the evidence.
witness — see something oneself.
purpose — reason for something.
right — what someone can justly expect or claim.
loyalty — faithfulness.
dispute — argument or quarrel.
reliable — able to be depended on or believed.

Why is history important?

History is a study of human *society*. It looks at how societies changed over many centuries of time. History is about *developments* that took place in the past. History studies how people in the past organized their lives, their work and their societies. It is about the tools that they *invented* and improved to help *develop* their society. It is also about how people's *cultures* and beliefs changed their societies.

To improve the way we live, we must understand how our lives came to be as they are. If we want to help to build a better future, we must understand the things that shape the world we live in. A careful study of history will help us to do this.

Studying history

The people who study and write about history are called historians. Studying history is a lot more complicated than just finding out and writing down what happened in the past. If it was as easy as that, all historians and all history books would agree and tell the same story. But they do not.

In fact, historians have many different *opinions* about the past. They usually agree about *facts*, for example, about whether a certain *event* did or did not happen. Usually, facts like that can be easily *proved* or *disproved*. Most disagreements are over
- what facts and events were important,
- how these facts should be *interpreted*.

Activity. *Selecting* facts. Each pupil in your class and the teacher write down what happened in your last lesson. It is impossible to write down everything you all said and did during that period. So only write down what you think were the most important things you saw and heard. The teacher will ask some of you to read your *accounts* to the class. You will probably find that the accounts are very different. Then the teacher will read her or his account. This will certainly be very different from yours.

Historians select information

Historians studying the past have the same sort of problems as your class did in the activity above. Historians also have to select the facts that they think are important. They leave out a lot of facts that they think are less important.

Historians select information which helps them answer the questions about the past that they believe are important. Different historians ask different questions about the past. Our knowledge of history grows and improves as more historians ask new questions about the past and find new information to answer these questions.

Historians interpret the past

The following example shows the differences that historians can have when they interpret the past. All historians try to be truthful. But their ideas about society *affect* what information they select and how they interpret this information. All historians have ideas about society and why events happen at particular times in particular societies. Problems of selection and interpretation mean that there can never be a history that contains all facts and all interpretations and is accepted by everyone.

Example. Interpreting events. Imagine that this event is reported in a newspaper: 'Workers broke the machines that they were using in a factory and afterwards ran away.' These are the facts. No one disagrees about them. If people study the event, they may disagree about what the event meant. One person may say that the workers were destructive and ungrateful, and that the government needed strong laws and more police to make workers behave properly. Another may say that the workers were badly trained. A third may say that the workers had been badly treated and were struggling bravely against employers who had paid them low wages.

All historians try to make sure that they have examined all the information as carefully as possible. They must all be prepared to change their interpretations if they find new *evidence* that does not agree with their ideas. When historians are studying evidence, we say that they are doing **research**.

Sources

What do historians use in their research? They can use
- documents,
- interviews,
- oral histories,
- archaeology.

What are documents?

Most documents are written records.

We can learn about pre-colonial times from the diaries, letters and reports of missionaries, travellers, traders and administrators. They can tell us a lot about the people among whom the writers lived, even though those people did not write.

Documents for colonial times include: letters, photographs, films, diaries, note books, pamphlets, posters, newspapers, records of court cases, and descriptions of events written by people who were there.

Discussion. You have documents about your own history, for example your birth certificate and your school reports. What could someone learn about you if they read
- your birth certificate?
- your school report?

What other documents do you have at home? What do they tell you about your family history? What do they tell you about the history of your community?

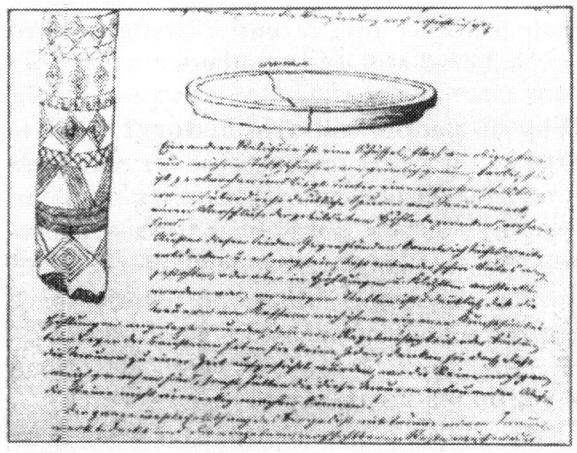

Historians use documents, like this page from the diary of a German called Karl Mauch, who visited Zimbabwe in 1870. He has drawn a stone dish and post he found at Great Zimbabwe.

What are interviews?

In an interview, a historian questions people and records their answers. Historians record interviews on a tape recorder and then write out the information.

In the drawing, a historian is asking an old man to talk about the past. The old man remembers events that happened more than 50 years ago. He is describing them to the historian.

Activity. Interview an older relative. Ask her or him to describe what you were like as a small child. Write down the information you get from your interview.

Documents and tape-recorded interviews are made at the same time as the events that they record, or they are made by people who took part in the events. They are first-hand or **primary sources** of history. Historians do not write them. The people who wrote them did not think that what they were writing or telling would be part of history one day.

Documents and interviews are sources of history. They are not histories. Many of the writers and speakers described what they heard and saw without understanding its meaning. They mixed their own opinions with facts. They could not see that their experiences were part of a *pattern*. Some were *biased*. A few did not tell the truth. People might have told lies or left out facts for all sorts of different reasons. Some wanted to please someone or harm someone else. Some wanted to make other people see things the same way they did. Some simply forgot or made mistakes.

Activity. Here is an example to help you understand bias.

Tendayi from School A and Agnes from School B are describing the same netball match.

Talk about these questions in your class.
What is Agnes's opinion of the match?
What is Tendayi's opinion of the match?
Why are their opinions different?
What fact did Agnes leave out?
What fact did Tendayi leave out?
Can you think of reasons why they left out these facts?

Everyone takes sides. Historians must understand this. They must be *critical* of primary sources. They must compare each piece of evidence with all the other evidence they have. They must *judge* all the evidence together.

Activity. Interviews and selection. Choose a recent important event, for example local celebrations of our first Independence Day, or an incident that happened during the liberation war. Interview several people who *witnessed* the event. Write down the information. Compare the different accounts. Are they primary or secondary sources? Write a group report on the event, selecting information from the accounts you have collected.

Oral histories

Traditions are people's beliefs and customs. Traditions are passed down from parents to children, from elders to young men and women. Stories about a people's past which are passed down like this are called oral histories. Most people did not write down their histories until recently. Histories were remembered and told to others.

Why do people tell oral history?

Oral histories are remembered for many different reasons. Most oral histories trace the story of a ruler's family back to their ancestors. Many tell of the great deeds of the chief or ruler's ancestors. Many oral histories leave out the names of ancestors who did not do anything great. Those who were weak or bad are often forgotten.

The *purpose* of many oral histories is to show that one particular family has a *right* to provide a chief to rule over the land. When a chief's family is very close to the ancestors, many people believe that the chief can work with the ancestors to bring rain and fertility to the land.

The purpose of oral history is not to tell history as it is taught in schools. The purpose is
- to help build a united society,
- to increase people's *loyalty* to the chief,
- to help everyone accept authority,
- to prevent or help solve *disputes* over land.

Discussion. Why do oral histories help to unite people? Talk about other reasons why people keep their traditions.

Activity. Draw pictures to show some traditions of your family or your community.

Historians use oral histories

Oral histories are not primary descriptions of events. The people who repeat traditions were not there or even alive when the events happened. Oral histories are **secondary sources** of history.

Many oral histories are remembered by only one or two mediums. They might tell the same story in the same way or they might tell it

Elders tell children the story of the people's past. This is called oral history.

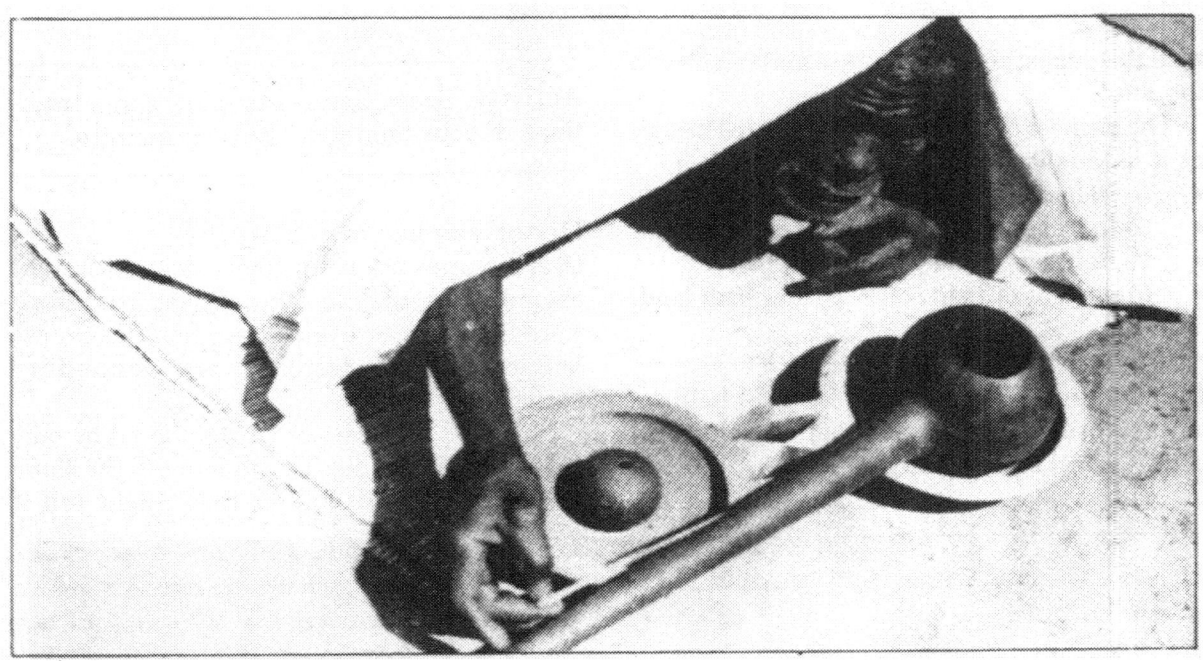

In some countries, a few people have the special task of remembering and retelling traditional history. In Zimbabwe spirit mediums do this. They are special because people believe they are called by the ancestors to keep and retell the story of the people's past.

differently. Historians must compare all the oral histories to judge how true they are. Historians must compare the oral histories of the winners and the losers in wars and disputes.

Discussion.
1. A ruler's oral history is often different from those of ordinary people. Can you think of reasons why?
2. The people who lose a war describe it differently from the people who win. Why?

Oral histories do not give us the **dates** of the events they describe. But we can work out how long ago an event happened. We can count the number of generations (parents and grandparents) between the story-teller and the ancestor who saw the event. A generation lasts for about 25 years.

Everyone forgets a little or changes a little or adds a little when they retell an oral history. So oral histories which are more than ten generations old are not very *reliable*. And a single oral history is not reliable. Historians must use
- many oral histories,
- oral histories from different places,
- oral histories which are not more than six to ten generations old (150 - 250 years),

to get a true description of the past.

Historians cannot give a true description of the past if they use
- only one oral history,
- oral history which is ten to 20 generations old (250 - 500 years).

Discussion. Remember everything we have learned about traditions. Why is one, very old oral history not enough evidence for a historian to use?

What is archaeology?

Archaeology is another way of studying the past. It examines the things that people of the past left behind them. These things may be
- tools,
- seeds from the people's crops,
- bones from the animals the people herded or hunted,
- the bones of the people themselves,
- remains of the people's houses and villages,
- pieces of pottery that the people left or threw away.

A person who studies these objects is an archaeologist. The objects are **physical evidence.**

Many objects were left behind long ago. They are buried in the soil. Archaeologists dig them up, or excavate them. This photograph shows archaeologists excavating a zimbabwe near Harare.

Different groups of people might live on the same piece of land at different times. After many years, their things might get mixed up in the soil. So archaeologists must be very careful. They must be sure that everything they find was made by the same people and used at the same time.

Archaeologists often find charcoal in their excavations. They can send such charcoal or bones to special laboratories. There, they can be tested to find out how old they are. Archaeologists can give us dates for things up to 5 million years old.

Archaeology cannot tell us people's names, language, stories and traditions, or songs and music. These things leave no remains behind them. But archaeology can tell us about how people lived thousands of years before anyone could write. It can tell us
- how people organized their society,
- what food they grew,
- what animals they kept and hunted,
- what tools they used,
- what crafts and trade they had.

Archaeology needs careful research and very large excavations. It is expensive. Little archaeology has been done in Africa. There is a lot of work to be done and new information to be uncovered by future archaeologists.

Summary. Historians use information from documents, interviews, oral histories and archaeology when they write history books. History books are **secondary sources.**

A historian writing a history book
- does research,
- examines every piece of evidence,
- compares all the evidence,
- chooses the evidence that she or he thinks is important,
- judges all the evidence together.

Remember that historians, like everyone else, might be biased.

2. Explaining history

In this chapter:
We will discover that there are many ways of describing and explaining history.
We will look at the main ways.
We will learn about Karl Marx's theories which help us to understand the development of human history.

You will need to know the meanings of these words:

support — increase the strength of, or be loyal to or give help to, or provide with necessities.
interests — well-being or profit or advantage.
experiences — what a person has lived through.
system — organized set of ideas or ways of doing things.
benefit — gain from.
restore — give or bring back.
achievement — something done, that people can be proud of.
exploit — use things or other people for one's own gain.
oppress — treat or rule over others cruelly or unfairly.
analyse — examine critically and study all the parts of.
factor — one of the facts or influences leading to a result, or one part of a bigger whole.
approach — way of coming nearer understanding an idea, person or thing.
distribution — dividing and spreading out over a wider area, or delivery.
theory — a set of rules for understanding or explaining something.
material — physical or made of matter.
define — say exactly what something is.
oppose — be against or completely disagree with.
conflict — battle or struggle.

History books

Whether they intend to or not, most history books help to change society or help to prevent change. In the last chapter, we saw that oral histories may be biased. They describe events in a way that *supports* a particular group or family. Most history books can also be biased (whether the writers know it or not). Most history books support the *interests* of a particular group in society.

Most history books support the interests of the people that control the society. This is because most historians come from the same group as the rulers. The ruling group can usually afford more and better education. They can also afford to pay for research to be done.

Let us now look at some different sorts of history.

Political history

Political history is the story of powerful people in society — the rulers, the leaders and the heroes. Political history looks at
- the deeds and decisions of those who have power,
- leaders who have tried to get power,
- wars and disputes over power.

Most writers of political history do not think that the *experiences* of ordinary people are very important.

From the earliest times, people in every sort of society have told or written about the lives of their heroes, great leaders and rulers. Most oral histories are about political history. Most history books, even today, are about political history.

In recent times, there have been two main sorts of political history in Africa — colonial history and nationalist history.

This is a colonial poster about Great Zimbabwe. Why is the man shown kneeling? Who is the Egyptian woman who looks like a ghost? Why is a foreigner shown at Great Zimbabwe? How does this poster support colonial history?

Definitions
Colonialism. A *colony* is a country which is settled and ruled by another country. For example, Britain *colonized* Zimbabwe. This means that Britain took control of the area that is now Zimbabwe. British people came to live in Zimbabwe as rulers and *colonizers*. The *colonial* period is the time from *colonization* to independence.

Nationalism is the desire of people to rule themselves. Many countries in Africa which were colonies fought *nationalist* struggles against the colonial rulers.

Colonial history

Colonial history was written by colonizers and their supporters. They tried to show that colonialism was a good *system*. Colonial history described what it called
- the deeds of white 'explorers' who 'discovered' Africa's wonders,
- the 'bravery' and 'dedication' of missionaries who brought 'civilization' and 'true religion' to Africa,
- the 'adventures' of 'pioneers' 'developing' 'new' lands and 'defending' themselves against 'local risings'.

Colonial history did not say very much about African people. It described them as 'backward' and 'uninventive'. It tried to destroy African people's pride in themselves and their past.

Discussion. Look at the words in inverted commas above (like 'explorers' who 'discovered' Africa's wonders). Make sure that you understand what all the words mean. Why are these words wrongly used? Why do these words give a false picture of colonization? Who *benefited* from descriptions such as these?

Nationalist history

Nationalist histories often describe the same events as colonial history but they see the past very differently. Nationalist histories show that
- Africa has a past to be proud of,
- 'explorers' discoveries' were known to Africans for centuries,
- Africa had civilizations, states, empires and religions as old and great as those of any other continent,
- the 'pioneers' land was stolen from Africans,
- 'local risings' were wars against oppression.

Nationalist histories describe
- the great leaders of the past and present,
- how Africans developed their own cultures,
- how Africans fought against colonization.

Nationalist history is important and good in many ways. It *restores* the truth. It gives people pride in their past.

Nationalist histories may also have weaknesses. Some describe only the great heroes and *achievements* of the past. Some leave out facts, such as
- that some African rulers *exploited* the ordinary people in their societies,
- that African states and empires often *oppressed* and exploited weaker states.

Just as most colonial historians belonged to an old ruling group, so most nationalist historians belong to a new ruling group. They support the interests of their group. They might try to give a false picture that a nation ruled by their group is united and contented.

Activity. Try to find an old history book that was used in your school a long time ago. How is it different from the books you use today? Can you tell whose interests the writer supported?

Book explores heroine's life
Staff Reporter

MBUYA Nehanda, the legendary spirit medium known as the mother of the liberation struggle, is to feature in a new book by a leading Shona novelist.

Mbuya Nehanda played a principal role in instigating the revolt against white settlers in the Mazoe area during the 1894-96 liberation war.

She and another revolutionary fighter, Kaguvi, were hanged by the British on April 27 1896. But her heroic role has made her the idol of modern-day Zimbabwean revolutionaries.

Compare these two documents about Mbuya Nehanda.

In the High Court of Matabeleland.

To the Sheriff of the Territory of Rhodesia, within the limits of the Matabeleland Order in Council of the 18th July, 1894, or his lawful Deputy Greeting.

The Queen against *Nianda*

in custody:

WHEREAS it appears of Record that at a Criminal Session of the High Court, holden before *Mr Justice Watermeyer* at *Salisbury* on the *Second* Day of *March* in the Year of Our Lord One Thousand Eight Hundred and *Ninety eight* the above named *Nianda* was duly convicted of the Crime of Murder and was sentenced by the Judgment of the said Court to be hanged by the neck until *she* be dead at such place of execution and at such time as His Honour the Administrator should be pleased to appoint:

And whereas it also appears of Record that His Excellency the High Commissioner has duly authorised and approved of the execution

Socialist history

Socialist history is usually very different from other sorts of history. Socialist historians believe that history is shaped mainly by ordinary people, and not just by leaders or powerful groups. They believe that all people are part of making history. They look at **social history**. They describe ordinary people in the past, such as peasants, workers and migrant labourers.

Socialist historians also study **economic history**. Economic history describes
- how people produce the food they eat and the goods they use,
- how people trade with one another,
- how people organize their crafts and industries.

Socialist historians do not simply describe events. They try to *analyse* events. They look at many events to understand their pattern. They try to find reasons for events and patterns. Often the causes of events and patterns are hidden. People do not always understand the *factors* that shape their history and society.

Other historians might share some of these *approaches*. It is not possible to be a socialist historian unless you agree with all these approaches.

It is also important to know what socialist historians do **not** believe. They do **not** believe:
- that history follows a pattern created by gods,
- that nature or climate or environment forces people to develop in a certain way,
- that people of different races are born with different abilities,
- that history is a muddle of meaningless events,
- that history is a great mystery that people cannot understand.

How do historians analyse the past?

They look at these factors:

1. Geography and **environment** — the sort of climate and countryside the people lived in, and how they affected people's lives.
2. Natural and human **resources** — the crops, animals, vegetation, crafts and industries, soils and minerals of the area; and the people who used them and their skills.
3. **Technology** — the tools and transport the people used to exploit their resources.
4. **Economy** — the production and *distribution* of the things people used.
5. **Social organization** — the relationships between all the different people and groups in a society.
6. **Relationships** between a society and neighbouring societies, communities or states. Relationships can, for instance, be peaceful or warlike, equal or unequal.
7. The influence of **the past** — the previous history of a people.

When we analyse any topic in history, we must discuss these seven factors. Come back to this list again and again as you read this book. Make sure that each factor has been discussed. We cannot understand any single factor by itself. Each factor has an influence on every other factor. No single factor by itself shapes the way that history develops. No single factor controls history.

Historical materialism

Historical materialism is a socialist *theory* of history. Many people consider that it is the most complete theory of history. Karl Marx and Friedrich Engels worked out the theory of historical materialism. Let us look at what the words mean.

Historical: Marx and Engels showed that we can only understand a society today if we understand the history of that society.

Materialism: Marx and Engels showed that everything in society is the result of *material* causes. We must study the material conditions in which people live to understand the ways they think and act, and their traditions, culture and beliefs.

Material causes

To understand material causes, we must look at four important parts of society:

1. The **resources**, or means of production. These are the things that people need in order to live a decent life. They include land, animals, natural resources like wood, water and minerals, seeds, crops, tools, houses and clothes and, in modern times, machines.

2. **Property**. We must look at who owns or controls the resources in a society. We must ask how they came to own or control these resources. Has one group captured, taken or bought the resources from the other people?

3. **Division of labour**. This means the way that work is shared out between people. We must look at how work is divided between
- women and men,
- farmers and craftspeople,
- traders and workers,
- those who work mainly with their minds (like teachers, historians, managers and officials) and those who work mainly with their hands (like farmers, peasants, labourers and craftspeople).

4. **Relations of production**. These are the links between different people in society. We must look especially at the relations between the people who work and the people who own the resources. Are the relations freely chosen, or do they involve inequality, exploitation or force? Are there slave and slave-owner, servant and master, worker and employer, trader and customer?

Karl Marx

Marx and Engels

Karl Marx was born in Germany in 1818. He studied history and philosophy at university and then became a journalist. He became editor of a newspaper. In 1849, he was deported from Germany because he criticized the government in his newspaper. He spent the rest of his life in terrible poverty as a refugee in London. He earned very little money. Often he could not afford food and medicines for his family.

For the next 34 years, until he died in 1883, Marx studied and wrote about the workings of the capitalist system. In his greatest book, *Capital*, he showed what a strong and evil system it was. In explaining the capitalist system, Marx showed that the ownership of resources by one class led to oppression in capitalist societies. From his studies of European history, Marx described how European modes of production changed from slavery (in ancient Greece and Rome) to feudalism, and then, in the 19th century, to capitalism.

Marx was interested in all history. He studied the development of early classless societies. He tried to describe the modes of production of ancient Germany and the countries of eastern Europe. He collected information on the traditional societies of India, China and Peru before capitalism. He described their mode of production as Asiatic. But in Europe at that time, there was very little information about this, and people in Europe knew almost nothing about the history of Africa.

Marx worked very hard to build workers' movements that would destroy capitalism. They would take over the resources from the capitalists and so introduce socialism. He showed how socialism, when it was

Friedrich Engels

complete and successful, would lead to the classless society of true communism. He wrote *The Communist Manifesto* to show the road towards communism.

Friedrich Engels was born in 1820, also in Germany. He never went to university. He joined his father's business, which owned factories making cotton cloth. This gave him wealth, and time to study.

Engels was Marx's closest friend in England. He gave Marx money when Marx was very poor. They wrote many books together, including *The Communist Manifesto*. They worked together helping to build political parties everywhere in Europe to bring about workers' power, socialism and communism.

Engels was particularly interested in the very early development of human society. Like Marx, he supported Charles Darwin's theory of evolution. In his own writings, he showed that history too evolves. He also wrote about the importance of labour in people's physical and social evolution.

After Marx's death, Engels continued to study information on traditional classless societies. He wrote about primitive communal and lineage societies in books like *The origin of the family, private property and the state*. Engels died in 1895.

Make a list of the resources you can see in this drawing.

Classes

When a historian has studied these four important points, he or she can see that often the people in a society are divided into classes. A person's class is decided by his or her control or lack of control of the resources.

An owning class is a group of people who own the resources that are needed to make goods. A working class is a group of people who produce the goods. If they do not own the resources which they need, they have to give some work to the owning class, or give part of the goods they produce to the owners.

The working class provides the owning class with wealth. The owning class does not work for this wealth. It gets this wealth through owning resources and exploiting the working class.

We can *define* the classes in a society by finding out
- who owns the resources,
- how the work is organized,
- the relations between workers and owners.

Classes are never decided by tribe, colour, race, culture or age, or even wealth. They are decided by the way production is organized.

When they analyse a society, historical materialists always ask these questions:
1. Are there different classes in the society?
2. How did the different classes develop?
3. How does the owning class benefit from the work of the working class?
4. How does the owning class force the workers to work for it?
5. Do the workers see that they are being exploited?
6. How does the working class free itself from exploitation?

What are the resources shown in these two pictures? Who do you think owns them?

Class struggle

Marx and Engels showed that in a society with classes, the different classes are always *opposed* to each other. Those with resources try to get more and more wealth from those who work. Workers struggle to get control of the resources. Class *conflicts* will continue as long as there are classes in society.

Modes of production

A mode of production is a way of describing a society at a particular time. It describes the society's
- way of owning resources,
- divisions of labour,
- relations of production.

In this book, we will study six different modes of production.

1. Primitive communalism (from the first people to the development of farming, chapters 6 - 10).
2. The lineage mode of production (developed farmers, chapters 11 - 12).
3. The tributary mode of production (African states, chapters 13 - 15, and 19 - 26).
4. The east African cities' mode of production, based on unequal trade (chapter 16).
5. The feudal mode of production (chapters 17 - 18).
6. The Asiatic mode of production (chapter 27).

We will learn more about modes of production in chapter 29.

Discussion. In what ways is political history similar to socialist history? In what ways is it different from socialist history?

3. Evolution

In this chapter:
> We will look at human beings as part of the animal world.
> We will find out about the theory of evolution.
> We will learn
> - what our ancestors looked like millions of years ago,
> - how we know about them,
> - how they changed.

You will need to know the meanings of these words:

extinct — that have died out or no longer exist.
process — a regular series of changes over a long time.
species — a type of animal or plant (for example, zebras, human beings).
isolated — placed apart or separated from others.
survive — continue to exist or still be alive.

Human beings are part of **the animal world**. People's legs, heads, eyes, teeth and other parts of their bodies are really very like the legs, heads, eyes and teeth of several other animals.

The animals that look most like human beings are the apes like gorillas and chimpanzees. We can see that we are related to these animals. We are also different from them in many ways. These are some of the important **differences**.

People
- walk on two legs all the time,
- do not have muzzles,
- have round heads,
- have bigger brains,
- have small teeth, all about the same size,
- do not have hairy fur.

Apes
- usually walk on four legs,
- have muzzles,
- have small heads,
- have smaller brains,
- have teeth of different sizes, some of which are very big,
- have hairy fur to keep them warm.

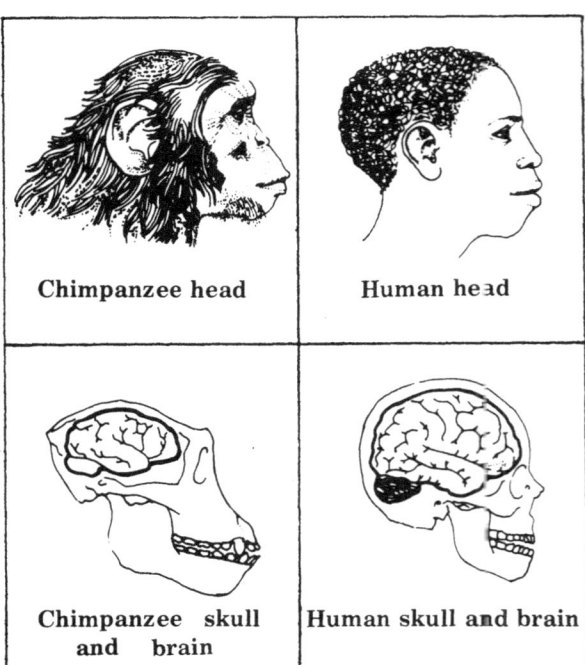

Chimpanzee head | Human head

Chimpanzee skull and brain | Human skull and brain

Models of stages in evolution — australopithecine, neandertal, chimpanzee.

Evolution

Most of the animals which lived on earth millions of years ago looked very different to the animals of today. Some of them became *extinct*. Others changed slowly over time into the animals we see around us today.

This *process* is called evolution. The scientist who first described how evolution takes place was called Charles Darwin. His ideas have been made much clearer by many later scientists.

How evolution works

There are slight differences within all *species* of animals. Some might be slightly taller, darker or heavier than their neighbours Such small differences are caused by chance.

Sometimes a few animals that had some of these chance differences were *isolated* from all other animals of the same species. Then the environment changed. The chance differences made this small group more suited to the new conditions. This group *survived* the new conditions better than any other animals of the same species.

The differences that made this group better able to survive were passed on to their descendants. The animals in this group were now quite different from the original species. A new sort of animal or species had evolved. The new species slowly increased in numbers. It spread out, and overcame and replaced the original species.

1. In Britain, there is a species called the Peppered Moth. Some Peppered Moths are light grey and some are dark grey.

2. Before 1850, there were many more light grey moths. The dark moths were easier to see and so birds ate large numbers of them.

3. Many factories were built in Britain during the industrial revolution. The smoke from the factories made trees, buildings and fences dark and dirty.

4. Now the light grey moths were easier to see. Birds ate most of the lighter moths, while the dark moths increased in number.

What is the chance difference in this example? How did the environment change? Which group of moths survived better after the environment changed? Why?

Darwin

Charles Darwin.

Charles Darwin was born in 1809. From childhood, he loved natural history, and collected things like fossils, shells and rocks. He started learning medicine, and then studied to be a Christian minister. He soon gave these up, and returned to his interest in natural history.

In 1831, he went on a five-year voyage of scientific research, on a ship called the Beagle, to many parts of the Atlantic Ocean and South America. He was able to collect fossils and study many species of animals. He found that every isolated island contained different but closely related species of creatures. He realised that these creatures could not each be a separate creation.

For the next 20 years, he collected facts to support his ideas. For three years, he wrote his great book, *The Origin of the Species,* in which he explained his theory of evolution. The book was published in 1859. It caused bitter arguments, especially with people in the Christian church who believed that god created all species. Almost all the scientists of the time saw the truth of Darwin's arguments. They supported his theories.

Darwin was a quiet, shy and peaceful man. He was often sick. He never joined in arguments over his ideas. His theory of evolution completely changed ideas in science and history.

Hominids

Millions of years ago, creatures lived on earth that were much more like humans than any ape. They are called hominids. We can see that hominids were not humans. Hominids were not monkeys or apes either. The last hominids died out many thousands of years ago. They are extinct.

How do we know about hominids?
We know about hominids because archaeologists have found and studied small pieces of their bones and teeth.

Most hominids' bones have been found in Africa. It seems that at least some of the earliest hominids lived in the woodlands and grasslands of eastern and southern Africa.

Archaeologists have found hominids' bones and teeth buried in the dried mud of ancient east African lakes. Hominids used to live beside these lakes. When they died, most of the bodies rotted or were eaten. They left no traces. But some of the bodies were covered by the mud of the lakes. Slowly, some of the bones and teeth turned to stone. We call such remains fossils. These lakes dried up many thousands of years ago. Archaelogists digging in the area found the fossil bones and teeth. By studying hominid fossil bones and teeth, archaelogists can tell
- how big the hominid was,
- how it walked,
- how it used its hands,
- what food it ate.

Some of these hominid fossils were also covered by the ash of ancient volcanoes. Scientists can tell how old this ash is. This tells them how old the fossils are.

Evolution of human beings

Scientists believe that people, hominids and apes all evolved from the same ancestor. This ancestor was not a person or a hominid or an ape. It was a creature we call *Ramapithecus*, or one very like it.

This ancestor lived millions of years ago. People, hominids and apes all developed in their own different and special ways. No scientist ever believed that people descended from apes. They do believe that people and apes had the same ancestor.

Over millions of years, as hominids evolved, they became more like people. They became more like us
- in appearance,
- in the sizes of their brains,
- in their teeth,
- in the way they walked,
- in the way they used their hands.

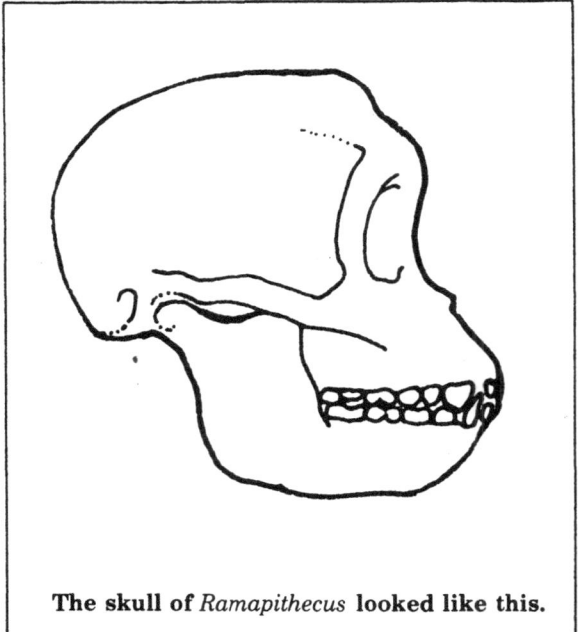

The skull of *Ramapithecus* looked like this.

Discussion. Look at the human body. How are we different from monkeys and apes? Think about our eyes, teeth, hands, arms, legs, feet, strength and speed, and the way we stand and move. How is each part of our body useful for the ordinary things we do each day?

Assisted answers. Fill in the missing words in these sentences.

1. Scientists believe that a creature called.......... was the ancestor of all people, hominids and apes.
2. A species is .... when all the animals in the species have died out.
3. The slow change of animal species is called ....
4. The extinct creatures that looked most like humans are called ....
5. .... are the remains of creatures that lived millions of years ago.

4. The earliest people

In this chapter.
We will learn about the evolution of hominids, from *Ramapithecus* to modern people. We will see how the appearance and tools of hominids changed over millions of years. We will find ways to imagine the great lengths of time that these changes have taken.

You will need to know the meanings of these words:
specialized — altered in some way for a particular purpose, able to do only a few things in a few ways.
task — a piece of work.
scavenge — look for and take what is not wanted by others.
skilled — having abilities or knowing how to do something well.
adapt — alter or adjust in order to live or do something better.
co-operate — work together.

Ramapithecus

The ancestor of all people, hominids and apes was *Ramapithecus*. It lived 14 million years ago. Archaeologists have found fossils of the jaws and teeth of ramapithecines. These fossils show us that ramapithecines were able to chew their food and move their jaws to grind up their food just as people can.

Australopithecus

The australopithecines lived from 5 million years ago to 1,5 million years ago. They were small creatures. When fully grown, australopithecines were about the size of a 12-year-old child today. They could walk and run upright just as we can.

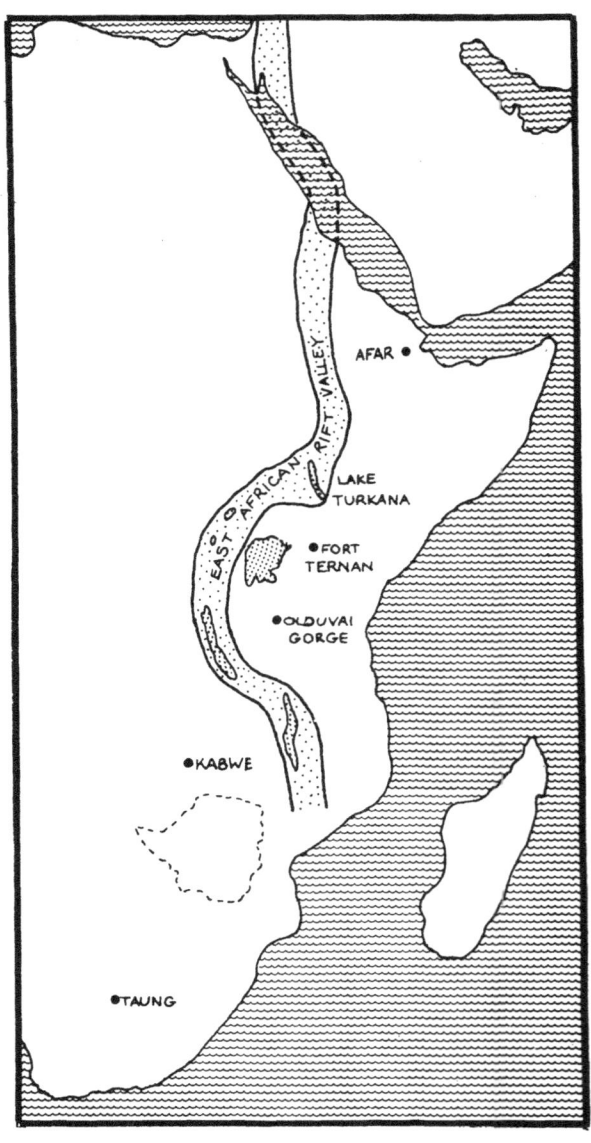

Fossil bones of hominids have been found at the places shown on this map. Some people call Africa 'the cradle of mankind' because so many fossil bones have been found in Africa.

One sort of australopithecine (*Australopithecus robustus*, also called 'Nutcracker Man') had very large jaws, back teeth and jaw muscles. With these, they were able to crunch and grind hard food like nuts. We cannot do this. They were *specialized* in a way that we are not.

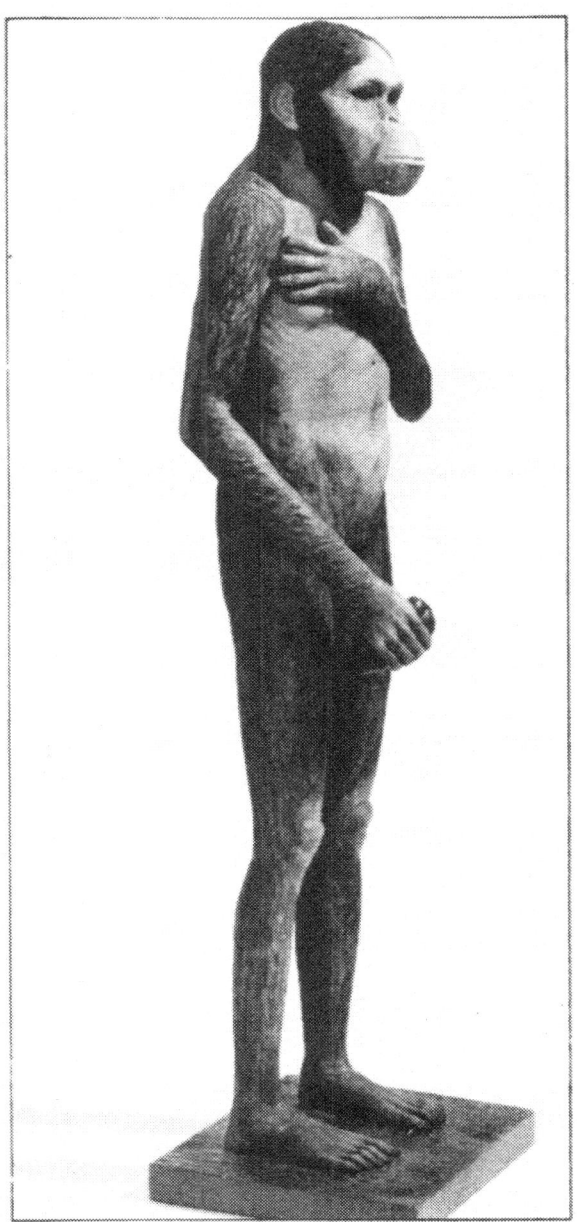

A model of *Australopithecus*.

The other sort of australopithecine (*Australopithecus gracilis*) was not specialized in the same way as *robustus*. They had small teeth, all about the same size. They were much more like our teeth. *Australopithecus gracilis* ate all sorts of different food like we do.

The australopithecines did not make tools, but they might have used sticks and stones to help them to do simple *tasks*.

Homo habilis

The habilines lived 2.5 to 1.5 million years ago. They are very important in human evolution because they were the first hominids to be able to talk, to use language.

They were also the first hominids to be able to make tools. Their tools are called Oldowan, because many of them were found at Olduvai Gorge. They were extremely simple tools. The habilines knocked a few small chips off a round stone or pebble to make a cutting edge.

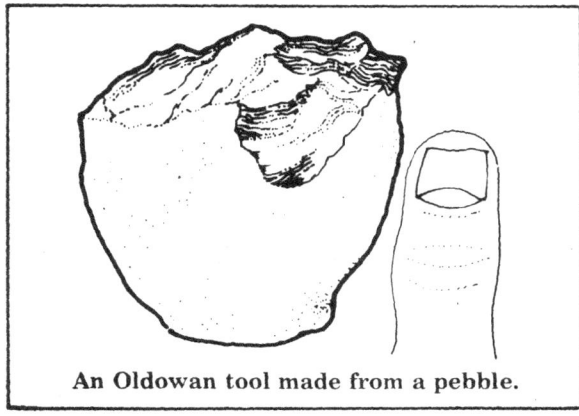

An Oldowan tool made from a pebble.

The habilines probably got most of their meat by *scavenging*, not by hunting. When they found an animal that had been killed by lions or hyenas, they drove these animals away or waited until they had finished eating and left. Then the habilines ate the remains. This was not a reliable source of meat. For many thousands of years, meat was probably only a small part of the hominids' diet.

Table of early hominids

Name(s) All the names in *italics* are Latin names.	*Ramapithecus*	*Australopithecus* (australopithecines, southern ape-man, *Zinjanthropus*, 'Nutcracker Man')	*Homo habilis* (habilines, 'handy man')
Date	14-8 million years ago	5-1,5 million years ago	2,5-1,5 million years ago
Found	India, Pakistan, Turkey. Kenya (Fort Ternan).	Ethiopia (Afar) Kenya (Lake Turkana) Tanzania (Olduvai) South Africa (Taung)	Kenya (Lake Turkana) Tanzania (Olduvai)
Appearance	Only jaws found. Grinding teeth like humans.	*A. robustus*: 1,5m tall 35-55 kg in weight, 530 c.c. brain. Very large grinding teeth. *A. gracilis*: 1,2m. tall, 24-45 kg in weight, 480 c.c. brain.	1,5 m tall, 40 kg in weight, 800 c.c. brain
Tools	No tools	Did not make tools but used sticks and stones.	Oldowan, stone choppers, scrapers, hammers.

Table of early hominids

Name(s)	*Homo erectus* ('standing man')	*Homo sapiens neandertalensis* (neandertals, *Homo rhodesiensis*, Kabwe or Broken Hill Man, 'man from Neandertal')	*Homo sapiens sapiens* (modern people, 'thinking man')
Date	1,5-0,5 million years ago	Perhaps as much as 0,5 million years ago. 100 000-40 000 years ago	Everywhere in world by 50 000 years ago
Found	Tanzania (Olduvai) China, Java, Transvaal, Algeria, Europe.	Zambia (Kabwe) Europe (Neandertal), Palestine, Central Asia	Everywhere
Appearance	Almost as big as modern people. 700-1200 c.c. brain. Very bony head.	Almost like modern people, average brain 1300 c.c.	People like us. Brain 1 000 – 2 000 c.c.; average 1 400 c.c.
Tools	Early Stone Age, handaxes, cleavers, flake tools, fire.	Middle Stone Age (very well made, large flake tools).	Middle Stone Age, Late Stone Age, Early Iron Age (A D 200 — A D 1100), Later Iron Age (A D 1100 — A D 1800). Modern technology.

Homo erectus

Homo erectus lived 1,5 to 0,5 million years ago. They made heavy, stone handaxes and cleavers. They could use these tools to chop down trees and branches, and to dig easily. By this time, people were *skilled* enough to make stone tools quickly and easily, whenever they needed them. This period is called the **Early Stone Age.**

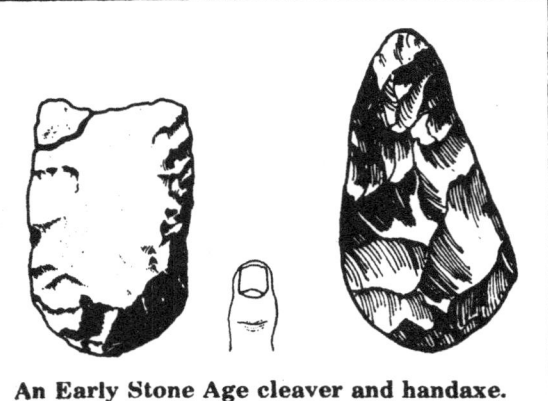

An Early Stone Age cleaver and handaxe.

Homo erectus learned to use fire. They used fire
- to drive animals away,
- to drive animals into traps,
- to protect their shelters at night,
- to keep themselves warm,
- to cook.

Because of *Homo erectus's* technology, they were able to live in many different environments. Archaeologists have found their fossil bones in many different parts of the world, such as
- open grasslands in Africa,
- forests in Java,
- windy plains in north China,
- frozen wastelands in north Europe.

Activity. Look in an atlas or on a wall map of the world. Find the places listed above where *Homo erectus* was found. What problems do you think they had in each of these environments? How were they able to *adapt* to all these environments?

What can we learn about *Homo erectus* from this drawing?

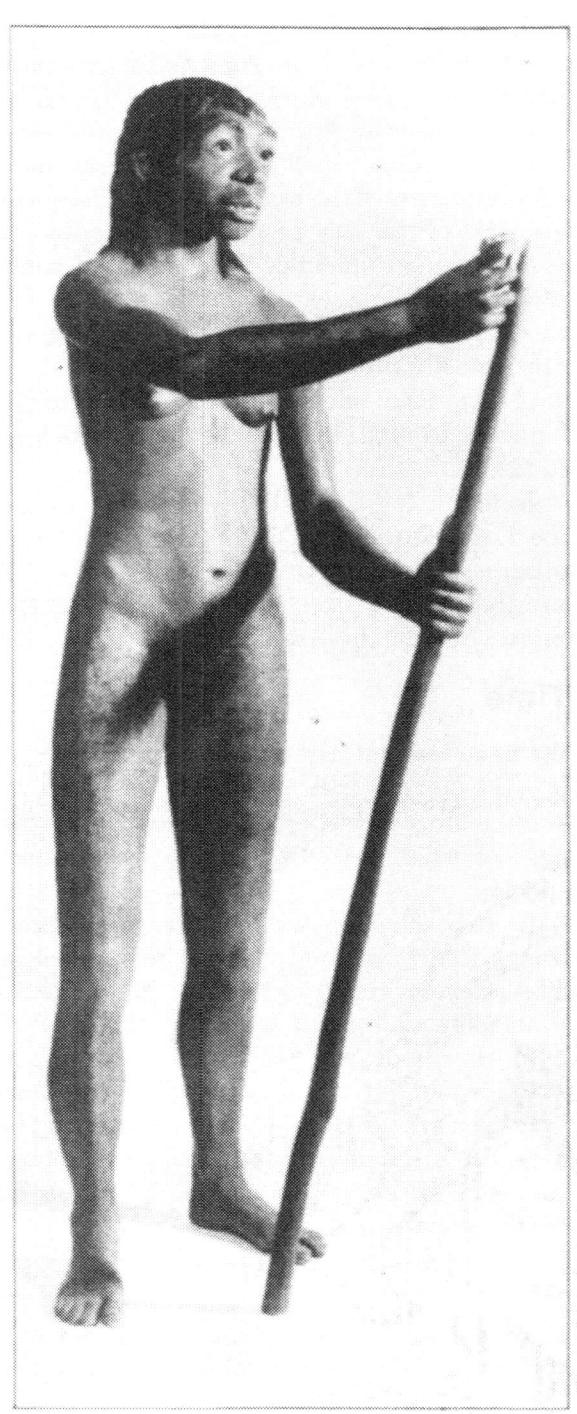

A model of a neandertal woman.

Homo sapiens neandertalensis

If we saw one today, we would know that a neandertal, from 100 000 years ago, was a human being. We might think that it was ugly and frightening because it had a heavy bony brow, low forehead, and jutting jaw. Neandertals were not exactly like people today but they were truly human beings.

Neandertals looked after their sick and injured. Neandertals with badly broken bones were cared for by others until their bones healed When a neandertal died, the others buried him or her in a special burial place, in a carefully dug grave, lined with stones. They were buried with flowers and food. This shows us that the neandertals had developed a **culture** that believed that there was another life after death. They believed that the things of this life could be used after death and could be taken to the world of the dead.

We can also see cultural development in neandertal tools. These tools belong to the **Middle Stone Age**. Stones were carefully shaped so that, when they were hit at a certain spot, one large flake was knocked off. This sort of flake made a very sharp tool. Flakes were also carefully chipped all round their edges to make tools of a lot of different shapes. Each shape was designed for a particular sort of work, for example to cut wood, strip bark, straighten spears or scrape hides. All of the tools made for one particular job looked almost the same. This shows that neandertals had a clear idea of the tool they wanted before they started to make it. They all agreed that certain shapes were best for particular jobs. They had the skill to copy such shapes exactly.

Large groups of neandertals *co-operated* on game drives. This means that together they drove whole herds of animals over cliffs, or into lakes or marshes where the animals were trapped and easy to kill. Then they shared out the meat.

The skull of a neandertal was found many years ago in Kabwe in Zambia. It was named *Homo rhodesiensis* or 'Rhodesian Man' by the scientists of the time. It was also called 'Broken Hill Man'. (At the time it was found, Kabwe was called Broken Hill and Zambia was called Northern Rhodesia.)

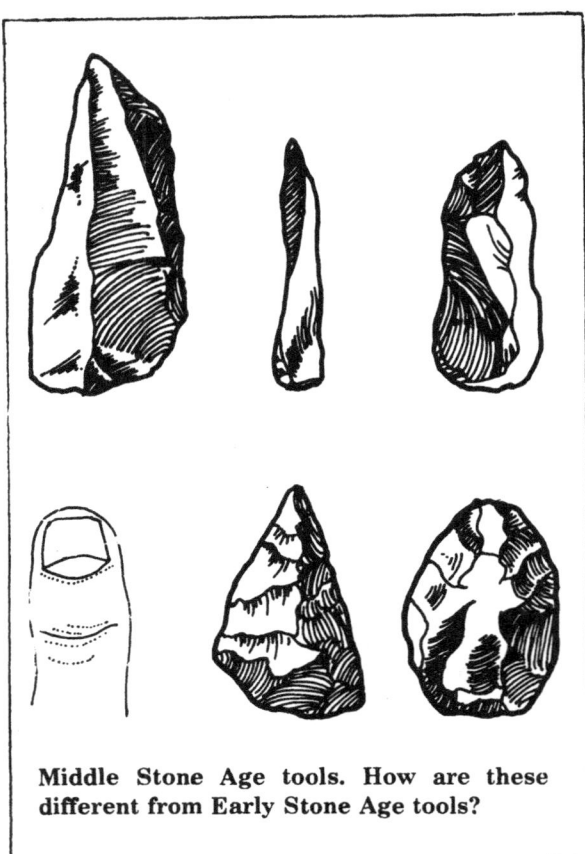

Middle Stone Age tools. How are these different from Early Stone Age tools?

Homo sapiens sapiens

We are called *Homo sapiens sapiens*. The earliest true people had spread throughout the world by 50 000 years ago. They continued to make **Middle Stone Age** tools. As they improved their skills, they developed **Late Stone Age** tools. (We will study the Late Stone Age in chapter 6.)

The bodies of *Homo sapiens sapiens* have not changed very much in the thousands of years since they first evolved. People have developed some small physical differences in different parts of the world. These differences are part of the way people have adapted to various environments. You can see small physical differences in people of different races. Most Africans belong to the Negroid race, most Europeans belong to the Caucasoid race, Khoi and San people belong to the Khoisanoid race, and Chinese people belong to the Mongoloid race.

In technology, people progressed through the **Late Stone Age** to farming. They then progressed to the **Iron Age**. Today, we could say that people's technology belongs to the Space Age, or the Atomic Age.

Time

We have learned that everyone has a history. It is the story of their own past. But when we study history as a subject, we learn about the past of whole societies, and of the human species.

In this chapter, we have learned about things that happened millions of years ago. This is a very, very long time ago. It is difficult to imagine such great lengths of time.

In this book, we will learn about many changes that happened in the past. In modern times, we are used to very fast changes in our lives. But in the distant past, change happened very slowly. Very little changed for tens of thousands of years.

Discussion. Rapid changes in society. What important changes have happened in your lifetime? How has the world changed since your grandparents' childhood?

Activity. To help us imagine slow change over hundreds of thousands of years, let us look at hominid evolution. Let us pretend that the 5 million years from the first australopithecines until today, happened in one year.

Draw a calendar for one year in your exercise books. Imagine that 5 million years happened in this one year. Mark these things on your calendar:
- 1 January: the first *Australopithecus*,
- 1 July: the first *Homo habilis*,
- 15 September: the first *Homo erectus*,
- 1 December: the first *Homo sapiens sapiens*.

On this 5-million-year calendar, you are about one second old. You can see how long the evolution of *Homo sapiens sapiens* has taken. You can see how slowly life changed.

Source-based question. Look carefully at the drawings of Oldowan and Early, Middle and Late Stone Age tools. Answer these questions.
a) What changes can you see in the size of tools?
b) How did the use of tools change?
c) What do all these changes tell us about the people who made them?
d) Are tools oral, physical or documentary sources of history?

Essay. As hominids evolved, they made better tools. Describe the changes in their tool-making. You should
a) describe and name the tools used by each kind of hominid,
b) explain how the tools were made,
c) explain what the tools were used for,
d) say what the tools tell us about the hominids that used them.

Dates

In Christian countries, many historians measure time according to the birth of Christ. For years before the birth of Christ, they add the letters BC ('Before Christ') to the date. For dates after his birth, they add the letters AD ('*Anno Domini*'. This is Latin for 'in the year of our lord, Christ').

Class Activity. With your teacher's help, make a time chart or frieze to stick on the wall of your classroom. At the end of each chapter, write the dates and important details of what you have learned on to cards. Stick the cards in the correct place on your time chart. The time chart will help you to see
- changes that happened slowly,
- changes that happened quickly,
- the different changes that happened at the same time.

You can also draw pictures to illustrate your time chart.

Assisted answers. The importance of fire in human evolution.
Fill in the missing words in the paragraph.
The first hominids to learn how to use fire were .... They could live in cold areas because they could make fires to keep themselves .... Their shelters were safe because fire frightened .... away. They could eat many new kinds of food because they could .... on fires. They used fire to drive animals into traps, so their hunting was more successful and they could eat more .... In all these ways, fire helped them to .... to many different environments.

5. The development of human society

In this chapter:
We will ask: What makes human society different from groups of other animals?
We will see the ways that early human societies evolved.

You will need to know the meanings of these words:

defend — protect from danger or attack.
prepare — get ready.
advantage — better position, or something which is favourable.
reason — connect a series of ideas logically to reach a conclusion.
stalk — get closer to something without it knowing.
ambush — lie in wait and make a surprise attack.
selfish — caring too much for oneself and not enough for others.
communicate — pass on or share information or ideas.
efficiently — doing what is necessary with as little time, labour and resources as possible.
disadvantage — worse position, or something which is unfavourable or harmful.
social — living in organized groups or societies.

How are people different from monkeys and apes?

We are different from monkeys and apes in many ways. Here are some important differences:
- Monkeys and apes often move on four legs. We stand up most of the time.
- Apes can run fast over long distances. We can walk for long distances. We can run quite fast for short distances.
- Apes can use their teeth to fight with, and to bite and tear flesh. With our teeth we can eat all sorts of food, such as fruit, nuts, seeds and meat. Our teeth are no good for fighting.
- Apes can use their hands for simple tasks, such as picking fruit from trees. Some can use simple tools, such as putting sticks down holes to collect insects to eat. We can use our hands for more complicated tasks. We can pick up and use very small objects. We can make complicated tools.

A chimpanzee pushing a stick into a termite nest to collect termites to eat.

- Apes *defend* themselves by running away or climbing trees or using their teeth. People and apes can defend themselves by throwing stones or by breaking off branches to hit or frighten enemies. Only people can make wooden spears or clubs or stone points to defend themselves. They make these before they meet danger. They *prepare* themselves for danger.

From these differences we can see that people are weak compared to apes, but people's skills give them *advantages* over other animals.

Reasoning

People have one very great advantage over other animals. Human brains have developed so that we can *reason*. We can understand problems and solve them. We can think of what might happen in the future and plan ahead.

Tools

Apes can use simple tools. For example, they can use stones to break open nuts and bones.

Early hominids also used simple tools like this. The important difference was that early hominids learned to use simple tools to make more complicated tools. They could use one stone as a hammer to knock chips off other stones.

Early hominids made many kinds of stone tools. They made sharp flakes to cut the bark from trees. They used the bark to make string and bags. They cut down trees and branches using bigger and heavier stone tools. With big flakes, they sharpened branches to make spears, digging sticks and clubs.

Early hominids used tools to dig holes for traps. They covered the holes with branches and grass. Animals did not see the traps and fell in.

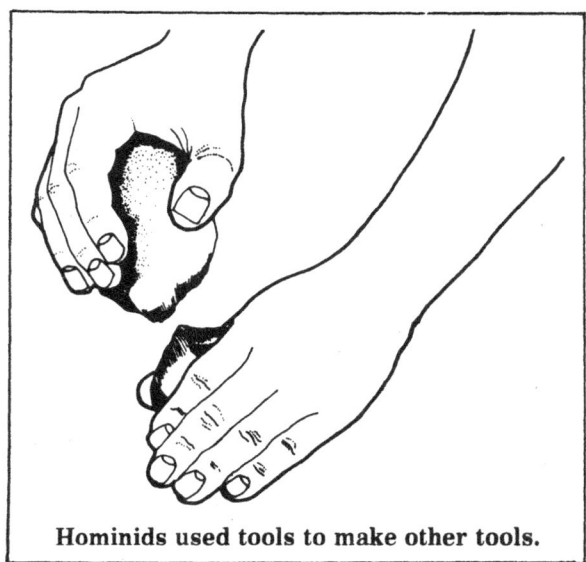

Hominids used tools to make other tools.

Tool-making such as this needed reasoning and planning. No ape can use tools to make other tools.

Discussion. What is a tool? What tools do you need for each of these tasks:
- cooking vegetables?
- making a desk?
- building a classroom?

What tools do you need to make these tools?

Sharing and working together

Many animals live in herds or groups. All monkeys, baboons and apes do. Mother apes share their food only with their babies. An adult ape has to beg or fight to get food from another ape. Lions, jackals and wild dogs all live in open country and hunt big animals. They co-operate in hunting, and share the meat from the animals they kill.

Hominids also lived together, in groups or societies. They shared and co-operated much more than any of these animals. Within their group, they shared all their food. No one had to fight or beg.

All the members of a habiline group sharing the meat of an animal.

Within their group, hominids shared out all the work between them. This gave them a very big advantage over most other animals. It made everything much quicker and easier to do. Very soon, work was divided between men and women.

Women looked after and taught the children. Near the camp, they collected insects, fruit and plants to eat. Perhaps they made baskets and bags. Then they could carry food back to the camp at the end of their day's work. The older and weaker women, and those with very young babies stayed in the camp all day, looking after the children.

Men did the hunting. They made spears and traps to kill animals. They formed hunting teams. They travelled far to find the animals. They learned the habits of animals, where to find them, and how to *stalk* and *ambush* them.

At the end of the day, women and men shared the food they had gathered. Everyone had to co-operate and trust everyone else. No one could be *selfish*. No one could keep food for themselves. The group could only stay together if everyone shared. The group could survive dangers and hardships only if everyone was united.

The group punished anyone who did not work and share with the others. If they had to, the group forced such a person to leave. Then the person would die because it was difficult to survive alone.

Advantages of sharing

When hominids learned to take food to their camp and share it with others, society made great progress. Old, weak and sick hominids did not starve and die. They stayed in the camp. They were fed by others.

Mothers were given food, so they were able to stay in the camp to look after the babies. This was very important. The babies of most other animals are strong enough to look after themselves a few weeks after birth. Like human young, hominid babies needed to be looked after for years. Hominid children could depend on their mothers for their food until they were at least six to eight years old. They did not have to search for their food like all other animals do. So they could grow healthy and strong.

This care gave children time to develop love for their parents and respect for the rest of their group. They learned how important their group was to their lives. These feelings made them want to remain part of the group when they grew up. Children also had time to learn all the skills that they needed in life. They learned

- how to hunt animals,
- what plants could be eaten,
- how to build shelters,
- how to make tools.

Language

To learn, to teach and to share knowledge needs language. Animals grunt and scream and growl, but these are not enough to *communicate* properly. People must have a language if they are going to make plans and discuss and agree.

We do not know when hominids first learned to speak to each other. Archaeologists cannot tell us because language leaves no physical evidence. We can get some idea by looking at hominids' skulls. From these we can find out the shape and size of the brain. Scientists believe that the habilines who lived 2 million years ago were the first hominids who were able to speak.

Activity. To understand how important language is, make groups of four. One of the four leaves the room. The other three choose a simple task for him or her to do. When the fourth person returns, he or she tries to find out what the task is, by doing various things. The other three may only grunt (for yes) or groan (for no).

Culture

Homo sapiens groups probably sang and danced and told stories together. They painted pictures of animals and hunting. They did not do these things only for enjoyment. These activities taught children how to behave properly. They taught what was right and wrong behaviour. This was the start of human culture. Only *Homo sapiens* has been able to develop culture.

Together the group had more knowledge than any one person could have. We call this 'group wisdom'. All members of the group shared this wisdom.

Early people began to
- share their knowledge,
- talk about their problems,
- think about and understand things in the same way,
- work out together how to solve problems,
- teach their skills to one another.

In these ways, they developed their culture and learned how to work most *efficiently*.

Discussion. What is culture?
What stories did you learn when you were a small child?
What did these stories teach you about right and wrong behaviour?

Technology

Technology is the tools people make and the ways they make them. We have seen how technology changed from the Early to the Middle Stone Ages.

Human beings first evolved more than 100 000 years ago. At that time, there were fewer people in the whole of Africa than live today in a small town. People lived in isolated groups. Each group was far away from any other group. This had advantages. Groups did not fight each other for food or land. It also had *disadvantages*. Groups could not meet to talk and share ideas about better ways of hunting or making tools. Such meetings are necessary for working out new inventions, and for new ways of doing things to spread from group to group. Because people were so isolated at first, developments in technology were very slow.

Adapting

People can adapt to all sorts of environments. They are able to do this because of their brains, *social* habits, language, skills and technology.

Because they can adapt, people are different from all other animals. All other animals are specialized. They can only live in one sort of environment. They can only eat a small number of different foods. They cannot change their habits or way of life. Many animals only live in one sort of area, in one part of the world.

People are different. They are not specialized. People are adaptable enough to live in all sorts of places and climates. Here are some of the ways that people are adaptable:
- People's teeth have evolved in a way that lets us bite and chew all sorts of food, such as fruit and nuts, vegetables, and meat.
- From very early times, people adapted to heat and cold. In cold climates, people learned to shelter in caves, to keep fires burning, to wear the furs and skins of animals, and to use furs as blankets to keep warm. In hot climates, people built shelters of grass and branches to give them shade.

People learned to adapt themselves to all sorts of different surroundings by changing
- the clothes they wore,
- the shelters they used or built,
- the food they ate,
- the animals they hunted and the ways they hunted them.

How have these people adapted to a very cold environment?

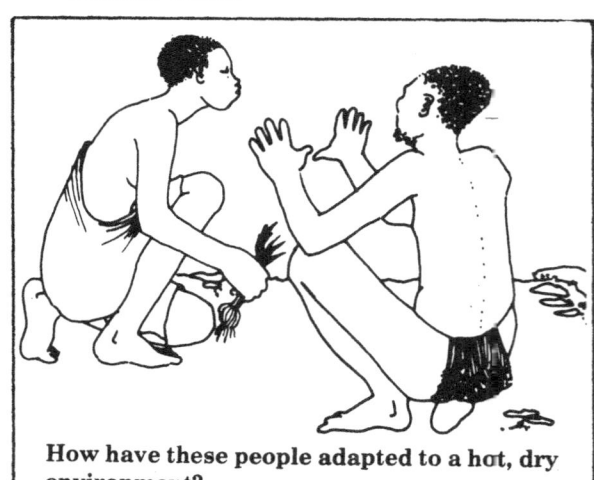

How have these people adapted to a hot, dry environment?

Assisted answers. Imagine that you are a child in a very early hominid society. Fill in the missing words in this description of your daily life.

Every day, the women of our group collect .... for all of us to eat. They carry these things in .... made from the bark of trees. The .... of our group go hunting. They make .... by covering holes with branches and grass. When an animal falls in, they kill it with their ....

On most days, I stay in the .... Here, the old people teach me and the other children to .... tools. Today, I am helping to build a new .... for people to sleep in.

At night, we all sing and tell .... I know one story about a man who did not share the meat from animals he killed. He had to .... the group.

Essay. Explain the importance of sharing food and work in early human societies. You should consider
a) how work was divided,
b) how food was shared,
c) why language was necessary for sharing in these ways,
d) the advantages of co-operation.

Essay. Compare apes and people under the following subheadings:
a) physical appearance and ability,
b) child-bearing,
c) social behaviour,
d) technology.

6. The Late Stone Age

In this chapter:
- We will discuss the primitive communal mode of production.
- We will look at how Late Stone Age people lived together.
- We will learn about their tools, clothes and shelters.

You will need to know the meanings of these words:

character — personality, or particular combination of a person's qualities.

trim — remove or cut off extra pieces, or make edges neat.

bore — make a hole by drilling or digging.

decorate — add to something to make it look more pleasing.

Summary. In chapters 4 and 5, we studied five million years of human evolution. We saw that as hominids and people evolved, changes took place in their bodies, societies and technology.

We ended chapter 5 by looking at *Homo sapiens sapiens*. At first they made Middle Stone Age tools. Middle Stone Age people
- lived together in groups,
- hunted animals,
- gathered wild foods,
- made tools of wood, stone and bone.

Late Stone Age society

As they improved their skills, people developed Late Stone Age tools. The Late Stone Age was the last period in history that people had tools made only of wood, bone and stone.

Society in Late Stone Age times was *communal*. This means that all healthy adults shared the work. Everyone worked who could. All the men did the same work. All the women did the same work.

There were no inequalities in the ownership of property. Almost everything was shared by the group. Only clothes and tools belonged to one person and to no one else. The only differences between people were in their skills, knowledge and *characters*.

Late Stone Age technology is called *primitive*. This means that all the tools were simple. They were made of materials that anyone could find and use. People made tools very quickly and easily. They could throw tools away when a task was done, and make new ones for a new task. Everyone knew how to make and use the tools they needed.

We can describe the mode of production of Late Stone Age groups as **primitive communalism**. All societies that depend on hunting and gathering for their food can be called primitive communal societies.

Discussion. How is a primitive communal society different from our society?

Late Stone Age technology

Archaeologists have found Late Stone Age tools all over Africa. They have excavated most of those tools from the floors of rock shelters.

Late Stone Age people made very small stone flakes and very sharp stone tools from these flakes. Many flakes were shaped like tiny knives. These are called blades. Other flakes were carefully *trimmed* and rounded to make scrapers, no bigger than your thumbnail. They are called 'thumbnail scrapers'. People trimmed some tiny flakes into crescent and triangular shapes.

We call all these tiny tools **microliths**. They were glued into wooden handles. The gum of trees was used for the glue. Microliths were also glued in the end of small straight sticks to make arrows. Many of these arrows were rubbed in poison, made from plants. The poison killed an animal much more quickly than a small arrow itself. Bows and poisoned arrows were new weapons of the Late Stone Age.

Late Stone Age people had other tools besides microliths. Hunters used sharp points made of bone for arrowheads and needles. Women *bored* holes through heavy, round stones. They fixed these on the end of their digging sticks to make them heavier and better for digging. They also used grindstones and hammerstones for preparing nuts and seeds for eating.

Dates

People in southern Africa began to make blades and microliths about 50 000 years ago. The people who made them were possibly the first *Homo sapiens sapiens* to live in southern Africa. They also still made Middle Stone Age tools, such as pointed stone spearheads and big cutting flakes. The new microlithic technology spread slowly. More and more people realised that microliths made good tools and weapons.

People from Kenya to Zambia made and used microliths for all sorts of tasks 19 000 years ago. It was only 10 000 years ago that

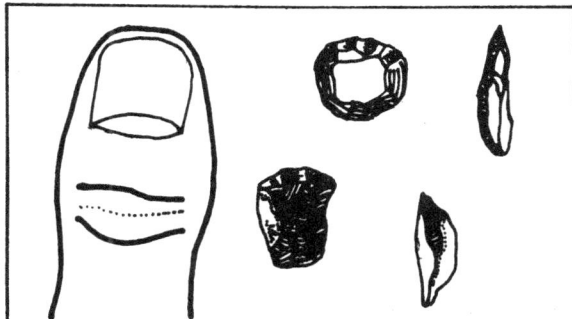

Late Stone Age microliths. Compare these blades and scrapers with the Early and Middle Stone Age tools in Chapter 4. What differences can you see?

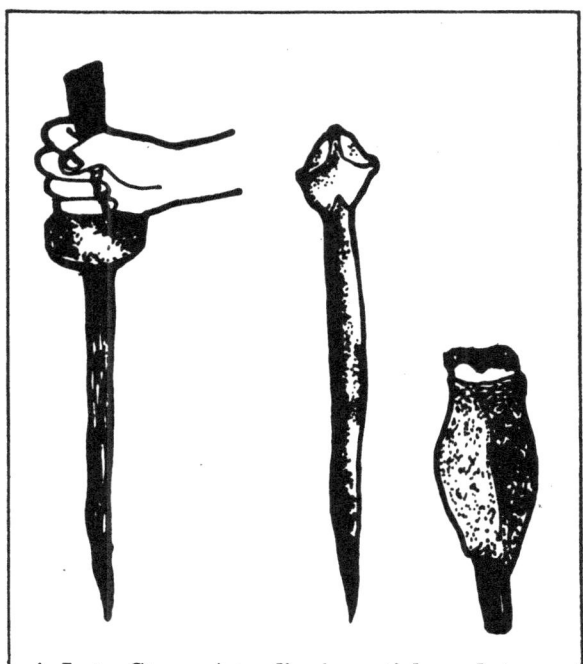

A Late Stone Age digging stick and two arrows.

everyone in southern Africa used microliths for all tools. Some archaeologists date the Late Stone Age from the time blades and microliths were first made — over 50 000 years ago. Other archaeologists date the Late Stone Age from when everyone made blades and microliths — less than 10 000 years ago.

A rock painting of Stone Age hunters.

What did Late Stone Age people look like?

Late Stone Age women wore long skin skirts and carried bags over their shoulders to hold the food they collected. They carried hard, pointed sticks to dig for roots and insects. The men wore small aprons made of animal skins. They *decorated* their bodies with painted patterns. They wore bead necklaces and bracelets made of ostrich egg shells.

The Late Stone Age people built small **shelters**. They used grass and small branches. Families sheltered from the sun in them.

Archaeologists have found skeletons that show that most Late Stone Age people looked exactly like us. We do not know what **language** they spoke. Some probably spoke a very early sort of Bantu language. Others probably spoke early sorts of San and Khoi languages.

The Late Stone Age people were probably the distant ancestors of the people who live in southern Africa today.

Guided answers. What kinds of tools did Late Stone Age people use? Fill in the missing words in the paragraphs.

The most important new tool of the Late Stone Age was the microlith. Microliths are made of .... They are much .... in size than Middle Stone Age tools. Microliths shaped like knives are called ....

Other materials were also used to make Late Stone Age tools. Microliths had handles made of .... They were stuck into the handles with .... made from .... Hunters used arrows and .... made of .... Hunters made arrowheads from microliths or .... The arrows worked better when the hunters rubbed .... on them.

To sew skins together, Late Stone Age people used .... made of .... They put heavy, round .... on the end of their digging sticks.

7. Hunter-gatherers

In this chapter:
We will look at hunter-gatherers today and hunter-gatherers of Late Stone Age times. Hunter-gatherers have a primitive communal mode of production.

You will need to know the meanings of these words:
edible — fit to be eaten.
grub — worm-like insect larva.
snare — catch animals in traps with nooses.
honour — respect, or give respect to.
network — an interconnected system, like a net.
obligation — something one must do, or what one owes to someone else.
territory — large stretch of land controlled or travelled by a person or people.
life cycle — stages in the life of a plant or animal.
mobile — moving or able to move easily.
preserve — prepare food so that it will not go bad or decay.
confident — completely sure.

A San hunter.

Hunter-gatherers today

We have learned why Late Stone Age societies are called primitive communal societies. We have found out that people in these societies lived by hunting animals and gathering other food. Some groups of people today live by hunting and gathering, such as
- the Pygmies or Twa in the tropical forests of Zaire,
- the Eskimos or Inuit in the cold northern part of North America,
- the Indians in tropical South America,
- the Aborigines in the semi-desert of Australia,
- the San in the Kgalagadi desert of southern Africa.

Activity. Find these places on the map of the world.

These groups of modern hunter-gatherers do not all live in the same way. They live in very different environments. They have different beliefs and cultures. But all these people have a primitive communal way of life. They organize their societies in similar ways. All of them use tools made of stone, wood and bone. They have solved the problems of living by hunting and gathering.

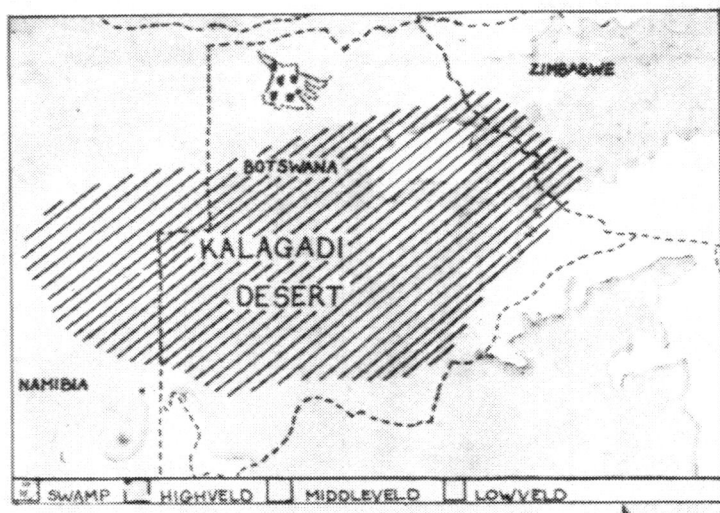

The Kgalagadi Desert.

The San

Today, hunter-gatherers live in the Kgalagadi desert and around its edges, in Botswana, Namibia and the western edges of Zimbabwe. Most of these people speak one of the San languages. Some speak a Khoi language. A few speak a Bantu language.

The San are descendants of Late Stone Age people. Unlike most other Stone Age people, they never became farmers. They remained hunters and gatherers. They kept the Stone Age technology. Over many centuries, they adapted their society, their way of life and even their bodies to the hard conditions of the dry lands in which they live. Today, they are small people with light, yellowish skins.

Scientists study these people to learn about the hunting and gathering way of life. The way that the San live today is similar to the way that Late Stone Age people lived, but not exactly the same.

Most San people today live in the Kgalagadi desert.

Late Stone Age people

The life of most Late Stone Age people was different to the life of the San in many important ways. Late Stone Age people lived in different environments from the San. There were different plants to eat. There were many more animals of many different sorts to hunt. Their life was much easier than that of the San. They could choose all sorts of different ways of getting their food. Different groups could specialize in different ways of hunting and gathering.

How do we know about the Late Stone Age people of long ago?

Our knowledge about the Late Stone Age way of life comes from
- archaeology,
- rock paintings,
- studying San life today. We must always remember that the Late Stone Age people were not San, and that the San are not Late Stone Age people. But both were hunter-gatherers, so we can learn more about the Late Stone Age by studying the San.

Work

Life for a hunting-gathering group was easy. The bush had lots of animals and plant food for those who knew where to look and what to look for. Work was divided between women and men.

Women collected most of the food. Melons, berries, bulbs and other *edible* roots, honey, *grubs*, ants, lizards, tortoises, birds' eggs and small birds were all collected and eaten. The women provided most of the food for the group, often twice as much as the men. There was a lot of food to choose from. They needed to collect only the best and tastiest plants.

The **men** of the group *snared* and trapped small buck for most of their meat. The great excitement came when six to eight hunters went stalking large animals together. They used bows and arrows to hunt large animals such as sable, kudu, eland, buffalo and even elephant.

An animal killed in a hunt did not belong to the hunter who killed it. It belonged to the whole group. The meat was shared. The whole group *honoured* a man who was skilful in hunting large animals. He had the *honour* of sharing the meat out between everyone, when he brought it back to camp.

At the end of the hunt, everyone got some meat. The hunter gave the best bits to people he owed favours, or to men who had helped him most in the hunt. Every hunter shared out the meat he killed. In this way, a whole *network* of favours was created. Everyone remembered these favours and *obligations*.

Hunting big animals was not very important as a source of food. But, because of sharing, it was extremely important in forming the social relations of a group. It united the group. It gave some men the importance and respect that a skilful hunter deserved.

In one day, one person could easily collect or hunt enough food for four or five people. Getting food only took 15 to 20 hours of work each week. Children and young people did not work until they were 15 to 20 years old. Older people also did not need to work. This meant that almost half the people in a group did not have to work at all. Everyone could spend many days
- resting in camp,
- talking and visiting,
- playing with the children,
- making ornaments to wear,
- making and decorating clothes and weapons.

Knowing the environment

Hunter-gatherers lived completely from the environment in a way we do not know today.

They did not store food for the future. The land was their storehouse. They did not have to wait for a harvest. Instead, they moved to the places where wild foods were ripening.

They did little to change nature, except for protecting some plants or burning off old grass so that animals came to graze the new grass. They did not need to alter nature to get what they needed.

Hunter-gatherers depended a great deal on their knowledge of the bush. A group moved over many hundreds of square kilometres during the different seasons. The members of the group knew the whole of their *territory*. They knew
- where the animals were moving to find new grazing,
- what food particular animals looked for in different seasons,
- every place where there was water and when the animals would go to drink there,
- every plant that provided good food, where it grew and when it would ripen,
- the *life cycle* of plants,
- how to protect plants so that the group could return to collect them year after year.

The environment provided the food, clothes, medicines and everything else the hunter-gatherers needed. Knowledge of the environment was the most important thing in life. People often went on journeys round their territory to see what the plants and animals were doing. These journeys gave knowledge, and knowledge gave success. Even hunting skills were not as important as knowledge of the environment.

Today, very few people have so much knowledge about the environment. It is difficult for us to imagine how much hunter-gatherers knew about wild life and plants. Their survival depended on this knowledge.

Activity. Test your knowledge of your own environment. How many different species of plants grow near your school? How many can you identify and name? How many are useful? What are they used for?

Property

Hunter-gatherers had to be *mobile*. They had to move camp every few weeks. They moved
- when the best food nearest the camp was collected,
- when the animals moved away,
- when the seasons changed,
- when other plants ripened in different parts of their territory.

Because they moved round such a lot, people could not have many possessions. They kept only what they could carry easily — their weapons, skin clothes, blankets and baskets. They had as few of these as possible.

Every family had the same sort of possessions. The hunter-gatherers did not believe

The people in this rock painting have been gathering wild food.

that things were the private property of one person. We might say that such people were poor. They did not think this about themselves.

Each group had its own territory, with its own waterholes and river pools. A group's rights to its resources were respected by all other groups. People also agreed that, if times were hard or if the herds gathered in one area, groups could camp or hunt in another group's territory.

Discussion. Do you think hunter-gatherers were poor? Was their life unhappy? Imagine that you are a hunter-gatherer. What do you like about your life? What do you dislike about your life?

Society

Most families had a father, mother and one or two children. A group was usually six to eight families, about 25 people altogether.

Most men in the group were equal. Some had more knowledge and skills than the others. Such men knew about
- animals and plants,
- their people's culture,
- the stories and legends of the people's origins and past,
- medicine and magic,
- how to paint and what the paintings meant.

The group gave more respect to men with knowledge like this. Such respect was given to a man who deserved it. It could not be passed on to his wife or children or family when he died.

Because groups were small, men did not marry women from the same group. Marriage was arranged so that the women came from another group. After a woman got married, she went to live in her husband's group. This gave men power over women. It became the usual pattern of life.

At certain times of the year, 20 to 30 groups met together. More than 500 people gathered. Young men found young women to become their wives at such gatherings.

A rock painting of a dance.

The gatherings of groups were a special time for story telling, singing and dancing. These gatherings strengthened the culture that all the groups shared. In Late Stone Age times, groups gathered in the big, painted caves that we know today.

People could decide to leave their group and join another group. A family might leave their group because they fought with other members of the group or because they felt they were treated unjustly.

Groups did not always keep the same people in them. They did not all stay the same size. Groups in rich territories grew in size. Groups in poor areas became smaller, because only a small number of people could live off the poor resources.

Change

We have seen in this chapter that hunter-gatherers knew a great deal about their environment. They were aware of how to grow, tend and harvest plants. They also knew how to *preserve* their food by
- drying and smoking meat,
- drying and storing nuts and seeds.

In the next chapter, we will see that many groups began to use this knowledge to become farmers. Other groups had the same knowledge, but chose not to settle down and become farmers. They remained hunter-gatherers. They were *confident* that the environment could provide everything they needed.

Guided answers. Compare the lives of San people today and hunter-gatherers of long ago. Fill in the missing words in the paragraph about the San people. Then write your own paragraph to explain how hunter-gatherers' lives long ago were different.

The San people live in a harsh environment, in the .... desert. The climate is very ...., so not many plants grow there. There are fewer .... to hunt.

Essay. Describe the life of a Late Stone Age group under the following subheadings:
a) Men's work,
b) Women's work,
c) Children and old people,
d) Culture.

---

8. Rock paintings

In this chapter:
- We will look at some rock paintings.
- We will find out what rock paintings tell us about Stone Age people.

You will need to know the meanings of these words:
observe — learn about by watching.
admire — have great respect for.
visible — able to be seen.
kinship — closeness in character, as if belonging to the same family.
trance — half-conscious, dreamlike state.
vision — something one thinks one sees, especially something that is not real.
supernatural — not existing in ordinary nature.

The paintings

All over southern Africa, we can find paintings done by Late Stone Age people. They painted pictures in rock shelters and in caves in hills. Some of the paintings may be more than 6 000 years old. Some are only 1 000 years old. These paintings tell us a great deal about Late Stone Age society.

Rock paintings are great works of art. They give us the same enjoyment that other works of art in museums give. They deserve respect and protection.

The artists

Looking at the paintings, we can see that the painters were very skilled. They *observed* the ways of animals very carefully. The paintings are full of life.

The pictures were all painted with crushed earth of different colours. The powders were mixed with animal fat or vegetable gum, to

A woman using a grindstone to prepare food.

Rock painters were very skilled.

45

make them stick to the rock surface. For brushes, the painters used feathers, animal hairs, or the crushed ends of sticks or plants.

What rock paintings can teach us

Rock paintings are primary sources of history. They show us
- the animals that the people most *admired*, such as kudu, sable, zebra, buffalo and elephant,
- how people looked and behaved,
- the clothes they wore,
- the tools they used,
- the sort of beliefs they had.

Many paintings show family groups of mother, father and one or two small children, resting in camp. Their baskets, bags and bows and arrows are carefully laid out around them. Other paintings show men going hunting or women collecting or preparing food.

The paintings were not done for pleasure or to decorate the rocks. The pictures are not only records of daily activities. They also show the culture and beliefs of the society.

A family group.

Paintings were part of the people's religious life.

Paintings were a very important way for the Stone Age hunters to make their beliefs *visible*. From the paintings, the beliefs could be shared with all the society. Children could learn from the paintings. By studying rock paintings carefully, we can also learn much more about the way our Late Stone Age ancestors thought about their world.

Hunters.

People in trances saw visions, such as the strange creatures in the paintings.

People believed that by painting animals their spirits became much closer to the animals' spirits. Hunters felt *kinship* with the animals they hunted. They had great respect for the spirit of an animal they killed. It was important to them to show this relationship through pictures.

Studies of the San people's beliefs help us to understand still more about the rock paintings. The San believe that some people have great powers to heal people, to control wild animals, and to bring rain. Such people dance until they are able to go into a *trance*. People believe that, when someone is in a trance, his or her spirit leaves the body. Dancing, trances, spirit travel, healing and rain-making are very important in San society.

Many strange Late Stone Age paintings show people dancing or lying on their backs or bleeding or with their hair standing up. These people are probably in trances. Other paintings probably show the *visions* that people saw in their trances. They saw things like the spirits of animals or the creatures that they believed brought the rain.

Group project. There are rock paintings in many parts of Zimbabwe. Visit a painted rock shelter as a group. Study the paintings.
How many animals are shown? What species? In what groups?
How many women are shown? How many men? How many children? In what groups? How are they dressed? What are they doing? Are there any *supernatural* creatures or activities shown? Try to find explanations for any strange scenes that are shown.

Write out the information you have collected. Put your group report on the classroom wall, or in the school library, or show it to your local museum.

Guided answers. How did Late Stone Age people paint on rocks? Why did they do these paintings?

The sentences below are in the wrong order. Rearrange them to answer the questions above. You should make two paragraphs.
One reason was to show their daily life.
The artists painted on rocks with feathers or animal hairs or the ends of sticks.
Many paintings show the spirits of people and animals, and the religious beliefs of the Late Stone Age people.
They crushed the rocks and soils, and mixed them with fat or gum.
The painters probably wanted to share these beliefs with everyone in their society, especially the children.
Late Stone Age people made paint from different coloured rocks and soils.
Late Stone Age artists probably had many reasons for painting their pictures.
This made the colours stick to the rock surface.
Hunting was an important part of Late Stone Age life and hunters wanted to show their respect for animals by painting them.

9. The change to farming

In this chapter:
We will ask How did farming first develop? We will look at the advantages and disadvantages of farming.

You will need to know the meanings of these words:

reject — refuse to accept.
companion — someone who lives or works with you.
nourishment — healthy food.
secure — reliable, or safe from danger.
unrest — disturbance or trouble in a society.
permanent — lasting or staying in one place always.
fertile — very productive land that grows good crops.
investment — putting money or labour into something that will give a profit in the future.
erosion — the washing away of the soil by rain or river water.
irrigation — putting water on the land.
fallow — land left uncultivated for one or more seasons.

How did farming develop?

Farming developed from the knowledge of hunter-gatherers. In chapter 7, we saw how much hunter-gatherers knew about their environment. They understood how to protect plants and encourage them to grow. Farming developed from such knowledge.

Farming was not a sudden invention. It developed slowly.

Stone Age societies had the knowledge to farm. But they needed a reason to change from hunting and gathering to a new way of life. Some groups began to farm. Some groups *rejected* farming. Some herded animals but grew no crops. Some groups tried farming only in good seasons.

What activities can you see in this painting of village life?

At first Stone Age people were not very interested in settling down in a village and starting to farm. Hunting and gathering had too many **advantages**.

- As hunters and gatherers, people had an easy life with very little work to do.
- Hunting was exciting and brought men honour and respect.
- People could choose when to hunt or gather food.
- People could change groups if they did not like their *companions*.
- Hunters and gatherers got an immediate return for their work. At the end of a hunt, hunters had the dead animal for meat. At the end of a day of collecting, gatherers had food ready to eat.

Disadvantages of farming

Compared to the life of a hunter-gatherer, farming has many disadvantages.

- Farming is harder work.
- Farming is less interesting.
- Farmers have to work regularly for long hours at fixed times of the year.
- Farmers get a delayed return. They have to wait for a long time after planting before they can harvest any food.
- Farming requires a new way of thinking. It requires planning. Farmers have to plan what food to plant. They do not harvest until many months later. They have to store food to feed themselves between harvests.
- There was little variety of food. At first, farmers only knew about one or two crops. People did not like eating the same food all the time. Often the food provided the wrong sort of *nourishment*. This made people weak. They got diseases more easily.
- Farming was less *secure*. Crops often failed because of drought or disease. Farmers could not be sure that they would harvest enough food.
- Farming caused new diseases. Village water often became dirty because it was used by many people for a long time. The water attracted insects and mosquitoes. These brought disease.
- Farming caused social *unrest*. The first farmers built villages of *permanent* houses. When people lived in villages it was difficult for a family to move away and join another village. There were more arguments between people. People had to develop new ways to settle disagreements. They had to find ways of uniting the people of their village.

Farmers have to store food. Grain can be stored in bins like these.

The first farmers settled down in permanent villages. What is the woman in this drawing doing? What is the structure behind her? Why is it built on stones? What is the woman using the pots for? Why are the pots different shapes?

Advantages of farming

The main advantage of farming is that people can get more food from less land. A farmer can grow more food on a piece of land than nature provides on the same piece of land. Instead of hunting and collecting food over a vast territory, people can grow all the food they need on a much smaller piece of land.

People no longer have to move round. They can settle down and build houses that last. They can live in bigger groups, in permanent villages. They can do this anywhere, not just in very *fertile* environments such as lake, river and sea shores. Because people do not have to move, they can have more possessions.

Land can be an *investment* for farmers. This means that the harder people work to improve their land, the better their crops. The way that farmers use and improve their land depends on the soils. Farming can be intensive or extensive.

Definitions

Intensive farming. Farmers can improve land with fertile soils in many ways. They can cut down trees and bushes, and burn them. They can collect stones and move them off the land. Often, they pile the stones up to make walls. These walls hold soil and water, and prevent *erosion*. Farmers can dam rivers and dig *irrigation* channels to lead water to the fields. With hard work, farmers can improve the soil year by year. They can continue to grow good crops on the same piece of land.

Extensive farming. In many parts of Africa, the soils are not very fertile or rich. The rain washes the soil foods away. Where there is plenty of land, the farming is not intensive, but extensive. Farmers plant crops on cleared land for a few years until the soil becomes exhausted. Then they clear new land. They leave the old lands to lie *fallow* until the soil recovers. Sometimes there is no new land left near a village, and so the village moves a few kilometres to fresh lands.

Discussion. What does a traditional farming family need in order to farm? (In other words, what are their means of production?) Make a list.

Assisted answers. Imagine that you are a hunter-gatherer. Explain why you do not want to become a farmer. Start with paragraph 1. Complete the other paragraphs yourself.

1. We get our food by hunting and gathering. When I collect fruit and insects, we can eat them the same day. When the men go hunting, we can eat meat the same day. But if I become a farmer, I will have to work and wait for some months before I can harvest and eat the food I grow.
2. We do not have to work very hard to get enough food for our group ....
3. We know a lot about the plants and animals of our territory. We know that we will always get enough to eat from our environment ....
4. If I want to, I can spend some days playing with the children and telling stories ....
5. We eat many different kinds of food ....
6. If we do not want to stay in our group, my family can join another group ....

---

10. The first farmers

In this chapter:
We will look at the ways in which early farmers produced the things they needed. This period is also called the Early Iron Age.
The first farmers had a primitive communal mode of production.

You will need to know the meanings of these words:
domesticate — tame and bring under human control.
temporary — lasting only for a short time.
texture — how something feels when you touch it.
migration — movement of a group or society to a new and distant place.
criticize — find faults.
introduce — give knowledge of something for the first time, or bring something for the first time.
experiment — test or try something.
rarely — very seldom or hardly ever.

Dates

It is very difficult to say when farming first started in southern Africa. Farming did not start suddenly. It was a slow process of change. Scientists cannot tell us when farming started. They very seldom find the remains of the first crops that people grew.

We know that Stone Age people in northeast Africa had settled in villages and made pottery by 6000 BC. There were farming villages near Lake Victoria by 400 BC and in parts of Zambia by 100 BC. By AD 200, farming had started in many parts of Zimbabwe, in southern Mozambique, and in the lowlands of Natal.

The change to farming in southern Africa probably started about 400 BC, when Late Stone Age people started to herd flocks of sheep. By AD 500, the process of change was still not complete. Many groups still lived by hunting and gathering until about AD 1100.

Technology

The first farmers did not need many tools. They cleared land by burning down trees. They used sharpened sticks to dig and weed. Their tools were still simple and easily made.

With only simple tools, early farmers had to choose land carefully. They chose open land with few trees and light soils. They were able to cultivate only a small area. They could store only a small amount of the grain they harvested. The stored grain probably rotted after a few months.

Discussion. Before they had iron tools, why could farmers only cultivate:
- open land with few trees?
- light soils?
- small pieces of land?

Think of ways that farming could change once farmers had iron tools.

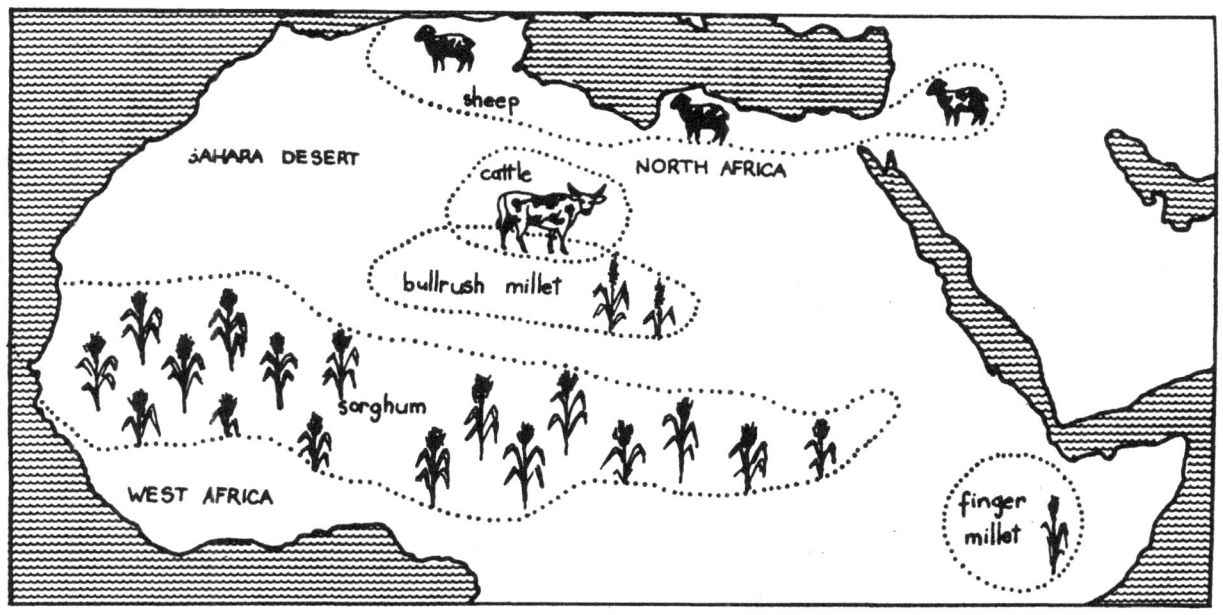

The first crops grew wild in the grassland of west Africa. Wild sheep and cattle lived in North Africa and the Sahara.

Crops

The first farmers grew sorghums, millets and cow peas. These once grew wild in the grasslands of west Africa. Early farmers protected these wild grasses. In this way, they developed the crops we know today. The crops gradually spread from west to east and southern Africa.

Animals

The wild ancestors of sheep, goats and cattle lived in south-west Asia, North Africa and the Sahara. Early farmers in these areas tamed the animals. They penned them up, kept them away from wild animals, and bred them to give better meat and milk.

There were no wild sheep, goats and cattle in east and southern Africa. Like the first crops, *domesticated* animals gradually spread to east and southern Africa. In southern Africa, Late Stone Age herders had domesticated sheep by 400 BC.

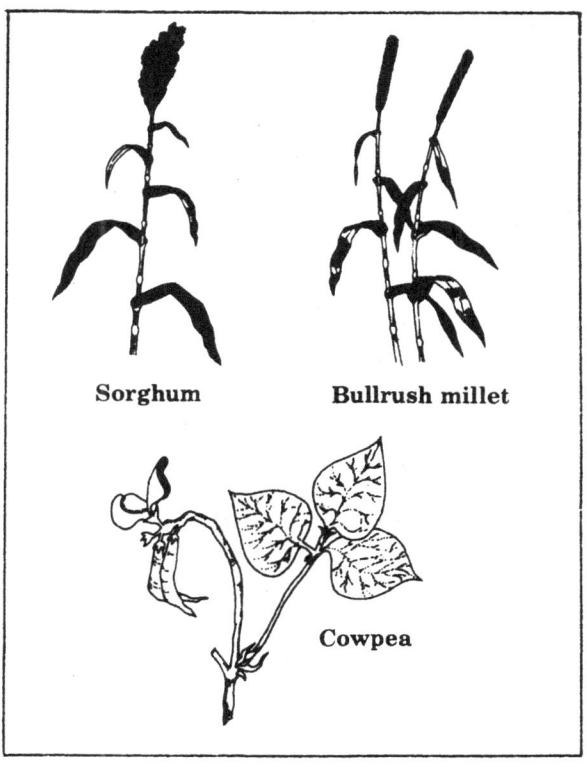

The first farmers used digging sticks like these to clear and weed the land.

Discussion. In chapter 7, we learned about hunter-gatherers' knowledge of their environment. How did farming develop from this knowledge? What did people need to know to be able to domesticate plants and animals?

Houses

The first farmers built only *temporary* shelters. Like the Stone Age hunter-gatherers, they made shelters with grass roofs and grass walls, and poles at the corners. These shelters were so small that people used them only to sleep in at night.

Later, people started to make proper houses. They used many more poles. They tied the poles together and plastered them with mud daga.

Pottery

When people began to settle in villages, they were able to develop pottery. Farmers needed pots to store and cook their grain crops. They needed pots to brew the beer that they made from grain. They ate and drank from pots.

The early farmers designed and made beautiful pots. They carefully drew patterns in the wet clay before the pots dried. They burned the pots in a fire to harden them. This is called 'firing' the pots.

The first pottery was very carefully designed, decorated and fired. Skilled craftworkers must have made this pottery. They must have spent a great deal of their time making pots to become so skilled. They probably worked for many different villages. They were semi-specialists.

Different sorts of pottery

The first farmers in southern Africa made many sorts of pottery with many sorts of

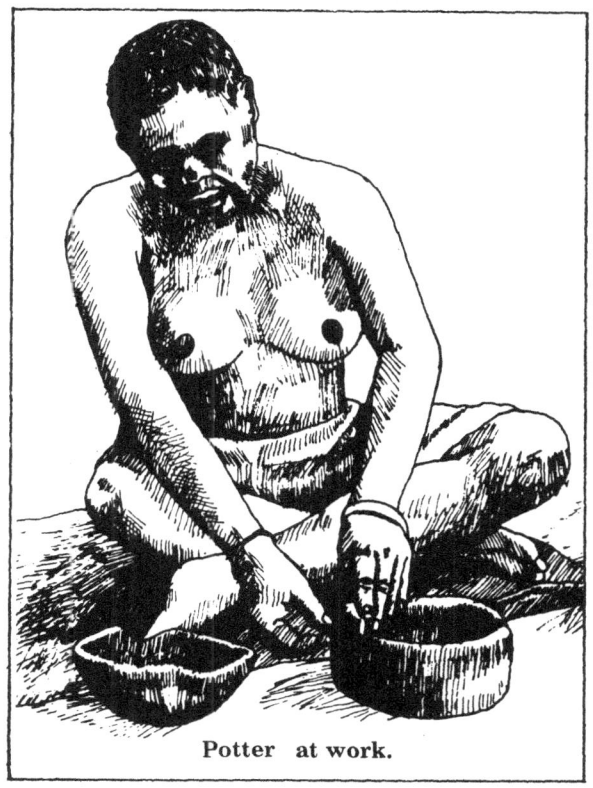
Potter at work.

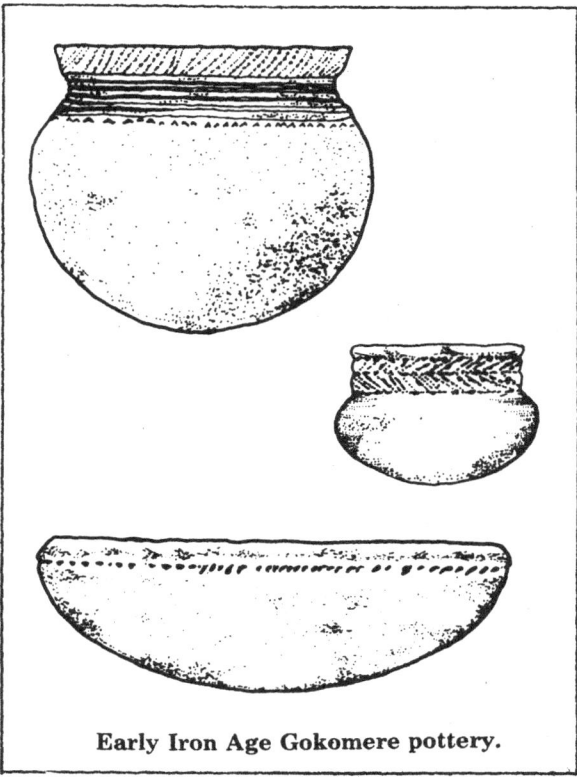
Early Iron Age Gokomere pottery.

patterns. Archaeologists compare and describe this Early Iron Age pottery. They draw maps to show where different sorts of pottery were made.

The different sorts of pottery show that there were cultural differences. Some of these differences may have been very small. Some may be invented by archaeologists. These differences may not be very important in understanding a people's history. Although groups in different areas made different sorts of pottery, they all had the same
- way of life,
- mode of production,
- technology,
- farming methods and crops.

Archaeologists have named some of the pottery made by the first farmers in southern Africa.
- Chinhoyi pottery of northern Zimbabwe,
- Gokomere pottery of southern Mashonaland and Matebeleland,
- Ziwa pottery of Nyanga and parts of Mashonaland,
- Dambwa or Kumadzulo pottery of Victoria Falls and south-west Zambia.

Project. Make a collection of traditional pottery or pieces of pottery. For each pot, describe the colours, shape, *textures*, decoration, tools used in decoration. Draw the different sorts of pots. Can you tell what each sort of pot was used for? How old is it? If you can, ask a traditional potter to tell you how pots are made and used.

Historical argument: Were there migrations?

Historians disagree about how farming spread in Africa.

1. Some historians say that farming was invented a few times in a few places in the world. They say that people *migrated* from those places and took the new invention with them. They say that farming spread through Africa in this way. Their explanation is called the **theory of Bantu migrations.** This theory says:
- Few important changes take place inside any society. Instead, migrating people take changes with them.
- Farming spread to east and southern Africa when some people migrated from the areas of early farming (like the northern edge of the grasslands of east or west Africa, or Ethiopia or the Sudan or Egypt).
- Pottery, metalwork, crops, animals and village life were all brought to southern Africa by these Bantu people from the north, who were the ancestors of the Shona, Ndebele and other Bantu-speakers.
- The Late Stone Age people were the San. The Bantu-speakers drove out the San and settled in their land.

The evidence for this theory is that people in many parts of Africa.
- made similar pottery,
- grew similar crops in similar ways,
- herded the same animals,
- spoke Bantu languages.

2. Other historians *criticize* this evidence. They agree that domesticated crops and animals were *introduced* to east and southern Africa from elsewhere. But they say that:
- Things like this can spread from neighbour to neighbour, without large numbers of people actually migrating.
- The **bones** of most of the Late Stone Age people in Zimbabwe are just like those of Zimbabweans today. They were not San. There is no proof from bones that new people came to Zimbabwe.
- **Languages** grow and exchange words and sounds with each other in a slow and complicated way. We cannot say that Bantu languages started in any one place at one particular time. There is no proof from languages for the migration theory.
- The **pottery** of the first farmers only shows that pots made by neighbours were more alike than pots made by potters working far apart. So there is no proof from pottery that new people came to Zimbabwe.

These historians explain the beginning of farming in another way. They say:
- All human societies are inventive and adaptable. All human societies can grow and change.
- Most changes come from within society itself. Changes are caused by the conflicts between the old and the new in society.
- Stone Age hunter-gatherers developed many different ways of living.
- Farming developed gradually, through *experimenting*. In this process, people gained knowledge and skills.
- Migrations of large numbers of people moving great distances will almost always destroy a society. People only migrate if there is a very powerful reason. Migrations rarely take place. So historians must have a lot of evidence to prove that a migration did happen.

These theories show different views of what people and societies can do. More evidence is needed before everyone agrees which theory is correct. This is one example of the way that our understanding of history grows and changes.

Iron and copper

Pottery was not the only craft that developed with the new way of life. Most farming villages were able to get a little iron. They made small iron arrowheads for hunting, so they no longer needed microliths. They also had a little copper to make bracelets and necklaces.

The knowledge of iron and copper smelting spread to southern Africa about the same time as new crops. We are not sure when or from where this knowledge came.

Copper and iron were not very important at first. People still used bone points on their arrows and made shell beads in the old way to decorate themselves. They still used sticks to dig up roots and bulbs to eat. They also used sticks to hoe their fields.

The first farmers were also the first people to make and use iron in eastern and southern Africa. So they are called **Early Iron Age** people.

The first farmers of Early Iron Age probably spoke Bantu languages. There were probably many different early Bantu languages. These Bantu languages were all related to each other. Scientists do not yet agree about how the Bantu languages are related to each other.

Discussion. The first farmers had a primitive communal mode of production. What does this tell you about:
- the way work was done?
- their technology?

Activity. Have a debate in your class. The topic is 'Farming was introduced to Zimbabwe by migrants from distant lands'. Choose one speaker to support this view and one speaker to oppose it. Everyone in the class should prepare their ideas carefully so they can take part in the discussion. Make sure that you give reasons for all your opinions.

Essay. What are the differences between hunting and gathering, and farming? Begin your answer by explaining how farming developed from hunter-gatherers' knowledge of the environment. Then compare hunting and gathering with farming, under the following subheadings:
a) work,
b) technology,
c) way of life,
d) art and culture.

Essay. Describe the pottery of the Early Iron Age farmers in southern Africa. Write short paragraphs to answer these questions:
a) How did Early Iron Age people make and decorate pots?
b) What materials did they use?
c) What were the pots used for?
d) Did everyone in Early Iron Age societies make pots, or only specialized craftworkers? What is the evidence for your answer?

11. Developments in farming

In this chapter:
> We will discuss the ways that farming societies had changed by AD 1100. The period after AD 1100 is called the Later Iron Age. We will learn how Later Iron Age farmers
> - lived and worked in family groups, called homesteads,
> - mined and traded iron, copper and gold.
>
> Later Iron Age farmers had a lineage mode of production. We will study this in chapter 12.

You will need to know the meanings of these words:

purely — entirely or only or without anything else added.

specialist — someone who makes their living or spends all their time doing one particular thing.

semi-specialist — someone who spends a lot but not all of their time doing one particular thing.

trade — exchange goods for other goods or for money.

compete — be in competition, or struggle to be better than or to get something from someone else.

dwelling — house.

smelt — separate metal from its ore. (The process of iron smelting is explained in this chapter.)

essential — absolutely necessary.

thresh — separate the grain from the chaff (waste) by beating it.

winnow — blow or shake the grain from the chaff in the air.

stunted — small because growth has been slowed down.

surplus — what is left over after what is needed has been used.

forge — hammer into shape when red hot.

establish — set up or start.

molten — melted or made liquid by heating.

luxury — something pleasing but not necessary.

ornament — something used to add beauty or decoration.

independence — not being dependent on or controlled by or influenced by others.

Changes

Between AD 500 and AD 1100, farming in southern Africa developed in these ways:

1. Farming became more skilful and efficient. People grew more and more different plants. They cultivated more and more land.

2. Few communities remained *purely* hunter-gatherers. Almost all groups began to farm. People could rely on farming for all the food they needed.

3. Cattle herds increased in numbers. People owned more and more cattle.

4. More and more people used iron for spears, axes and hoes.
5. People began to mine copper and gold.
6. Groups became less self-sufficient. People began to depend on *specialist* and *semi-specialist* craftworkers. They could no longer produce everything they needed themselves. They started to *trade*.
7. Society was changing. People were no longer equal as they had been in primitive communal groups. Powerful people became chiefs and rulers.
8. Communities grew bigger. The population of farmers increased. Groups of people began to think of themselves as members of a tribe. Different groups or tribes began to *compete* for land for farming, grazing and hunting. Different groups began to raid each other for cattle and grazing land.

These changes did not happen suddenly. They were gradual. By AD 800, southern African societies had begun to change in these ways. By AD 1100, the changes were complete.

We will now look at southern African societies after AD 1100. This period is called the **Later Iron Age.**

The homestead

Land was farmed by family groups. We call each family group and its *dwellings* a homestead.

The homestead grew all the food that it needed. The family got most of their meat from sheep, goats and cattle, not from hunting. They built their own houses. They made most of their own tools and clothes. They were almost self-sufficient.

Discussion. Are we self-sufficient in our lives today? How many of the things we use are made by semi-specialists and specialists? How many of the things we need are
- made by our families?
- got by exchange within our group?
- bought in markets or shops?

All the men of the village working together to catch fish.

Work

Men cleared the land for farming and built the houses. This was hard and heavy work. Sometimes, one family asked all the men in the village to help in such work. They organized communal work parties. All the men in the community joined together in communal hunting, especially in game drives.

Young men herded the cattle and protected the fields from animals such as baboons. Men made the farming tools and the spears, arrows, snares and nets for hunting.

Some men were specialist craftworkers. They *smelted* iron and copper and wove cloth. They traded these things with other communities.

Women did a lot of the *essential* work. They looked after the babies and brought them up. They planted, hoed and weeded the fields. They reaped, *threshed* and *winnowed* the grain. They stamped and ground the grain to make meal. They prepared the food for the whole homestead. They made beer to reward the communal work parties. Many women made pottery.

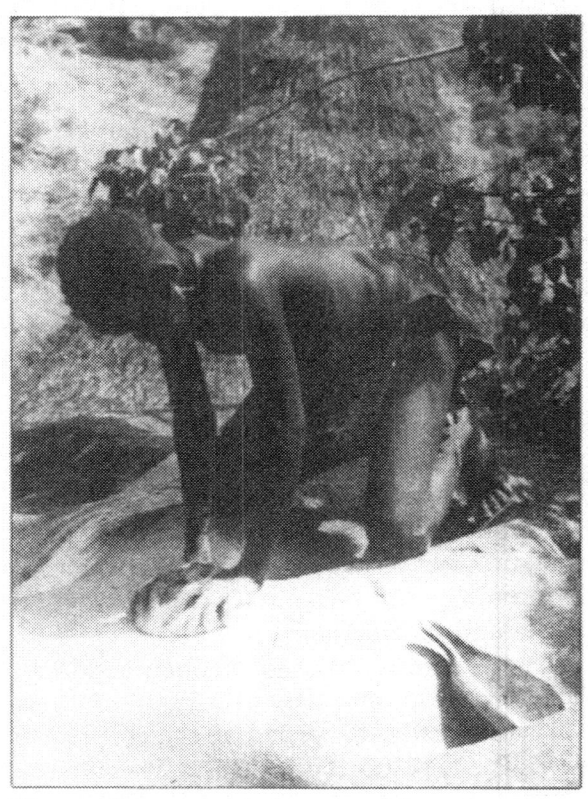

Women did much of the essential work, such as grinding the grain.

Communal threshing.

Houses

People no longer lived in small grass shelters. Each homestead had several houses. There were separate houses for the head of the homestead, for each wife, and for the growing boys and girls. There were other houses for cooking and eating. There were storage bins for the different crops. In some homesteads, each woman had her own bins. There were also pens for animals.

Land

There was enough good farming land for anyone who wanted to use it. Most of the land could only be used for extensive farming. Farmers planted crops on the same piece of land for a few years only. When the soil lost its fertility, farmers could not control the weeds. The crops became weak and *stunted*. Farmers then had to clear new lands.

The land belonged to the whole community. People said:

A homestead could use a piece of land for as long as it wished. When the family moved, that piece of land again belonged to the community. Another homestead could cultivate it.

No one could buy or sell land. No one could give land to relatives outside the homestead. Land did not belong to one person or family. Land was not private property. No one could become rich and powerful because they owned large pieces of land.

Cattle

For many centuries, farmers had kept sheep, goats and cattle for meat and milk. Gradually, the number of cattle increased.

When a homestead was successful, with many women working in the fields and good crops, the homestead had more food than it could eat. The *surplus* food could not be stored because grain stored in bins rotted after a few months. It was much better to exchange surplus grain for cattle. These cattle had calves, and herds increased even more.

Iron

By AD 1100 many communities had heavy iron tools and weapons. Iron smelting needs great skill. Ordinary people could

- help to build the iron smelting furnace,
- burn wood to make charcoal,
- dig, carry and crush the ore,
- *forge* the raw iron.

But ordinary people could not smelt iron. Iron smelting needed the skill of a master smelter. People could only learn iron smelting skills by training for a long time with someone who was already a smelter. Not every community, certainly not every homestead, had a master smelter.

Iron ores can be found in many places. But the best ores are much rarer. Iron smelting industries were *established* in places with the best ores. Here, smelters learned their skills. They moved to communities that needed their work for a short time. They often carried iron tools with them. They traded these with communities that had no smelter.

With iron axes and iron hoes, it was much easier and quicker to clear and till the land. But most homesteads could not make their own iron tools. They had to trade for iron tools or get master smelters to come and make tools for them.

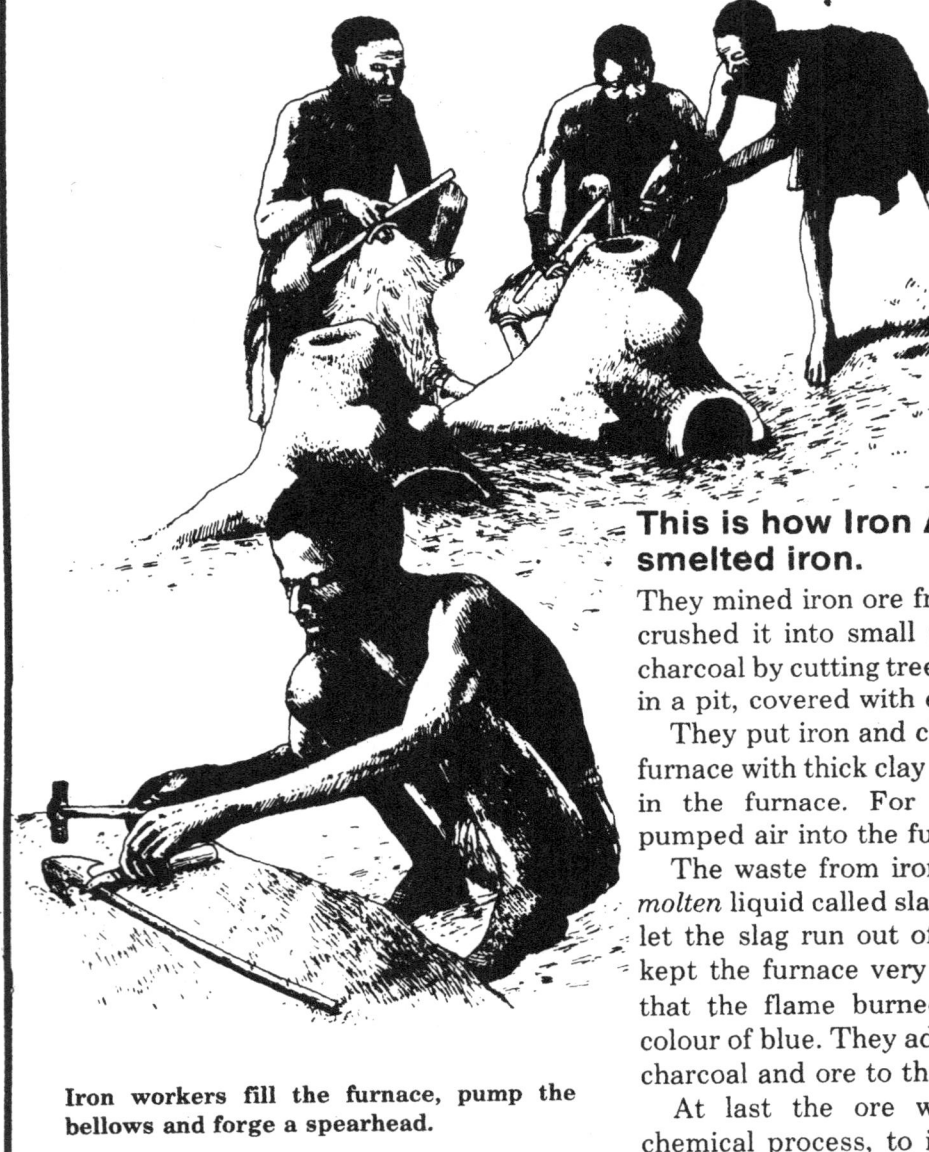

Iron workers fill the furnace, pump the bellows and forge a spearhead.

This is how Iron Age people smelted iron.

They mined iron ore from the ground and crushed it into small stones. They made charcoal by cutting trees and burning them in a pit, covered with earth.

They put iron and charcoal into a small furnace with thick clay walls. They lit a fire in the furnace. For many hours, they pumped air into the furnace with bellows.

The waste from iron smelting is a hot, *molten* liquid called slag. The iron smelters let the slag run out of the furnace. They kept the furnace very hot. They checked that the flame burned exactly the right colour of blue. They added more and more charcoal and ore to the furnace.

At last the ore was changed, by a chemical process, to iron. A big lump of raw iron (called bloom) was taken out of the bottom of the furnace. The bloom was taken to the forge. There people heated it again and again on the forge fire. Each time they heated it, they hammered it while it was red hot. Eventually, it split into separate pieces. They reheated and beat each piece again and again until it was the shape of the tool they needed.

Copper

Copper ore is only found in a very few places in eastern and southern Africa. Copper was smelted like iron. People made copper needles and wire. With the wire, they made necklaces and bracelets to wear on their arms and legs. These were *luxuries,* not necessities, but people liked them very much. Communities traded these luxuries.

Pottery

Most pottery of the Later Iron Age was simpler than the pottery of the Early Iron Age. The shapes of the pots were easier to make and there was much less decoration on them. The pots were not as hard and well fired as before. This shows that each homestead now made its own pottery. It was no longer made by semi-specialists. A homestead did not need to make pots very often, perhaps only every year or two. The potters had little chance to practise their skills.

So, by studying the changes in the pots, we can tell that the organization of production changed.

Archaeologists have given names to various styles of Later Iron Age pottery in Zimbabwe.
- Leopard's Kopje pottery is found in southern Matebeleland.
- Round Harare, many graves grouped together in large cemeteries were filled with pots. These are called Harare pottery.
- Musengezi pottery is found in the north. Many people were buried in caves with this pottery. It has more decoration than other Later Iron Age pottery.

Gold

Gold is carried in rivers that flow over gold deposits. Villagers who lived near these rivers dug for gold. They spent a few weeks each year, when they had no crops in the fields, looking for gold.

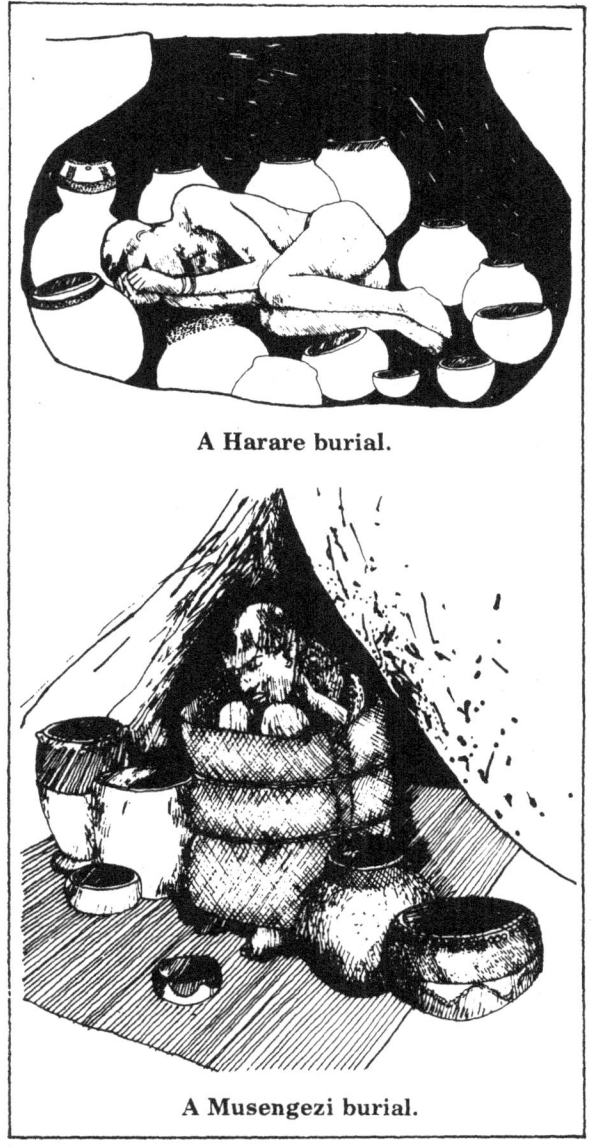

A Harare burial.

A Musengezi burial.

The men took mud and gravel from the sides and beds of the rivers. Some even dived for it in deep pools. The women washed the mud away to get the grains of gold. They used shallow, carved, wooden trays to do this.

Gold is very soft. The villagers could make it into *ornaments* without heating it.

Gold is found in rocks. Rain washes some of the gold into rivers, sand and mud. Here people can collect it. Other people dig mines into the rock to reach the gold.

Trade

From about AD 900, villagers began to trade their gold with foreign traders. Swahili traders came from
- the east African coast,
- the Zambezi river,
- towns like Sofala and Sena.

The foreign traders exchanged cloth and glass beads, from places like India and Arabia, for gold. This trade became more and more important as the Later Iron Age progressed.

At the beginning of this chapter, we learned that each homestead was almost self-sufficient. A homestead could produce most of the things that it needed, such as houses, wooden tools, seeds, clothes and pottery.

We have also seen that each homestead was not able to produce everything that it needed. Specialists made iron for tools and weapons. In many places, people could not get salt. Salt was traded over long distances.

How does trade change society?

Societies change when they start to trade and specialize. The organization of society becomes more complex. Trade and specialization help society to develop in many ways. But there are dangers.

Trade destroys the *independence* of a community. Instead of being self-sufficient, a community begins to depend on goods produced by specialists or in other areas.

If one group gets control of the trade, this group can force producers to sell their products at unfairly low prices. The same group can force people to buy goods at unfairly high prices. In this way, trade can become an **unequal exchange**. So trade can lead to inequality and exploitation.

A chief selling meal to a foreign trader.

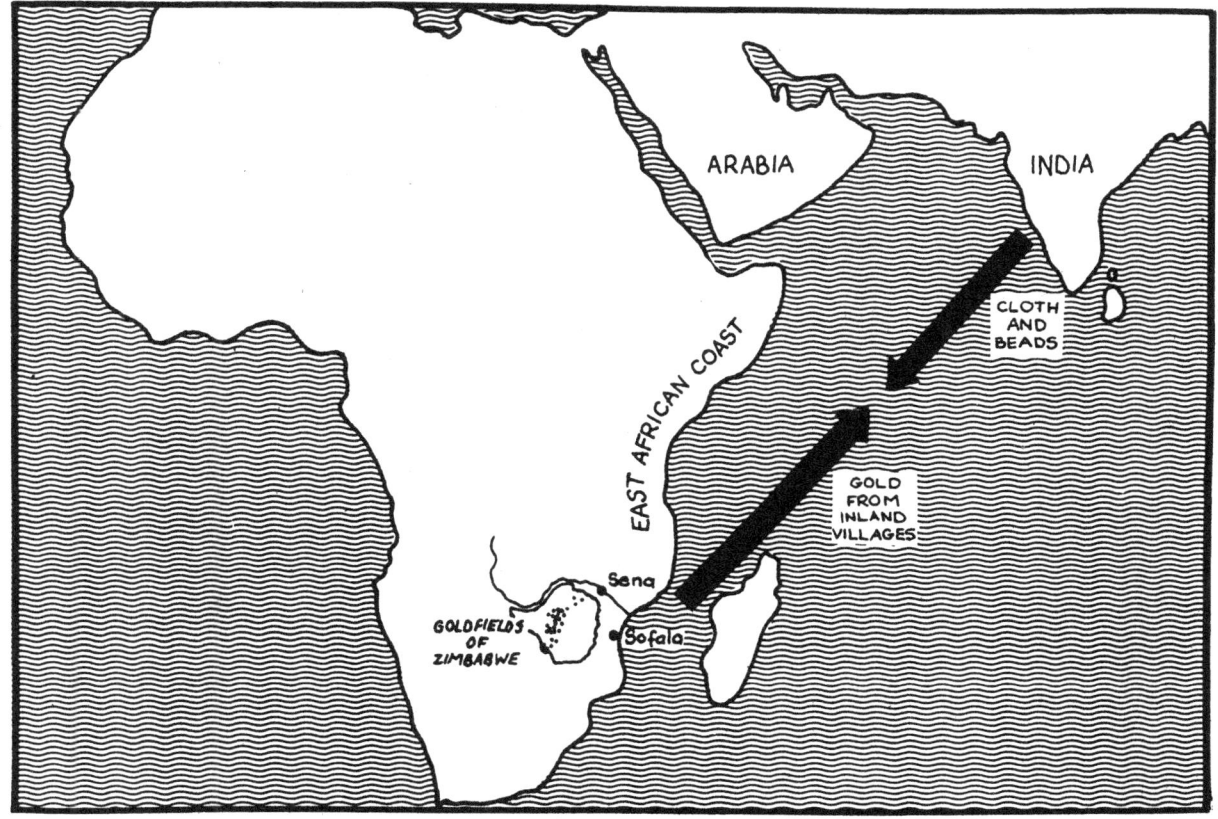
Early gold trade.

Assisted answers. What are the differences between the Early and Later Iron Ages in:
a) tools?
b) crafts?
c) cattle?
d) property?
e) population size?

Begin your first paragraph like this:
a) Early Iron Age hunters used iron arrowheads, but most tools were still made of stone, wood and bone. In the Later Iron Age,..................................

Project. Interview a traditional craftworker who knows how to do one of the following:
- smelt iron or copper,
- make pottery,
- wash for gold,
- weave baskets or mats or cloth.

Write a report on the craft.

Essay. Describe a homestead and its work, under the following subheadings:
a) members,
b) division of work by sex and age;
c) property,
d) products.

12. Lineages

In this chapter:
> We will see how Later Iron Age homesteads belonged to lineages.
> We will find out how work was divided in the lineage mode of production.
> We will discuss the start of inequality and exploitation.

You will need to know the meanings of these words:

senior — older, or more important or more powerful.
junior — younger, or less important or less powerful.
hide — animal's skin.
sacrifice — offer something to gods.
ensure — make sure or certain.
effect — result.
client — someone who depends on or is supported by a patron.
patron — a wealthy or powerful person who gives support or protection.
slave — a person who is owned by another person. (You can read about slavery in chapter 29.)
despise — feel scorn for, or consider worthless.

Lineage societies

By the start of the Later Iron Age, most people in southern Africa lived and farmed in homesteads. All homesteads belonged to a lineage. A lineage was like a very large family.

All the people in a **community** believed that they were descended from one ancestor. In the traditions of most communities, the ancestor was a great hero of very long ago.

In each community, there were many **lineages.** All the people in a lineage believed that they shared the same ancestor. They believed that this ancestor was related to the ancestor or founding father of the whole community.

Some lineages were *senior* to others. People believed that the ancestor of a senior lineage was closely related to the founding father (his brother or son, for example). The

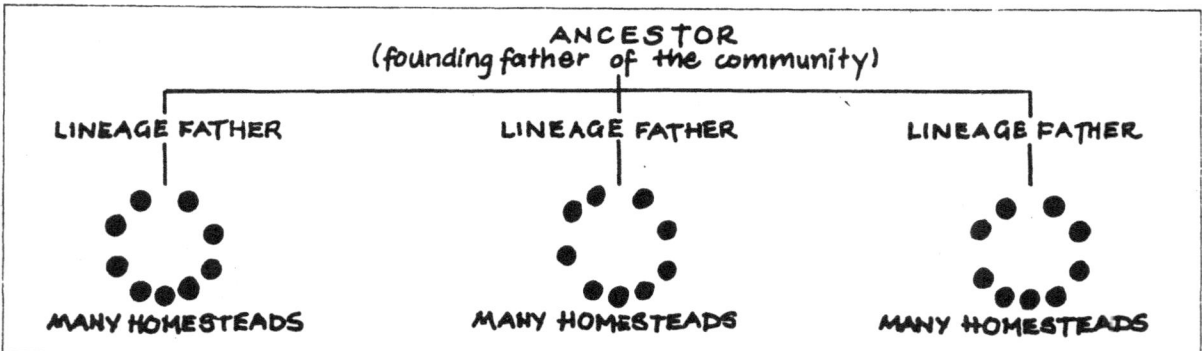

This diagram shows how a community was organised like a very large family. This is the sort of organization we call a lineage system.

ancestor of a *junior* lineage was believed to be only distantly related to the founding father (his grandson, cousin, nephew or son of his younger brother, for example). Chiefs were chosen from the most senior lineages.

The **men** of a homestead — the fathers, brothers and sons — all belonged to the same lineage. They shared their lineage with many other homesteads. A man could not marry a woman from his lineage. He had to marry a woman from another lineage. His wife came to live in his homestead.

Women kept the lineage they were born into, the lineage of their father. A married woman did not take her husband's lineage. Children had the same lineage as their father.

So everyone believed that they belonged to a single family. Each person belonged to a homestead. Each homestead belong to a lineage. Each lineage was part of a community.

To understand how these lineage relationships worked, we will look at cattle, bridewealth and marriage.

Discussion. What are the differences between a homestead and a lineage?

Cattle

Cattle provided milk, meat and *hides*. But they were also important in other ways.

- People *sacrificed* cattle to the ancestors to ask for rain and good crops.
- They sacrificed cattle to the ancestors at funerals.
- They used cattle as bridewealth in marriage exchanges. The homestead exchanged cattle for wives for the young men.
- Cattle were eaten at wedding feasts.

Herders took great pride in their cattle and decorated them with jewellery.

We can see that cattle had a **social value.** This was even more important than their economic value.

Cattle did not belong to the whole community like the land did. But very few cattle belonged to just one person. So cattle were not really private property. Most cattle belonged to the lineage. If anyone wanted to sell or exchange cattle outside the lineage, they had to ask the whole lineage.

The old men or elders of the lineage had a lot of power. They decided what happened to almost all the cattle in all the homesteads of their lineage. This gave the elders special power because cattle were so important in marriage exchanges. When a young man wanted to marry, he had to ask the elders of his lineage to give some cattle to the young woman's lineage as bridewealth. The elders of the young man's lineage and the elders of the young woman's lineage had to discuss and agree to this.

Discussion. Do you belong to a lineage? How far back can you trace your lineage? Who was its founder? How is it related to other lineages? Do you know any of your lineage's traditions?

Bridewealth and marriage
Bridewealth was very important in farming societies. It had many good points. It *ensured* that women were secure and respected. Bridewealth had social value.

When a young woman married, her homestead lost her labour. But her homestead got more cattle from her husband's lineage as bridewealth.

In a lineage society, one man could have more than one wife. This is called polygamy.

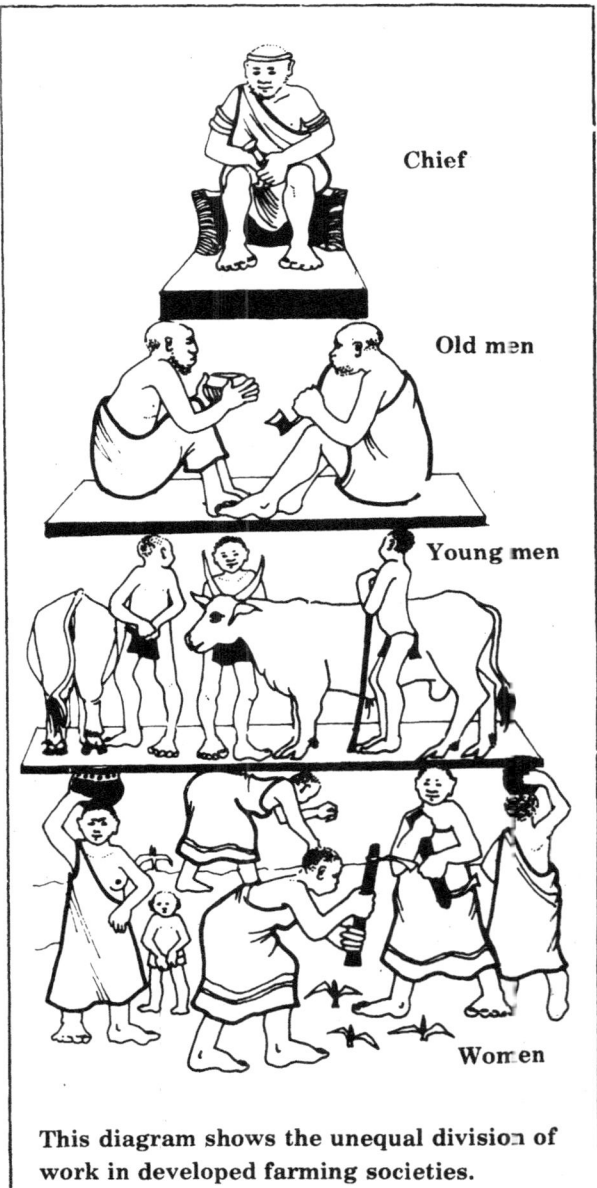

This diagram shows the unequal division of work in developed farming societies.

We have seen that the women did most of the work in the fields. So if the men married more wives, the homestead could grow more crops and buy more cattle. More wives also meant more children, so the homestead increased in numbers.

Activity. Draw your family tree. Show all the relatives and ancestors that you know about. How many generations back do you know about on your mother's side? How many on your father's?

Work and inequality

The lineage system had many important *effects*. It led to the first real inequalities between people. What were these?

1. Although the young men did all the work of looking after the lineage's cattle, the chiefs and elders controlled the cattle.

2. Lineages were not equal and marriage exchanges were not equal. A chief could ask for more bridewealth when a young woman of his lineage married. A senior lineage gave fewer cattle when their young men married women from a junior lineage. So senior lineages could increase their wealth in cattle more easily that junior lineages. More and more of the cattle belonged to the senior lineages.

3. Women did much of the work. They looked after the children and crops. They prepared the food. But they had few rights in their husband's homestead or lineage. Their children belonged to their husband's lineage. The work that the children did and the cattle they brought when they married benefited their father's lineage and not their mother's.

Inequality means that people with more power can exploit people with less power. The lineage system brought exploitation.

Discussion. Look at the three sorts of unequal relationships above. In each one, who had more power? Who was exploited? In what ways did powerful people benefit from the work of less powerful people?

Wealth

We can see that people were no longer equal. Chiefs had more wealth. This meant
- they had bigger and better-made houses,
- they had more land under cultivation,
- they had more wives to work in their fields,
- they ate more beef,
- they had more beer,
- they could organize more communal work parties because they had plenty of beer to reward the work parties,
- they could trade for more iron tools, copper jewellery and cloth.

In the same way, senior lineages lived better than junior lineages.

These differences did not set people completely apart. Everyone still did the same sort of work. Everyone shared in communal work. The wives of chiefs and elders worked in the fields. All young men, whatever their lineages, hunted together and herded the cattle.

Were there different classes in lineage societies?

Although people were not equal in a lineage society, they were not divided into separate classes.

There were not separate classes because no single group completely owned the resources. No single group had complete power over another group. People all believed that they belonged to a single family, the lineage.

Essay. Describe the features of a lineage mode of production, under the following subheadings:
a) control of resources,
b) division of work,
c) relations of production.

Re-read the discussion of material causes in chapter 2. It will help you to select the information you need for this essay.

The Khoikhoi

We have learned how farming societies of eastern and southern Africa changed and developed. These farmers were Bantu-speaking people with a developed Iron Age technology, organized in a lineage system.

This system also developed among peoples of different languages, race and technology. An example is the Khoikhoi or, shortened, the Khoi. The Khoi people look very much like the San. Many people believe they belong to the same race as the San. The Khoi languages also sound similar to those of the San. They are very different languages from Bantu. Many Khoi speakers remained hunter-gatherers, for example, the Khoi speakers in the Kgalagadi.

The Khoi are best remembered as herders of sheep and cattle. They never settled permanently in one place. They moved with their herds of cattle through the mountains and coastal plains of western Namibia and the southern part of South Africa. Every season they moved to different areas, to get the best grazing for cattle. Their movements followed a regular pattern.

They used the milk of their sheep and cattle for food. They killed their livestock only for religious sacrifices. They used their oxen to carry their belongings and mats when they moved. They used the mats to make their houses. They had a Late Stone Age technology. They made no metal tools themselves. They traded iron and copper jewellery with farmers.

Their society was organized in a similar way to the farming societies we have just studied. Like the farmers, the Khoi communities saw themselves as part of a large family descended from a founding father. They had chiefs, elders, and senior and junior lineages. A Khoi community under one chief could include many hundreds of people.

Khoi society was unequal. This inequality was increased because many Khoi had San *clients*. The San clients hunted and worked for Khoi *patrons* in return for meat, milk and protection. They were a separate class within Khoi society.

The Khoi lived in large groups of up to 100 people. They were able to live in much larger groups than any San hunter-gatherers because their herds provided a more reliable source of food than hunting wild animals did.

The Khoi usually stayed in one place long enough to build houses of mats and branches. They also developed crafts like pottery and the weaving of house and sleeping mats. Their camps were often quite big, with about 30 houses. The houses in the camp were laid out in a careful order. Each lineage lived together. Each house was placed in order of seniority. The houses were placed round the cattle which were herded into the middle of the camp at night.

Khoi society was destroyed three centuries ago by the early European settlers in South Africa. At first, the Khoi tried to survive as traders, trading goods between the Europeans and the Iron Age farmers. But they were soon driven from their traditional grazing lands. The Boers raided them, captured them and forced them to become *slaves*. The Khoi were *despised* and called 'Hottentots', by the Boers. In a few years, the whole of Khoi herding society vanished from South Africa.

The Khoi herders are an example of a very different people from ourselves. They had a very different technology but they developed social relations similar to those we know.

A painting of a Khoi camp.

Discussion. What are the differences between hunting and gathering societies (like many San societies), and herding societies (like most Khoikhoi societies)?

Discussion. What are the differences between equal societies, unequal societies and class societies? It will help you to look at chapter 2, where we discussed classes and class struggle.

Essay. Compare the primitive communal and lineage modes of production, using the following subheadings:
a) division of work,
b) co-operation,
c) control of resources,
d) units of production.

Chiefs and their families had more possessions than other people.

71

13. Ruling classes

In this chapter:
- We will see how classes first developed in southern Africa.
- We will discuss the ways the ruling class began to control cattle, iron production, gold mining and foreign trade.
- We will describe the tributary mode of production.
- We will look at the way traditions supported the new rulers' power.

You will need to know the meanings of these words.

tribute — goods, money or labour given to or demanded by a ruler or ruling class.
porter — someone who carries things.
expedition — a number of people travelling together for a particular purpose.
trample — tread on or crush underfoot.
highveld — level grassland more than 1 200 metres above sea level.
lowveld — level grassland less than 900 metres above sea level.
management — the way that something is controlled or organized.
armed — supplied with or carrying weapons.
collapse — fall down suddenly.
worthwhile — resulting in enough benefit to be worth doing or producing.
coral — hard substance made by tiny creatures in the sea.
possessed — occupied or dominated by a spirit.
initiation — being introduced into or allowed to become part of a group.

The first classes

In chapter 12, we saw how inequalities and exploitation began to develop in lineage societies. We saw that senior lineages became more powerful and owned more and more cattle. But the society was not divided into classes. Now we will see how classes began to develop in farming societies.

Chiefs and senior lineages increased their power even further. They gained control of important resources:
- larger herds of cattle,
- iron working,
- gold mining,
- foreign trade.

As a result, inequalities increased. Also people could now be divided into two classes — a ruling class and a class of farmers and villagers. The ruling class controlled many resources.

The ruling class were chiefs and senior lineages who gained control of cattle, iron production, gold mining and trade. With their increased power, they exploited the rest of the people in new ways. People had to produce surplus food to give to the ruling class as *tribute*. Here are some of the ways that ordinary people worked for the rulers:

- In many villages, there were rulers' fields. Everyone had to spend part of their time cultivating these fields. All the crops from these fields belonged to the rulers.
- Young men were often away from their homesteads. They herded and guarded the rulers' cattle herds.
- Young men also spent part of the year building the rulers' houses.
- Women spent some of their time digging and carrying clay for the rulers' houses. They helped to make and decorate the daga work.
- Men went as *porters* and guards on trading *expeditions*.
- Hunters had to give one tusk from every elephant they killed to their ruler.
- People who washed for gold had to give part of each day's washings to their ruler. If they found a large lump of gold, they had to give it to the ruler.

We can see that these changes meant a new way of organizing production. We can call it a **tributary mode of production** because the farming class gave food and labour to the chiefs as tribute.

In this chapter, we will see how farming societies developed a tributary mode of production.

Cattle

In chapter 12, we learned that cattle had great social value. They were important for sacrifices, bridewealth and feasts. So those who controlled the cattle had a lot of power in their society. They had control over people's most important activities.

As the number of cattle increased, it became more and more difficult to find

Rulers depended on other people's work. At Great Zimbabwe, craftworkers produced beautiful clay pots and stone dishes like these for the ruling class.

enough good grazing near the villages. The cattle had to be kept away from the growing crops, which they might *trample* and eat. To overcome these problems, all the cattle were brought together in large herds. Young men were put in charge of the herds.

The young men took the cattle far away from the fields to good grazing lands. They protected the cattle and the grazing lands from attack by other people. They moved the cattle quite long distances each season. In summer, the cattle grazed the new grass on the *highveld*. In winter, the young men moved them to the bush grazing of the *lowveld*. The disease-carrying tsetse flies that lived in the lowveld were no danger in winter.

This *management* of cattle was easiest when all the cattle were under the control of a single manager. In this way, a few people gained control of more and more cattle. Eventually, most of the cattle belonged to what people called the rulers' herds.

The young men who guarded the cattle were *armed*. It was easy to organize them into raiding parties. Strong raiding parties stole cattle from weaker people. These stolen cattle were not divided up among the young men. They became part of the rulers' herd, because the ruling class organized the raiding parties.

Iron

Exercise. Choose the correct ending for each sentence.
1. The best iron ore was mined
   A. in many places.
   B. in a few places.
2. Iron smelting skills were known to
   A. a few people.
   B. many people.
3. Iron tools made farming
   A. easier.
   B. more difficult.

Iron hoes and axes became even more important to farmers. They were almost as important as cattle. Iron tools began to have social value. They were used as sacrifices to the ancestors, and as bridewealth.

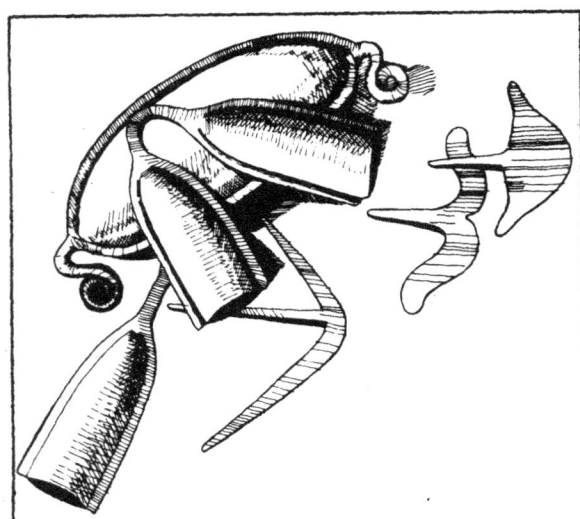

Iron craftworkers made gongs and axes for their rulers to use in ceremonies.

The ruling class gained control of iron production. They demanded food and work as tribute from the farmers. The rulers rewarded them with tools. We can see that control of iron production gave the ruling class more power over the farmers.

Gold

Exercise. Answer these questions.
Who were the first people to collect gold?
How did they collect the gold?
Did they collect gold all year round?
What was the gold used for?

Gold was not very important to farmers because
- it was too soft to be used for making tools,
- copper for making beautiful ornaments was easier to find.

The people who really wanted gold were foreign traders from the Indian Ocean. These traders sent the gold to India, which was a great world centre for gold trading. In India, the gold was made into jewellery and coins. The coins were used in trade throughout the world.

The traders wanted more and more gold. The gold that the village farmers washed from the rivers was not enough. The real source of gold had to be found.

Gold deposits were found in rocks in some parts of Zimbabwe. These areas are called goldfields. People dug **mines** into the rock. They cracked and split the rock with iron hammers and chisels or by lighting fires against the rock. In these ways, they made deep pits and tunnels.

Mining was hard and dangerous work. Many tunnels *collapsed* and killed the miners. Often, miners worked very hard, but found little gold. Few people wanted to mine. The

A miner sitting at the bottom of a mine. He hammers out the ore and puts it in a basket to be pulled up to the surface.

ruling class had to force or reward people to do this work. Only the ruling class could give rewards. They gave cattle to the miners for the gold. The ruling class organized gold mining because
- they controlled the foreign trade,
- they had enough cattle to exchange for gold.

Trade

For at least 1 000 years, foreign traders have wanted Zimbabwean gold. It was difficult for them to get it. This is what traders had to do:
- make sure that there was enough gold collected in one place to make an expedition inland *worthwhile,*
- collect a lot of trade goods to exchange for gold,

This drawing shows gold miners at work. At the bottom, people are crushing the ore and two women are washing the ore to get the gold. At the top is a trader buying gold from the chief.

- form an expedition from the coast, with men to guard the goods and guides to show them the way,
- pay tribute in towns and villages they passed through, for the protection of the rulers there.

Sometimes, the people inland formed their own expeditions. They took gold to the coast to exchange with the foreign traders. Then the inland traders had to pay tribute for protection and reward the porters, guards and guides.

Only the ruling class were able to
- organize expeditions to trade at the coast, or
- collect a lot of gold in one place inland to exchange with the traders' expeditions.

So the ruling class gained control of the foreign trade. In this way, they also gained control of gold mining.

What goods did the traders bring? They brought
- coloured and embroidered cloth, woven in India,
- glazed pottery made in China and Persia (Iran),
- glass beads, made in factories in India,
- a lot of beautiful but useless things, such as sea shells and *coral*.

Most of these goods were kept by the ruling class. The only goods that reached ordinary villagers were the beads. They were pretty, but not useful. They were not used for production or tribute or bridewealth. They were not necessary to society.

Discussion. Do you remember what we learned about trade at the end of chapter 11? How did trade encourage specialization in lineage societies?
How did foreign traders benefit from the gold trade?
How did the ruling class inland benefit from the gold trade?
How did ordinary villagers benefit from the gold trade?

How the new ruling class increased their power

The new ruling class were the old senior lineages and chiefs and elders. They had power because they controlled many of the things that were necessary to the life of the villagers. The ruling class also used many of the old traditions and *institutions* of society to strengthen their power.

Definition. The word 'institution' can mean many things. When we use it in history we usually mean social institutions. These are laws, beliefs and organizations that control the way people behave.

Some of the old institutions of lineage societies were changed slightly to support the new rulers:
- People asked the ancestors to increase the fertility of the land and to send rain. The rulers now took over these duties. This increased their power.
- People believed that spirit mediums spoke for the ancestors. Some spirit mediums were *possessed* by the ancestors of the rulers. These mediums now became very important. They spoke to all the people in a large area. The messages and importance of these mediums added to the power of the rulers.
- In some communities, there were *initiation* schools. In these schools, all young men or all young women of all lineages were taught the traditions of their society. After this, they were considered to be adults. Initiation schools taught children about the rulers' power.
- Other communities had brotherhoods or secret societies. People of all lineages belonged to them. Some of these societies served a particular god. Others had particular duties, such as keeping order, or hunting. They all became servants of the ruling class.
- In other communities, everyone of a particular age belonged to an age grade. These also served the ruling class.

The rulers used initiation schools, secret societies and age grades to encourage loyalty and support for the ruling class.

Ruling class life

The ruling class now became separated from the rest of the people. The ruling class had a different way of life.

The families of the rulers no longer worked in the fields. They got their food from the villagers' tribute.

Village life

Life for ordinary people was not very different from before. The ruler now decided what land a farmer could cultivate. But there was still enough land for everyone. The one big change was that the rulers took part of each homestead's food, time and work. In return, people benefited in these ways:

- A powerful ruler gave protection and safety to everyone in the community.
- People were proud of being members of a powerful community.
- With good management, the community's cattle herds increased. People knew that these cattle provided bridewealth for their young men. Also, cattle were killed for everyone to eat at important festivals.
- Many people got glass beads as a result of the gold trade.
- Because the people paid the tribute, the rulers had a lot of food. They used some of this to support craftspeople. These craftspeople made iron tools and weapons, copper jewellery and cloth. So such goods were better made and easier to get than before.

As we can see, the tributary mode of production gave far greater benefits to the rulers than to the ordinary people. The ordinary people were exploited by the rulers.

Did ordinary people feel exploited?

People did not understand that they were exploited by the ruling class. They still felt that they were part of the same great family as their rulers. The ruling class never controlled the land. People still believed it belonged to the ancestors and that they could farm it as they wished.

It was in the interests of the ruling class to keep the support and loyalty of the rest of the people. The rulers knew that they depended on other people's work. Everyone knew that a ruler's power did not reach very far from his town. People knew that they could move out of reach of a harsh ruler. They could join another community somewhere else. This prevented the ruling class from behaving harshly.

Essay. Describe the beginning of the gold trade between Zimbabwe and foreign traders. Your description should include the answers to these questions:

a) Who produced the gold? How did they produce it at first? How did their methods of getting the gold change? Why did they change?

b) Who wanted the gold? What did they bring to exchange for the gold? Why did they want the gold?

c) Who benefited from the gold trade? Did the producers benefit? Did their rulers benefit? Did the foreigners benefit?

14. The state

In this chapter:
We will ask: What is a state?
We will look at
- the relations between states,
- early African states.

You will need to know the meanings of these words:

create — produce or make or bring into existence.
feature — distinctive or special part of something.
capital — main town or city of a state.
enforce — use force to make sure that something is done or obeyed.
confiscate — take away by force or by right or authority.
governor — someone who rules or controls, on behalf of a higher ruler.
invade — enter as an enemy.
slight — small, not very much.
ally — a person or group which supports another.
corrupt — rotten or dishonest, or accepting favours dishonestly.

What is a state?

When a society is divided into separate classes, the ruling class has to *create* organizations which help it to control the rest of society. A community or country with such organizations is called a state.

All states have some things in common:
1. The society is divided into separate **classes**. This is the most important *feature* of a state. (A state may also have people of different races, customs, tribes, cultures and religions. But this does not always happen.)
2. A state has many **officials** to manage it. These include religious specialists like priests or mediums. Other officials are soldiers, builders, tribute collectors and traditional historians. All officials work for the state and support the power of the ruling class.
3. A state has a definite **territory** under its control. It defends its territory against enemies. Some states were very small. In the past, many cities were independent states. Most early states had a territory that stretched about 50 to 100 kilometres from the town that the ruler lived in. This town was the *capital* of the state. Today, most states are nation-states. These have very big territories. They are separate and independent countries.
4. A state takes part of the **surplus** produced by some classes, such as farmers, traders and craftspeople. This surplus is sometimes called 'tribute' and sometimes 'tax'. The state uses this surplus to support the ruling class, state organizations and officials.
5. A state makes **laws** to control society. A state may use force to make sure that people obey the laws; to collect tribute and taxes; and to keep order. The state uses law courts, soldiers and police to *enforce* its laws.

Relations between states

In history, we study the relations between different classes in a society. We also study the

The ruling class and officials consult with the ruler of an east African state at his capital.

relations between different societies or states.

A powerful state can exploit weaker states. It can do this in many ways. A powerful state can demand tribute in crops, cattle or crafts from a weaker state. If tribute is not paid, it may raid the weaker state and *confiscate* the goods.

A powerful state may place members of its ruling class at the head of a weaker state. It may send officials as *governors* of the weaker state. In this way the powerful state makes sure that the weaker state obeys it.

A powerful state may send a great many of its people to settle in the weaker state, and take control of its land, economy and production. This is called colonization. The weaker state becomes a colony of the stronger state. (We discussed colonization in chapter 2.)

A strong state together with the weaker states that it exploits are called an empire. The empire is usually given the name of the state in control, for example the British empire.

Early states in Africa

States developed in Africa in the same way as they did everywhere else. A state developed within a society to meet the needs of that society to grow and organize. Each state developed in very small steps.

States did not develop because of new technology. Nor were they copied from other societies. A very few states grew because one group *invaded* another group and became a ruling class.

The power of states in Africa was often *slight*. Many states lasted for only one or two centuries. This is a short time in world history. Many states in Africa shared the same weaknesses:

1. The land was the most important means of production or resource. Many African states did not control the land. These states could only increase their power by getting more people to give the state part of their labour, as herders, soldiers, builders and miners. People's work was the state's strength. But if people felt that the state was oppressing them, they could move away to new lands. So the state's power was limited.

2. In many states in Africa, disputes broke out when a ruler died. Often, the senior families of the ruling class each wanted one of their members to be the new ruler. Each family tried to find *allies* to help them. Some asked other groups in the state to support them. Some called on allies from other states. Some even asked complete outsiders, such as the early Portuguese invaders, to help them in their fight. Such disputes always divided and weakened the state. Often *corrupt* people gained control of the state, as a result of disputes. Such people owed too many favours to those who had helped to put them in power.

15. Great Zimbabwe

In this chapter:
We will study the state which had its capital at Great Zimbabwe.
We will discuss
- the lives of the ordinary people,
- the lives of the ruling class,
- the *architecture*,
- its relations with other states,
- the end of the state at Great Zimbabwe.

The state at Great Zimbabwe had a tributary mode of production.

You will need to know the meanings of these words:

architecture — art or science of building; style of building.
unique — being the only one of its kind, or having no others like it.
courtyard — space enclosed by walls.
royal — belonging to a king or queen.
treasure — collection of wealth or valuable things.
mason — someone who builds with stone.
altar — flat-topped block for sacrifices or religious ceremonies.
mould — form into shapes or patterns.
symbol — mark or sign that shows or stands for something else.
privacy — being out of public sight.
represent — stand for, or be a sign of.
mortar — a mixture or cement for joining bricks and stones.
fortification — strengthened building for defence.
advertise — make something generally or publicly known.
prestige — importance or influence.
route — way taken for travel between one place and another.

Great Zimbabwe was the centre of a very early African state. It was one of the greatest African states. It had a tributary mode of production.

The architecture of Great Zimbabwe is *unique* in the world. It was created by the people of Zimbabwe, alone and unaided.

Because Great Zimbabwe is so old we have no reliable traditions from the time that it was built. We know about it from its archaeology and architecture.

Dates

Great Zimbabwe did not happen suddenly. It had a long history. Early Iron Age farmers lived at Great Zimbabwe over 1 500 years ago.

From about AD 900, people in eastern Botswana and south-western Zimbabwe were developing class societies. People were organized to work together. They built the first towns in southern Africa. (We will learn more about these towns in chapter 21.) About AD 1100, Later Iron Age farmers built a village on the hill at Great Zimbabwe. By AD 1200, the whole population at Great Zimbabwe was organized to do communal building work.

The settlement on the hill was surrounded by a high wall made of granite blocks. This stone wall was built in about AD 1200. About 100 years later, the ruler's home was moved from the hill to the valley below. In the valley, the ruler's home was enlarged again and again. More and more houses, *courtyards* and stone walls were added. Soon after AD 1400, a single, huge, outer wall was built round the whole group of buildings. It is called Imba Huru which means 'the Great Enclosure'.

During all this time, other members of the ruling class were building more and more homes in the valley round the ruler's home. Each was surrounded by its own stone wall. About AD 1450, the power of Great Zimbabwe ended.

For over 200 years, Great Zimbabwe was probably the largest city anywhere in Africa, outside Egypt. It was the capital of a well-organized, wealthy, powerful and long-lived state.

The lives of ordinary people

About 10 000 ordinary people lived in the valley at Great Zimbabwe. They lived outside the stone walls that we see today. Their houses were built of wood and clay. These houses fell down and were buried long ago. Archaeologists have excavated only very few of them.

What work did ordinary people do? Some were farmers. Their land lay round the city. Many farmers had a very long walk to their fields every day. Not everyone had land or farmed. There was not enough land within reach of the city for everyone to farm.

Some men were herders. They were away from the city for many months of the year, moving the ruler's herds from one grazing place to another.

Some people were specialist craftworkers. The rulers provided houses and food for these craftspeople.

Copper was brought to Great Zimbabwe from the mines of Hurungwe, in the north of Zimbabwe. Craftspeople made copper beads and wire bangles. Everyone wore at least a few. Craftspeople beat some copper into ornamental spears and axes, to be used in ceremonies.

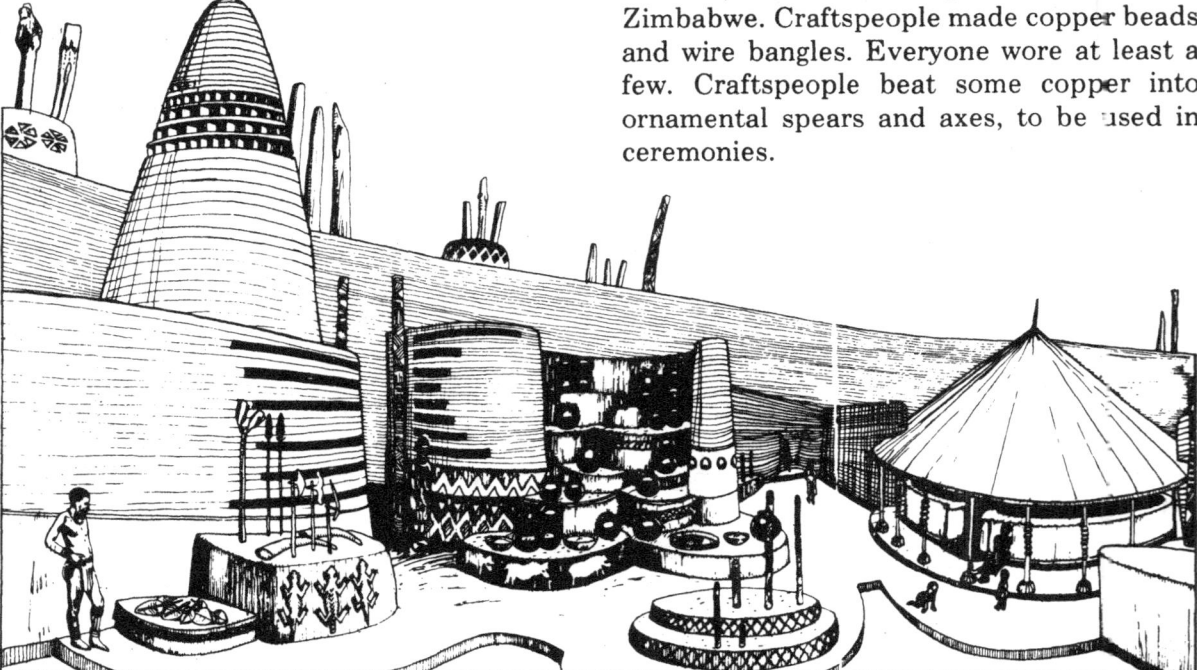

This drawing shows the Great Enclosure, as it might have looked more than 500 years ago.

In this photograph, we can see the Great Enclosure and other walls of the city.

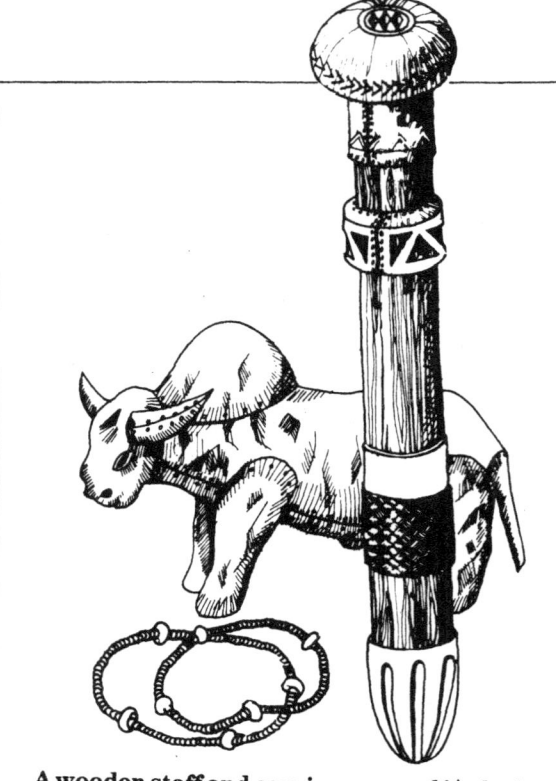

A wooden staff and carving covered in sheets of beaten gold.

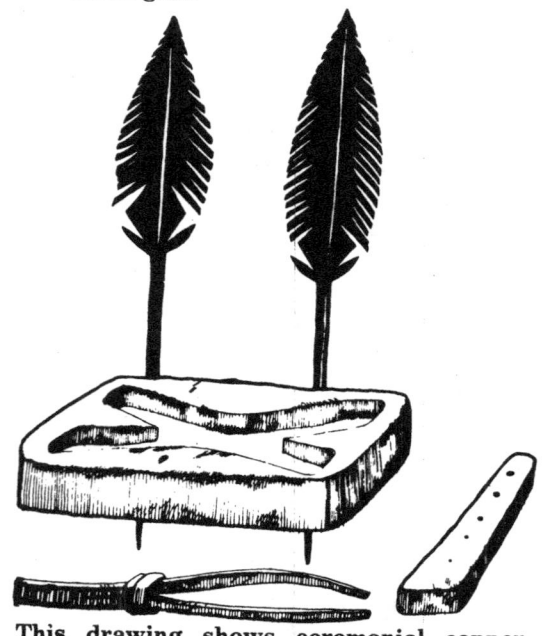

This drawing shows ceremonial copper spears and the tools that coppersmiths used to make copper wire for jewellery.

Gold was brought from the goldfields of Matebeleland and northern Mashonaland. Craftspeople made some of the gold into beads and jewellery for the ruling class. They beat some gold into thin sheets to cover wooden carvings and the handles of spears and axes. A lot of the gold was traded with foreigners.

Iron workers worked at furnaces and forges outside the Great Enclosure. Archaeologists found almost 100 kilograms of ceremonial hoes and axes in a *royal treasure*. They also found small bars of iron ready to be forged into tools. Such items were given to the ruler as tribute, perhaps by the iron workers, or perhaps by townspeople or tributary people from further away.

Cotton was woven into cloth to wear and to use as blankets.

Some people were carvers in wood and stone. They made the eight famous Zimbabwe birds and many very big, flat, ceremonial dishes. They carved these from a soft local stone called soapstone. There were probably many more carvings in wood and stone. These have now been destroyed and lost.

A few *masons* worked throughout the year, fitting stone blocks in to build walls round the ruler's homes.

For a few weeks each year, all the men and cattle herds returned to Great Zimbabwe. This was probably a time of ceremonies and religious feasts. Many cattle were given to the city people to be sacrificed and eaten by everyone. Many were probably given as rewards for labour. The bodies of many cattle, killed as sacrifices, were found on an *altar* inside the Great Enclosure.

When the men were at home and the fields had no crops, the men helped the stonemasons for a few weeks. They carried stones and split them. The stone blocks were used to enlarge the stone walls surrounding the homes of the ruling class.

Cattle being sacrificed on an altar at Great Zimbabwe.

The Eastern Enclosure on the hill looked something like this more than 500 years ago.

Discussion. The builders of Great Zimbabwe.
Who built the walls?
What time of year did they build them?
How were they rewarded for building?
What did they do the rest of the year?
How long did they spend building?
Who were the walls for?
Were the builders slaves?

Ruling class life

The ruling class was very small compared with the rest of the population. There were about 40 stone enclosures in the city. Each one surrounded the homestead of a family of the ruling class. There were about 300 members of the ruling class at Great Zimbabwe.

Spirit mediums were also members of the ruling class. The small enclosures on the hill were probably their homes and spirit houses.

The ruling class lived in houses with very thick walls of clay. The walls were polished, and painted and *moulded* with all sorts of designs. Inside, hearths, pot-stands, seats and bed-platforms were all made of the same polished clay. The houses and courtyards were surrounded by walls of stone. The stone walls were the *symbol* of the ruling class.

The stone walls hid the ruling class from everyone else. They lived in complete *privacy*. Probably no ordinary people ever saw the way the ruling class lived behind the stone walls. Inside many walls, there were narrow twisting passages. These made the stone enclosures even more private.

Most important entrances held tall carvings, made of stone or wood. These carvings were probably of the animals that *represented* the owners' lineage.

In the courtyards, there were many altars, platforms and towers. These held more carvings, all made to honour the lineages and ancestors of the owners.

The rulers ate the beef from their cattle herds. The rest of the people ate meat from sheep, goats or wild animals. The ruling class drank a lot of traditional, thick beer, made from grain.

The rulers' pottery was much more finely made and decorated than other people's pottery. It was so polished that it looked as if it was made from metal. It was used more for drinking than for cooking or eating.

The ruling class wore gold and copper bangles on their arms and legs. The jewellery was so heavy that the ruling class obviously did little work. They also wore heavy, decorated cloth brought by foreign traders. They hung such cloth inside their houses. Inside, too, were pottery and glass from China, Syria and Persia, brought by traders.

Architecture

During the 250 years of the city's power, the style of building developed and changed.

The stone walls were all built of granite blocks. Millions of blocks could be made from broken slabs of granite. Such slabs lay on the many bare granite hills all round the city. The builders did not use *mortar* to keep the blocks together.

Masons hammered blocks into the exact shapes that were needed. This is called dressing the blocks. The masons used hard hammerstones to dress the blocks. They made drains for rainwater through the later walls.

Why are the walls so big?

There has been a lot of discussion about this question.

The great walls did not hold up roofs. They were not built for shelter from wind or rain. The houses inside gave all the shelter that was needed.

The walls gave privacy. But much smaller walls made of poles or clay would have given the same privacy.

The stone walls look like *fortifications*. But a careful look at the layout of the walls shows that they were not fortifications. Soldiers standing on top of the walls or at the doorways would have had no protection from spears and arrows. Some walls were built on the top of cliffs. The cliffs are such strong natural defences that no one could attack them successfully. So the walls were unnecessary for defence. Some places that could be attacked and entered easily have no wall to protect them. The houses of the ordinary people had no

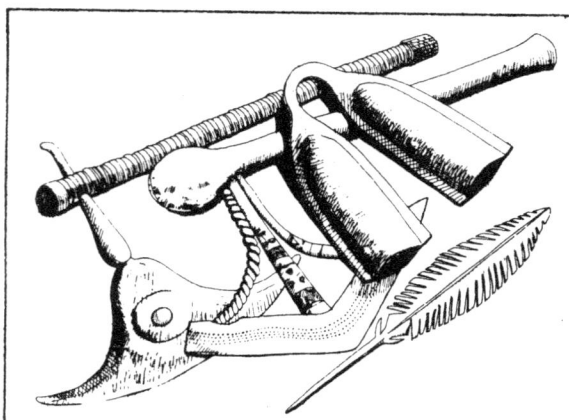

Decorated iron and copper axes and spears used by the rulers of Great Zimbabwe and Kame.

The blocks of the earliest walls were laid in lines that went up and down. We call these lines 'courses'.

As the masons became more and more skilled, they carefully matched the blocks. So the blocks in each course were the same size. Courses in the later walls were exactly straight and horizontal.

protection. The ruling class was so small that it would not have survived an attack that defeated the rest of the city. Anyway, the city was so big and strong that no one could have defeated it.

The stone walls did have a very important purpose. This was to show the power of the ruling class to the city and to the world. The great walls *advertised* the state's power, wealth, skills and organization to everyone who saw them. The walls gave the ruling class and everyone in the city pride in the state's achievement. This was enough reason to put such work and skill into building them.

States like Great Zimbabwe

The culture developed at Great Zimbabwe spread throughout the area shown on the map. The ruling classes of societies in this area built stone walls round their homesteads. They wanted to show that they were members of the same class as the rulers at Great Zimbabwe itself. In this way, they could share the same *prestige*.

Masons from Great Zimbabwe probably visited other areas. They taught stone workers in these areas how to build stone walls. In this period, there were about 60 small zimbabwes all over Zimbabwe. There were also a few in Mozambique. The rulers who lived in them copied the culture of Great Zimbabwe in every way. They had the same houses, pottery, jewellery and food. There may have been seven or more independent states. Each of these states probably

- had its capital at a large zimbabwe,
- had a territory that stretched about 70 kilometres in every direction from the capital,
- sometimes traded with Great Zimbabwe,
- sometimes received foreign goods from Great Zimbabwe,
- sometimes paid tribute to Great Zimbabwe,
- sent members of their ruling families to live at Great Zimbabwe for a time, to strengthen their links with Great Zimbabwe,
- sometimes had members of their ruling families married to members of the ruling class of Great Zimbabwe.

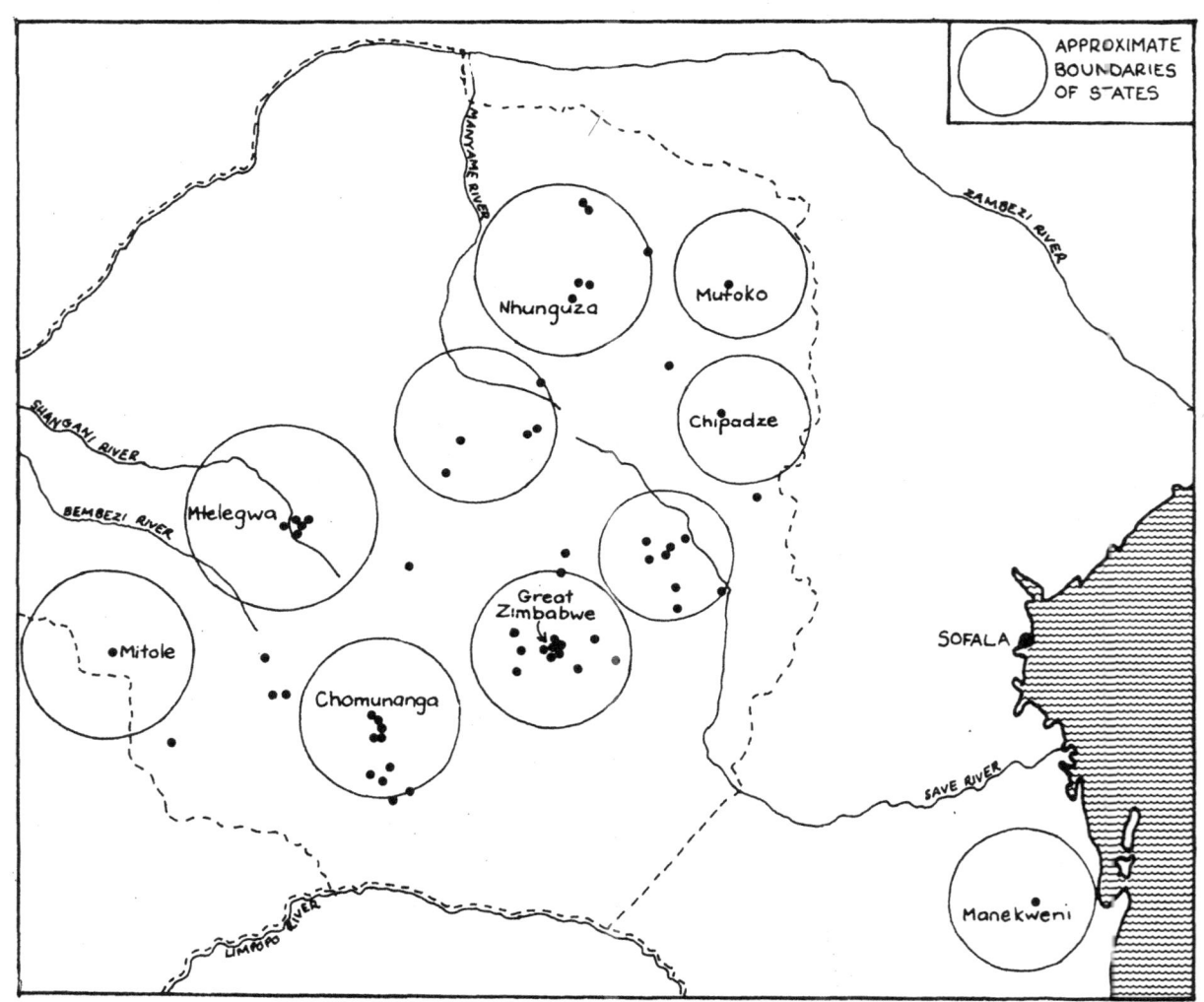

The culture of Great Zimbabwe spread. Other zimbabwes were built at these places.

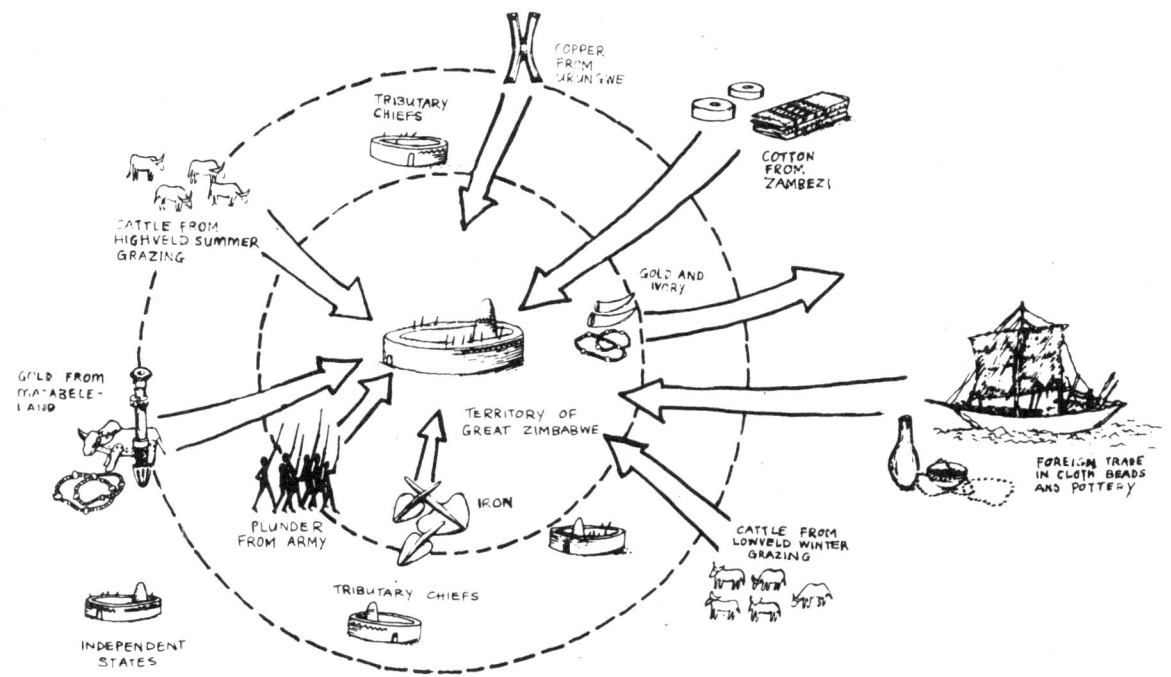

This diagram shows the economy of the state at Great Zimbabwe.

The end of Great Zimbabwe

Archaeologists cannot tell us yet why Great Zimbabwe lost its power. When we think about this, we must remember that states are very complicated organizations. It is difficult to keep a state strong. All states eventually change and weaken. There can be all sorts of reasons for this.

Great Zimbabwe was extremely successful for over 200 years. It overcame all its problems of land and herd management. In the end,
- did the institutions of the state fail to satisfy the needs of the people?
- did the land become worn out and infertile?
- did new states become powerful and take over some of the trade?
- did foreign traders take new *routes* to these new markets?

These are some of the questions that archaeologists and historians still have to answer. More research is needed to give us the answers.

Project. Write to your nearest museum and ask for a list of zimbabwes near your home or school. Visit one.

As a group, make a plan of the walls. Describe the enclosures. Say what they may have been used for.

Are there different styles of walls?

Is there any decoration?

Write a report using all the information you have collected. Illustrate your report. A well prepared report may interest your local museum.

Source-based question. Read this description of Great Zimbabwe, and then answer the questions below. The description was written by a Portuguese called Joao de Barros, in 1552. De Barros did not see Great Zimbabwe himself.

❝ There are mines in a district called Toroa, which by another name is known as the kingdom of Butua, which is ruled by a prince called Burrom, a vassal of Benomotapa, which lands adjoin that aforesaid, consisting of vast plains. These mines are the most ancient known in the country. They are all in the plain, in the midst of which there is a square fortress of masonry within and without, built of stones of marvellous size. There appears to be no mortar joining them. The wall is more than twenty-five spans in width, and the height is not so great considering the width. Above the door of this edifice is an inscription, which some Moorish merchants, learned men, who went thither, could not read, neither could they tell what the character might be. This edifice is almost surrounded by hills, upon which are others resembling it in the fashioning of the stone and the absence of mortar. One of them is a tower more than 26 metres high.

The natives of the country call all these edifices Symbaoe, which according to their language signifies court, for every place where Benomotapa may be is so called. They say that being royal property all the king's other dwellings have this name. It is guarded by a nobleman, who has charge of it. They call this officer Symbacayo as we should say keeper of the Symbaoe. There are always some of Benomotapa's wives therein, of whom this Symbacayo takes care. When, and by whom, these edifices were raised, as the people of the land are ignorant of the art of writing, there is no record, but they say they are the work of the devil, for in comparison with their power and knowledge it does not seem possible to them that they should be the work of man. Some Moors who saw it, to whom Vicente Pegado, who was captain of Sofala, showed our fortress there and the work of the windows and arches, that they might compare it with the stone work of the said edifice, said that they could not be compared with it for smoothness and perfection. The distance of this edifice from Sofala in a direct line to the west is 720 kilometres, or thereabouts, and it is between 20° and 21° south latitude. There are no ancient or modern buildings in those parts, the people being barbarians, and all their houses of wood. ❞

(Note: Great Zimbabwe is 480 kilometres due west of Sofala, 20° south of the equator. The Conical Tower is 10 metres high today.)

a) How does de Barros describe the 'fortress'?
b) Do you think this fortress is Great Zimbabwe?
c) In what ways is de Barros's description accurate?
d) In what ways is his description inaccurate?
e) What reasons can you think of for the inaccuracies?
f) Who actually visited the fortress?
g) What was the fortress used for when the report was written?
h) Why do you think people thought it was the work of the devil?

Essay. Write a short history of Great Zimbabwe. Include information on:
a) its dates,
b) who built it,
c) the materials and building methods used,
d) its purpose,
e) the town and territory,
f) the organization of society.

16. East African city-states

In this chapter:
We will study a group of city-states that developed on the east African coast.
We will see how different these states were from Great Zimbabwe.
We will look at
- the history of trade between east Africa and Asia,
- the effects of this trade,
- the different classes in Swahili societies.

These states developed a mode of production different from any other that we have studied. It combined
- exploiting workers on farms owned by the ruling class, with
- exploiting inland people who produced gold and ivory, through unequal exchange.

You will need to know the meanings of these words:

shrine — a holy or sacred place.
merchant — a trader.
practice — way of doing things, or usual method.
status — social position or importance.
reef — ridge of rock just above or below the surface of the sea.
harbour — place of shelter for ships.
mangrove — tree with very hard wood that grows in warm, shallow sea-water.
factory — building and machinery for producing goods.
warehouse — building used to store goods.
partner — someone who shares in an activity or business.
port — town or place with a harbour.
orchard — area of land planted with fruit trees.
ward — area or district of a city or town.
elect — choose, especially by voting.
hereditary — inherited from one's parents.
alliance — uniting to achieve a shared aim.
monopoly — absolute control of something by a single person or group.
remote — far apart or far away.
industry — manufacturing on a large scale.
raw materials — materials in their natural state.
manufacture — things made for example by craftwork.
export — send goods to another country.
agent — someone who acts for someone else.

The people

The people of the east African coast are called the Swahili. The name comes from the Arabic word for sea-coast, 'suahel'. The coast was also called 'the land of Zanj'. 'Zanj' means black people. The names Zanzibar and Azania come from the word Zanj.

Swahili is a Bantu language. The Swahili people of the coast were African. At first, all the Swahili were farmers. Most of them continued to be farmers. Some began to trade as well as farm.

Swahili *merchants* became Muslims. The Swahili also began to use the laws and business *practices* of Islam. This helped them to establish trust and understanding with foreign traders. They built many mosques in each town for people to pray in.

Sometimes groups of people fled from wars in Persia and Arabia. They went to settle on the east African coast. Many of them worked in the mosques or became teachers of Islamic law. Some foreign traders married Swahili husbands or wives. But foreigners always remained outsiders in Swahili society. They had no power in the government of the cities.

Islamic religion and culture had a strong influence on Swahili society. Some Swahili groups even took the names of Arabic or Persian towns. For example, one Swahili group became known as the Shirazi. Shiraz is a town in southern Iran (formerly Persia). They did this to give themselves more *status*.

The Swahili changed and adapted the Islamic religion to fit in with their traditional beliefs. Their tombs were of a unique Swahili design. They used traditional African trumpets called siwa in ceremonies and festivals.

Muslims worship Allah in buildings called mosques. This photograph shows the ruin of a mosque on the east African coast.

Islam

Followers of Islam are called Muslims. Muslims believe in a single god, Allah. Muslims worship in mosques.

Allah's prophet, Mohammed, told the world about Allah. Mohammed lived in Arabia, until he died in about AD 632. He purified the ancient religion of Arabia. His writings are in the Koran, the holy book of Islam. He taught in the Arabic city of Mecca. The great *shrine* of Islam is at Mecca. All Muslims try to visit Mecca during their lives.

Project. Try and find out as much as you can about the religion of Islam. Invite a Muslim believer to give a talk to your class about it. What other sources can you use?

A Swahili tomb with traditional carved coral

A traditional Swahili trumpet, called a siwa.

The beginning of trade

The east African coast stretches from Somalia, through Kenya and Tanzania, to Mozambique. The coast is sheltered from waves and storms by a line of coral *reefs* and islands. Zanzibar, Lamu and Kilwa are some of the islands along the coast. Voyages along this sheltered coast were easy.

Trading ships used a wind called the monsoon to sail between Asia and Africa. The monsoon blows from India towards Africa from November until March each year. It blows in the opposite direction from April until August. Ships could not sail in June and July because there were too many storms then. They had to wait in the *harbours* for the right winds. If they missed the right monsoon, they had to wait for many months.

Travel by sea was much quicker than travel on land. The small sailing boats of the Swahili could travel 50 kilometres a day. On land, a trading expedition could not walk more than 10 kilometres a day. Some big ships could sail across the ocean. They could travel 150 kilometres a day. A voyage from India to Africa took two or three weeks.

Discussion. What have we learned about the geography and environment of the east African coast?
How did these factors influence the development of trade?

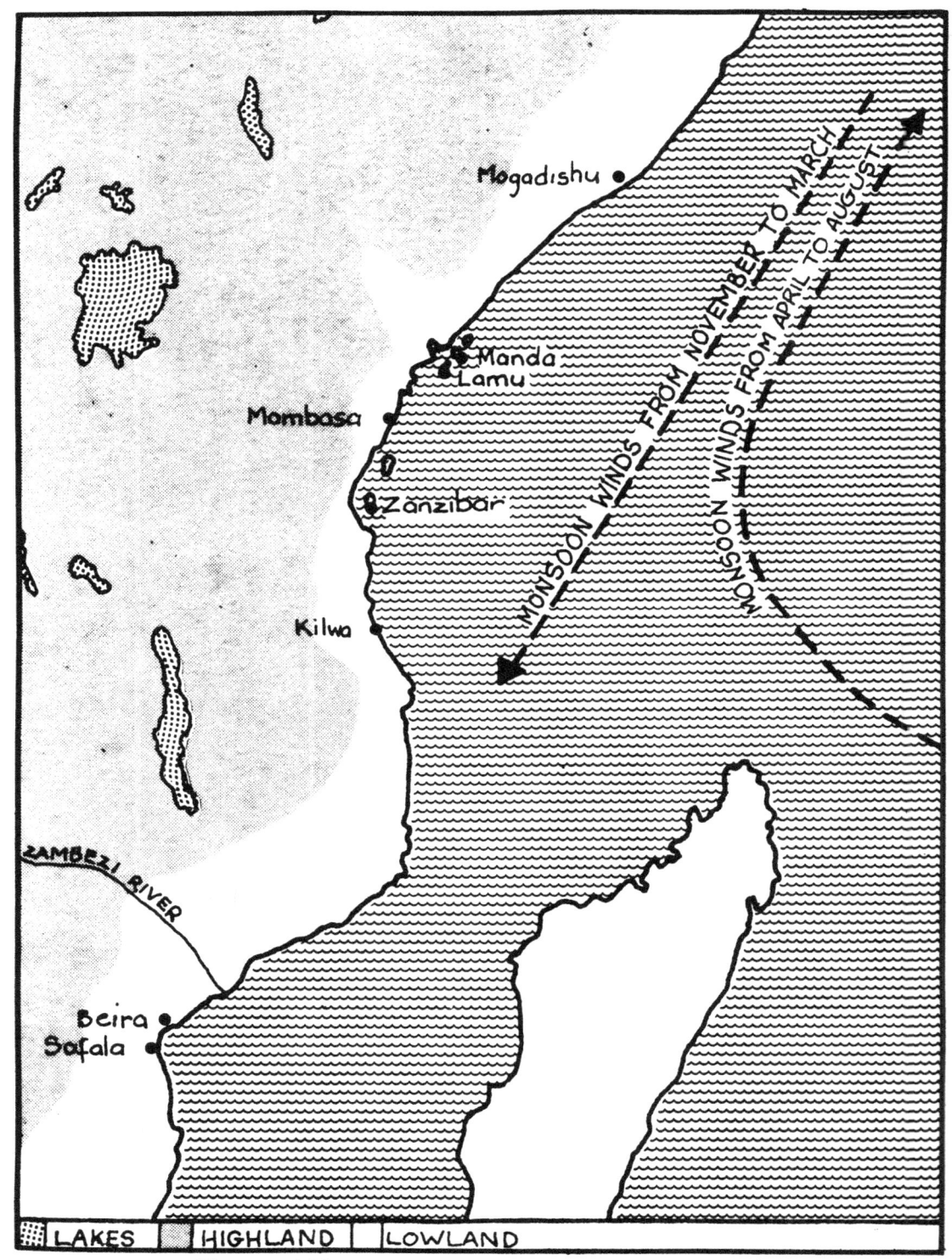

The east African coast. Look also at the map in chapter 11.

At first, the east African traders exchanged
- cowrie shells that were used for money,
- shell beads,
- tortoise shells,
- products of local industry, such as iron smelting,
- *mangrove* poles which were used to build the roofs of houses in desert lands in Asia,
- criminals and prisoners-of-war who were taken to be slaves in Asia.

The foreign traders brought
- cloth made in *factories* in India,
- pottery called porcelain, celadon and faience made in factories in China and Persia,
- glass beads made in factories in India.

Trade became more and more important. From AD 900, great wealth came to the coast. This was when the cities of Asia found out about the ivory of Africa and the gold of Zimbabwe.

All through the year, the Swahili traders collected goods from inland and along the coast. They made many voyages along the coast in their small boats to collect goods and bring them back to their cities. They stored the goods in the merchants' *warehouses*.

The foreign sailors and traders travelled in dhows from Arabia, Persia and India. They stayed with Swahili traders when they were in east Africa. They became *partners*. They bought all the goods that their Swahili partners had collected.

The Swahili built big sailing ships called mtepe.

Sources and dates

Historians use old documents and archaeology to learn about the city-states of the east African coast.

In about AD 100, a guidebook was written for the captains of ships which sailed from the Red Sea and Egypt. The guidebook was called *Periplus of the Erytheaen Sea*. It described all the *ports* of the Red Sea, Arabia and east Africa. The most southerly African port mentioned was called Rhapta. Archaeologists have not yet found the remains of Rhapta. It is still buried by sand and mud on the Tanzanian coast.

The earliest town that archaeologists have found is Manda, on an island in the north of Kenya. Manda grew up in the 9th century.

Later, trading ships travelled further south. In the 12th century, Kilwa became the biggest and best known town in east Africa. Kilwa is on an island in southern Tanzania. It continued to be important until the 15th century.

Some of the east African trading towns and cities are now ruins, such as Manda and Kilwa. Others grew and developed. Many important towns today have remains of the early trading cities in them, such as Mogadishu, Mombasa and Zanzibar. Villages, called mji, all along the coast have the remains of mosques and stone tombs from the days of the great overseas trade.

Traders came from Arabia and India in dhows.

The city-states

The east African city-states were very different from the state at Great Zimbabwe.

The east African city-states were very small. Their territories were single cities and the farmland round them. They rarely received tribute. They rarely had armies to control their territory or collect tribute. Their economies depended on trade, not on production from mines, cattle or craftspeople.

The ruling class was called the ungwana. They were all traders. The wealth of the ungwana came from trade between the interior of Africa and the markets of Arabia and India. Their food came from the farms round the city. This food was produced by the farmers, called the shenzi. The shenzi worked more as slaves of the ruling class than as free farmers. Many of their farms belonged to the ungwana. The crops the farmers grew belonged to the ungwana.

The ruling class (ungwana)

The ungwana's houses were built of blocks of coral, cut from the coral reefs off-shore. Mortar and plaster were made by burning coral. The roofs were made of coral supported on mangrove poles. The architecture of the mosques and houses was Islamic. In front of each house, there was a courtyard where the house-owner met guests. Inside, there was a beautifully decorated guest room where foreign traders could stay.

Islamic religion said that all women must live in complete privacy. The houses had no outside windows. This ensured the privacy of the women. *Orchards* grew in enclosed gardens behind the houses.

The coral houses were not just comfortable homes. Only an ungwana could afford to build a coral house. A coral house was a sign to everyone, including foreign traders, that the owner was an ungwana and a man of wealth. He could be relied on as a trading partner. An ungwana's house proved that he had the money to pay his trading debts. So coral houses were important for encouraging trade.

The lineages of the ungwana were called kabila. The houses of people in the same kabila were built close together. They formed separate *wards* of the town. Each ward of the town *elected* an elder, called a mzee, to a council. The council was headed by one of the mzee, called the sheikh or emir. He was the head of the town. Some sheiks became *hereditary* leaders. This happened particularly in towns which were threatened by inland people and needed strong leadership. We can see that the government of these city-states was organized through lineages, as in many other African societies.

Each kabila made its own separate agreements with chiefs of the inland peoples to exchange ivory, grain and other farm products for foreign goods. Sometimes whole cities made *alliances* with inland peoples. They did this to ensure the protection of the city from attack. The ungwana themselves never travelled or traded far from their towns. The rulers of the inland people did not allow them to. No single ungwana had a *monopoly* on any particular trade route or inland region.

Ungwana of today perform a wedding dance.

The ruin of a coral house on the East African coast.

The farmers (shenzi)

Most of the people in a town were shenzi. They farmed outside the town, on fields called shambas. Some shenzi worked on their own shambas and some worked on shambas that belonged to the ungwana. They produced meat, fish, coconuts and other food for the town and visiting ships.

The shenzi lived in different parts of the town from the ungwana. Their houses were made of pole and clay with thatched roofs. As we have learned, they were an exploited class. They had no say in the government of the town.

Relations between city-states

Each town was an independent city-state. The biggest cities were those that had the best harbours for trading. Examples are Kilwa, Mombasa and Mogadishu. At times, the biggest cities were able to take control of smaller and more *remote* towns, such as Sofala.

Sofala was near the present Mozambique port of Beira. It was the most southern port on the coast. Gold was carried from Zimbabwe to Sofala. But Sofala was out of reach of the monsoon winds and the overseas dhows. It was reached by very small boats. These boats could only travel in light winds and close to the shore.

Sofala was controlled by Mogadishu until the 13th century. During this time, Mogadishu was the most powerful city on the coast. Kilwa captured Sofala from Mogadishu in the 13th century. Kilwa made Sofala a colony. Then Kilwa grew rich quickly. In a few years, the Emir of Kilwa was wealthy enough to build the great palace of Husuni Kubwa. Mogadishu became poor and powerless after it lost the Sofala trade.

Husuni Kubwa was the greatest of all the houses on the east African coast. Built in about AD 1300 for the Emir of Kilwa, it had ornamental pools, courtyards and many domed reception rooms. It was as grand as any European palace of that time.

Unequal trade. Inland producers traded their gold and ivory with the ungwana. The ungwana then traded with foreign traders. Who benefited most? Who benefited least?

The effects of trade

Trade made the cities rich. But trade did not encourage local *industries* to develop in the cities. The only important industries that developed as a result of trade were
- making coins to help trade (Mogadishu and Kilwa made their own copper coins with the sheikh's name stamped on them),
- ship-building and repairing,
- house-building and the crafts that went with it, such as cutting and burning coral, carpentry, stone carving and plastering.

Industries did not develop because the foreign traders wanted *raw materials*. They did not want *manufactured* goods, such as local cloth or iron work. In return, foreign traders brought all sorts of factory-made cloth and pottery from Asia. This was good for the Asian industries. It allowed them to develop their factories and industries. It was harmful to the local industries.

The foreign traders knew the real value of gold and ivory on the world market. The ungwana did not. So the traders could cheat the ungwana and pay them less than the value of the gold and ivory. The traders exhanged cloth and pottery which were cheap to make, for ivory and gold, which they sold in Asia for great profits.

In the same way and for the same reasons, the ungwana were able to cheat the inland producers of ivory and gold. They did not pay the producers the true value of their goods.

The ungwana trading class grew very wealthy. They lived a life of luxury. They dressed in expensive silks and other Indian cloths. They owned rich ornaments from India and China. They were educated in the schools of Islam and knew a lot about the Koran, Islam's holy book. They wrote Swahili in Arabic letters.

The ungwana were not producers. The producers of food were the shenzi. The producers of the *export* goods were the hunters and miners of the inland villages and states. The ungwana were middle-men or *agents*. They were the link between the foreign sea-traders and the inland peoples.

Source-based question. Read the passage carefully, and then answer the questions below. The passage was written by a famous Arab traveller called ibn Battuta. It describes his journey down the East African coast in 1331.

"We arrived at Mogadishu, which is a very large town. The people have very many camels, and slaughter many hundreds every day. They have also many sheep. The merchants are wealthy, and manufacture a material which takes its name from the town and which is exported to Egypt and elsewhere.

Among the customs of the people of this town is the following: when a ship comes into port, it is boarded from sanbuqs, that is to say, little boats. Each sanbuq carries a crowd of young men, each carrying a covered dish containing food. Each one of them presents his dish to a merchant on board and calls out: 'This man is my guest.' And his fellows do the same. Not one of the merchants disembarks except to go to the house of his host among the young men, save frequent visitors to the country. In such a case they go where they like. When a merchant has settled in his host's house, the latter sells for him what he has brought and makes his purchases for him. Buying anything from a merchant below its market price or selling him anything except in his host's presence is disapproved of by the people of Mogadishu. They find it of advantage to keep to this rule...

Then I set off by sea from the town of Mogadishu for the land of the Swahili and the town of Kilwa, which is in the land of Zanj. We arrived at Mombasa, a large island two days' journey from the land of the Swahili. The island is quite separate from the mainland. It grows bananas, lemons, and oranges. The people also gather a fruit which they call jammun, which looks like an olive. It has a nut like an olive, but its taste is very sweet. The people do not engage in agriculture, but import grain from the Swahili. The greater part of their diet is bananas and fish. They follow the Shafi'i rite, and are devout, chaste, and virtuous.

Their mosques are very strongly constructed of wood. Beside the door of each mosque are one or two wells, 50 — 100 centimetres deep. They draw water from them with a wooden vessel which is fixed on to the end of a thin stick, 50 centimetres long. The earth round the mosque and the well is stamped flat. Anyone who wishes to enter the mosque first washes his feet; beside the door is a piece of heavy material for drying them. Anyone who wishes to perform the ritual ablutions, takes the vessel between his thighs, pours water on his hands, and so makes his ablutions. Everyone here goes barefoot.

We spent a night on the island and then set sail for Kilwa, the principal town on the coast, the greater part of whose inhabitants are Zanj of very black complexion. Their faces are scarred. A merchant told me that Sofala is half a month's march from Kilwa, and that between Sofala and Yufi in the country of the Limiin is a month's march. Powdered gold is brought from Yufi to Sofala.

Kilwa is one of the most beautiful and well-constructed towns in the world. The whole of it is built of wood. The roofs are built with mangrove poles. There is very much rain. The people are engaged in a holy war, for their country lies beside that of pagan Zanj. The chief qualities are devotion and piety: They follow the Shafi'i rite."

a) What is the purpose of the ceremony of the 'dish of food'? How did it help trade?
b) In your own words, describe the town of

Kilwa at the time that ibn Battuta visited it.
c) Why do you think ibn Battuta said that Kilwa was built of wood? (We know that the ungwana houses had walls of coral).
d) What are the meanings of Shafi, Zanj and Swahili?
e) Where do you think Yufi was?
f) Who do you think the Limiin were?

Discussion. What differences were there between these states and the state at Great Zimbabwe?

Excercise. In this chapter we have learned a lot of Swahili and Arabic words. What do these Swahili words mean:
Ungwana, shenzi, mji, mtepe, kabila, mzee, shamba, siwa?
What do these Arabic words mean:
Allah, mosque, Muslim, sheikh, emir, suahel, Zanj, Koran, dhow?

Discussion. What is unequal exchange? Does it happen today? How can we decide the real value of goods? Can we decide by looking at the price? Can we decide by calculating how much work was necessary to produce the goods?

Discussion. Elephants in Zimbabwe were hunted for their ivory. Through trade, a lot of this ivory reached India. How many times was a piece of ivory exchanged for other things, from the time it was cut from the elephant to the time it was placed as a bangle on an Indian's arm? List the different people it passed between.

Essay. Describe the trade between east Africa and Zimbabwe in the early 15th century. You should include:
a) products,
b) routes,
c) methods of transport,
d) methods of trade,
e) who the traders were,
f) who benefited from the trade.

17. Feudalism

In this chapter:
- We will look at the feudal mode of production in Europe.
- We will see how it began to change.
- This will give us a picture of Portuguese society at the time that the Portuguese began to come to Africa.

You will need to know the meanings of these words:

bound — tied to or under the control of something or someone.

monarch — supreme ruler, such as king, queen or emperor.

vassal — one who is given land by the monarch and in return must obey and defend the monarch

prince — male member of royal family, especially a monarch's son or grandson.

challenge — question or dispute or threaten.

citizen — a person belonging to or living in a city or country.

province — area of the country outside the capital.

Feudal classes

Feudalism existed all over Europe between the 11th and 14th centuries. All the land was divided into huge estates. Each estate was as big as some African chiefdoms. The estates belonged to a class of landowners called the aristocracy. Landowners were called knights, barons or lords.

The lords' land was farmed by serfs. Serfs did not own their farms. They were not paid any wages for their labour. The lord allowed serfs to farm as they wanted. He allowed them to keep part of their crops to feed themselves.

This diagram shows the classes in feudal society.

In return, they had to give tribute to their lord. As tribute, the serfs had to give part of their crops. Serfs also had to work on the lord's land for some of the time. If there was a war, some serfs had to be soldiers in the lord's armies. Serfs could never leave their lord's estate. They were *bound* to a particular lord. They were not free.

The lord was also not completely free. He was a *vassal*. This means that he was subject to a greater lord, called a duke, or a *prince*. Every lord was a vassal of the king or *monarch*. The lord and his serfs served in the king's army.

Knights, barons, lords, dukes, princes and kings were all landowners or aristocrats. The aristocracy exploited the serfs.

The king relied on each of his lords to keep order on their estates and to defend their lands. Very few officials worked for the king. There was no real central government.

Changes in the feudal mode of production

As trade developed, towns and cities grew up. There were traders and craftspeople in the towns who were no longer serfs. They were

This drawing was made in Lisbon, Portugal, in 1594. The Portuguese sailed to Africa in ships like these. Notice the cannons in the largest trading ship in the picture.

not bound to a particular lord as serfs were. They were the beginnings of a new class, called the bourgeois class.

The new, emerging class was not controlled by the aristocracy. It *challenged* the power of the king. It threatened the feudal system. To save the feudal system, each king took more and more power to himself. Kings began to set up organizations, with officials, law enforcers, tax collectors, and so on. These organizations were under the control of the king. The government became centralized under the king. The kings did this to control the rising power of the towns and their *citizens*. They tried to stop the citizens becoming free.

Each king's power grew until he was an absolute monarch. This means that he controlled almost all the power of the state himself. His orders were enforced by his own army. The king paid for the army from the taxes that the lords and the towns had to pay.

The king and his army protected the lords' lands. The lords still kept order in the *provinces* of the kingdom. They also kept their huge estates. But the king's armies, officials and government took over a lot of the lord's power.

Feudal Portugal

In the 15th century, Portugal was an absolute monarchy. Absolute monarchy was the last stage of feudalism.

Portugal was one of the smallest, poorest and most backward countries in Europe. Its agricultural land was poor. Its industries remained undeveloped.

The Portuguese were the only people to try and introduce European feudalism to Africa. Portugal was different from any part of Africa in many ways:
- technology,
- economy,
- environment,
- culture,
- religion,
- social system and, above all, in its feudalism and absolute monarchy.

We have looked at the feudal economy and organization of society that existed in Portugal. In the next chapter, we will learn about the Portuguese in Africa.

Essay. Describe the feudal mode of production. You should consider these points:
a) the different classes,
b) who administered and governed the country,
c) how armies were raised and organized,
d) land ownership,
e) town and country,
f) the life of a serf.

18. The Portuguese in Africa

In this chapter:
We will learn about the first Portuguese ships and soldiers that came to Africa.
We will see how Portuguese officials and settlers exploited African land and trade.
We will discuss the effects of this exploiation.

You will need to know the meanings of these words:

navigator — someone who works out and guides the route of a ship.
cannon — very large gun that is fixed or mounted on wheels or on a ship.
ruthless — having no pity or mercy.
enslave — make someone a slave.
resist — fight or act against, or oppose.
spice — substance made from a plant and used to add flavour to food.
scheme — a plan, often secret or dishonest.
outpost — distant or remote settlement.
impose — force on to, or establish by authority.
outlaw — someone who breaks the law and so has no legal rights or protection.
interfere — intrude into someone else's affairs.
dissident — someone who disagrees, especially with their government or ruler.
mercenary — professional soldier, or someone who is hired to fight for another.
outcast — someone who is rejected or homeless.
ambition — a strong desire for success.

Early Portuguese influence

The Portuguese were the first nation of Europe to make any contact with tropical Africa. In 1443, Portuguese ships first reached south of the Sahara. They gradually sailed

Vasco da Gama was the leader of the first Portuguese expedition to sail round South Africa to India.

further south, to the African kingdoms of Kongo and Ngola. In 1498, Portuguese ships sailed round southern Africa and entered the Indian Ocean. Very soon, they were making regular voyages to the cities of east Africa and India.

The Portuguese had good ocean *navigators*. Their ocean-going ships were heavy enough to carry large *cannons*. These cannons could destroy any other ships in the Indian Ocean. Portuguese ships could also destroy towns from the sea.

The Portuguese soldiers were *ruthless*. They attacked many towns. They took the wealth from these towns and then destroyed them. The Portuguese killed or *enslaved* any people who *resisted* them. They brought a new and terrible kind of war to Africa.

The Portuguese in west Africa

When they first came to Africa, the Portuguese saw that Africa did not need anything from Portugal. They decided to take part in the local trade between west African states. They carried African products in their ships between African ports and states. They were peaceful and equal partners of African traders and rulers.

The Portuguese made profits from carrying this trade. They used the profits to buy African gold, slaves and *spices* to take back to Portugal.

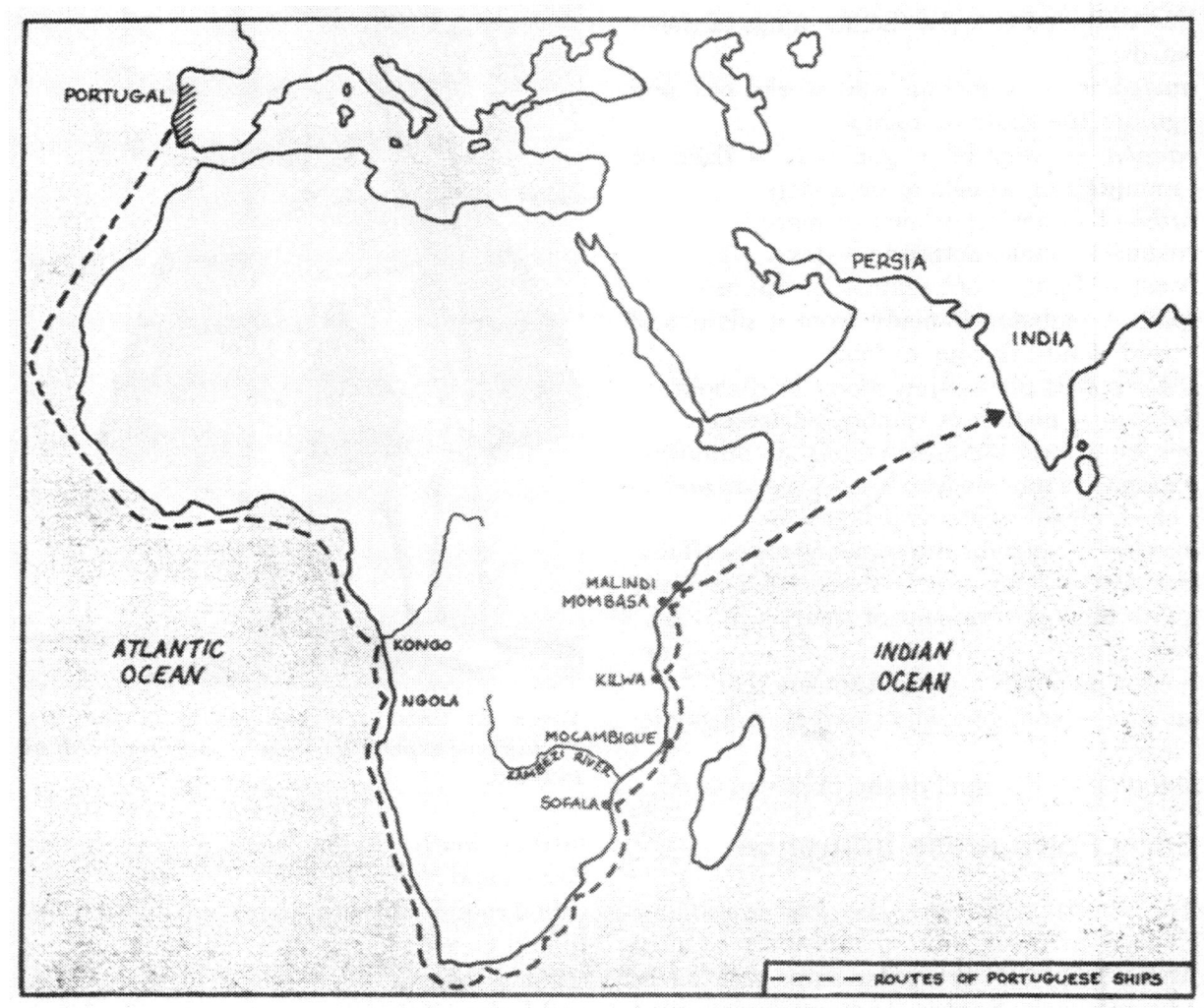

The Portuguese sailed to Africa and Asia.

The Portuguese in east Africa

When the Portuguese reached the east African city states, they found that trade between Africa and India had been going on for centuries. No Portuguese products were wanted by east Africa or India.

The Portuguese therefore decided to try and get the profits from the trade between Africa and India for themselves. They tried to force the Swahili traders and captains of the dhows and mtepes to work for them, or to pay taxes to them. With the heavy guns on their bigger ships, the Portuguese were able to destroy many coastal towns. Then they built forts and placed Portuguese soldiers in some of these towns. Kilwa was one.

This warfare and oppression failed to win trade for the Portuguese. Traders avoided the Portuguese ships by travelling secretly, in small boats close to the shore. They made new ports that the Portuguese could not reach.

The Portuguese then realized that they had to try and control the whole ocean with their ships. They also had to move inland and try to take over the inland trade at its source. They tried to take over some of the local systems of production.

As part of these *schemes,* the Portuguese built a fort at Sofala in 1505. Within a very few years, the first Portuguese entered Zimbabwe.

Discussion. Why did the Portuguese try to make money from ocean trade? Why did the Portuguese begin to settle in east Africa?

At first, the Portuguese traded as equals in Africa and India. In this drawing, Vasco da Gama is showing his respect for an Indian king.

Portuguese missionaries brought Christianity to Africa. This painting shows a Catholic church service in early Tete.

Portuguese settlements

The population of Portugal was always very small. Portugal was only able to send a very few people to Africa. Between 1500 and 1700, the settled population of Portuguese on the Zambezi river towns and in Zimbabwe was never more than 200 people.

Portuguese soldiers built forts and settlements in Africa and India. The Portuguese king said that these *outposts* were Portuguese royal land. He gave this land to a lord from Portugal to govern for him. The lord was called a viceroy. Each viceroy governed for a few years.

The viceroys governed in the same way as feudal lords in Portugal. They had to defend and settle their land for the king. In return, the king allowed them to exploit the land in any way they wanted. They had a monopoly of all trade. This means they had complete control of trade. They kept the profits from any trade they organized for themselves.

The viceroys were able to sell all the jobs in the lands they governed. There were many officials, such as local governors, fort captains, judges and tax collectors. All officials bought their jobs from the viceroy. The officials were not paid any salary. Instead they were allowed to keep part of the profits from their work. For example
- tax collectors kept part of the taxes they collected,
- judges kept part of the fines they *imposed,*
- traders kept part of the profits from their trading.

Exercise. Finish these sentences.
In African tradition, land belonged to .....
In feudal Europe, land belonged to ....
The Portuguese king said that the parts of Africa where his soldiers settled belonged to ....

Discussion. The Portuguese king gave African land to his viceroys to govern. To whom did this land really belong?

Sertanejos

Many Portuguese in Africa had no official jobs. They could not grow rich like the officials. Many stopped obeying the Portuguese king and viceroys. They began to break the official monopoly by trading on their own. They became almost *outlaws*. They were called 'sertanejos' which means 'men in the bush'.

Some sertanejos were nobles. Others were 'degredados', criminals who were sent to Africa instead of prison, as punishment. They did not obey Portuguese laws. They did not obey African laws and customs either. They *interfered* in local African trade and politics. Some sertanejos built up large African armies of their own.

The sertanejos with armies began to take part in local African wars. They helped African rulers or invaders or *dissidents*. These sertanejos were *mercenaries*. If the side they fought for was successful, they were given some land by the ruler they had helped. This land was usually
- far from the ruler's capital, or
- an area which was disloyal to the ruler, or
- an area which the ruler had recently conquered.

The ruler gave the sertanejo control over all the people who lived in the area.

Prazos

Lands were given by African rulers as rewards to sertanejos. These lands were called 'prazos'. The new Portuguese owners were called 'prazeros'. They were like feudal lords but they were vassals of African rulers.

The Portuguese king saw that the prazeros were becoming rich and powerful. He wanted them to be loyal to Portugal again. So he pretended that he had given them the prazos. He ordered the prazeros
- to help any Portuguese officials and armies in their area,
- to keep order in their prazos,
- to develop their land to benefit Portugal.

Africans on the prazos

The African people who lived on the land that was given to prazeros remained on that land. They farmed it as they had always done. The Portuguese called these farmers 'colonos'. They treated them as feudal serfs. Colonos had to pay tribute in crops and labour to the prazeros.

The prazeros also began to gather large numbers of slaves for themselves. The slaves were called 'chikundas'. Most of the people who became chikundas were *outcasts* from their own societies. They were people who had lost their villages, lands and cattle in wars. They looked for protection from a powerful chief or prazero. The chikundas formed the private armies of the prazeros.

Some chikundas became traders for the prazeros. They were called 'vashambadzi'. They took trading expeditions from the prazos to inland markets and rulers. Vashambadzi often spent many months away from the prazos, travelling and trading. Vashambadzi were allowed to do some trading for themselves. They kept the profits from this part of the trade for themselves.

The wealth of the prazos

The Portuguese king hoped
- that the prazos would become productive farms, worked by slaves,
- that the prazos would benefit the Portuguese state as well as the prazeros,
- that crops that Portugal needed would be grown on the prazos and sent to Portugal.

If this plan had succeeded, prazos might

This painting shows a chikunda.

have become the start of Portuguese colonies in Africa. The plan never worked. Transport to the markets was too difficult. There was no one to buy the crops or ship them to Portugal. The only productive work done for prazeros was the mining of gold. Some goldfields on prazos north of the lower Zambezi river were developed. This mining was done by women slaves.

The prazeros got their wealth from
- trade,
- tribute from colonos,
- raiding other people's villages,
- fighting as mercenaries.

People thought prazeros would rule in similar ways to chiefs. But they did not become part of African society or culture or politics. They did not have kinship ties to the people as chiefs did. Prazeros ruled by force and oppression.

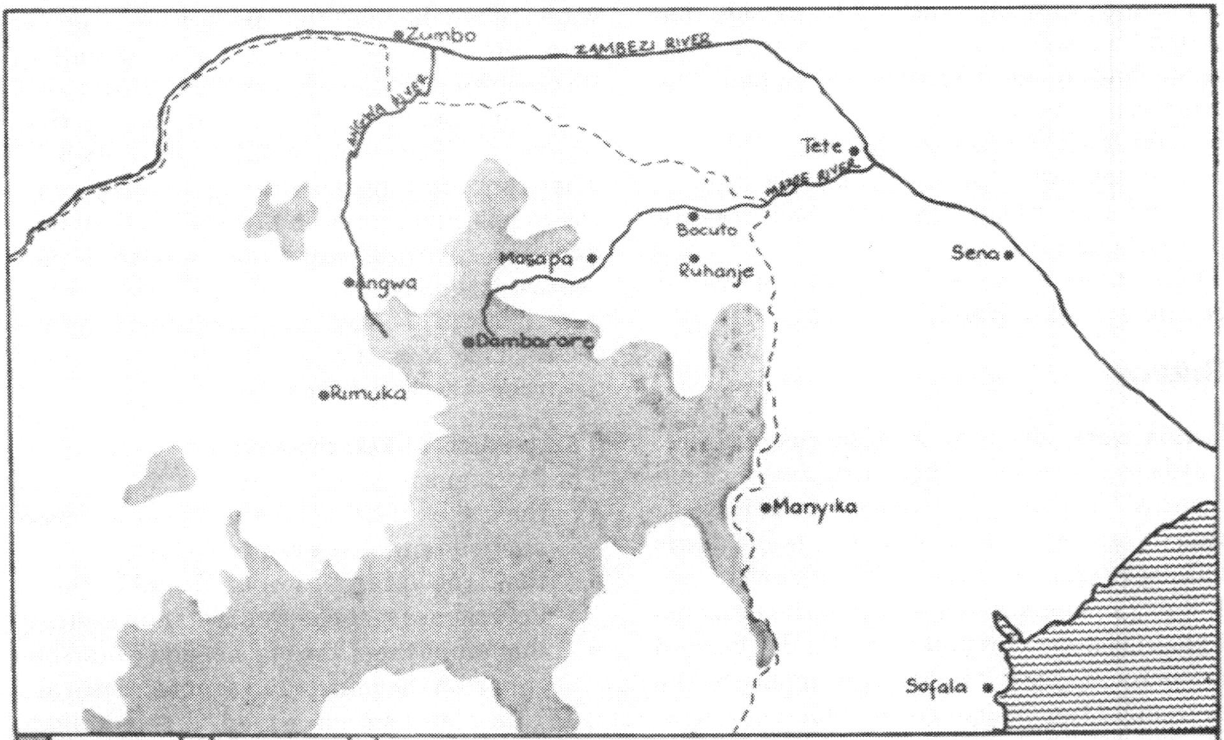

The Portuguese established market towns, called feiras, at these places.

How did the prazos affect Africa?

Prazos were a new sort of exploitation in Africa. They developed out of the feudal system of Europe. They had no place in African society. They were a destructive influence on any people they affected.

Prazeros were ruthless and oppressive. They also became corrupt and lazy. They did nothing to develop their lands or people. Many prazeros left their prazos to live in the Portuguese towns that grew up along the Zambezi and the coast. They lived off the work of their colonos, chikundas and vashambadzi.

Not many prazos lasted very long. The prazo system lasted longer than any single prazo did. The system ended when the real Portuguese colonization of Mozambique started in the late 19th century.

The Portuguese brought more than 500 years of corruption and suffering to Africa. Wherever they settled, the Portuguese caused great disaster for African societies and economies. In the end, Africans always defeated the Portuguese. Portuguese plans and *ambitions* for exploiting Africa all failed. We shall learn much more about this in Book 2.

Exercise. In this chapter we have learned new words. For each of the following words, say
a) what it means,
b) what language it comes from.
Prazos, sertanejos, colonos, degredados, chikundas, vashambadzi.

Discussion. What is corruption?
List the ways that the Portuguese system in Africa was corrupt.
Can you think of examples of corruption today? How can corruption be prevented?

Essay. Describe the prazo system, under the following subheadings:
a) Classes,
b) Land ownership,
c) Armies,
d) The life of a colono.

Essay. From the 15th century, the Portuguese rulers planned to develop Portugal by exploiting Africa.
a) Describe the different schemes of the Portuguese.
b) Explain why these schemes failed.

Many prazeros left their prazos to live in towns like Tete. This is what Tete looked like in 1859.

19. Mutapa origins and society

In this chapter:
- We will study the Mutapa state in northern Zimbabwe.
- We will learn about its *origins*, environment, people and economy.
- We will see that it had a tributary mode of production.

You will need to know the meanings of these words:

origin — source or starting point or beginning.
tempt — try and persuade someone to do something wrong or something that they would not usually do.
boundary — edge.
ingot — piece of cast metal of a particular shape.
rebellion — organized armed resistance to a government or ruler.
supervise — oversee or direct work or workers.
ambassador — a representative of one state sent to another state.
spy — someone who secretly watches and reports on the activities of others.
encourage — urge or promote or give hope to.
import — bring goods from another country.
rank — grade of importance.
page — boy employed to attend to the king's needs.

Great Zimbabwe and Mutapa

Great Zimbabwe was the first great state in southern Africa. At the end of chapter 15, we saw how Great Zimbabwe began to lose its wealth and power. At the same time, another famous state was developing in the north of Zimbabwe. This was the state ruled by the Mutapa lineage. It began sometime in 15th century and lasted until the 20th century.

The Mutapa state was always independent of Great Zimbabwe. It was in a better place than Great Zimbabwe for trading in gold. There were many more rich goldfields in the north of Zimbabwe than there were near Great Zimbabwe. The Zambezi river was a better route to the sea than the route from Great Zimbabwe to Sofala.

Origins of the Mutapa state

Even before the first Mutapas, the ruling class of the north had the same culture as the ruling class at Great Zimbabwe. Mutapa culture began at Great Zimbabwe. The rulers
- lived in similar houses,
- wore the same clothes and jewellery,
- used the same sort of pottery.

Their capitals were surrounded by beautiful stone walls like those at Great Zimbabwe. These walls were built by masons who learned their skills at Great Zimbabwe. When the Mutapas moved their capital to places without good building stone, they no longer had stone walls round their homes.

There are several zimbabwes near the top of the Mazowe river and its goldfields. The names of some of these zimbabwes are Ruanga, Nhunguza, Chisvingo and Pote. There are bigger zimbabwes at Zvongombe, west of Mount Darwin. In the Zambezi valley, there are three stone zimbabwes. Traditions say that the valley zimbabwes were the homes of the first Mutapa rulers.

Traditions about Mutapa origins

People have kept many traditions about the origins of the Mutapa state. Here is one of them. Read this passage and then answer the questions which follow.

> ❢ Nyakatonje lived in Dande in the Zambezi valley which, at that time, was called Mbire. He travelled to the country of Guruuswa taking with him some salt. When he arrived, he found Mutota living there. Mutota killed an ox to welcome him. When the meat was cooked, Nyakatonje added salt to his portion. Mutota saw him eating this and asked for some. When he tasted how good it was, he asked Nyakatonje where he came from and then set out with him as guide to find the land of the salt. With him went his son Nebedza (also known as Matope) and his daughter Nehanda, as well as Zvimba and Mutota's friend (or brother) Chingoo.
>
> They journeyed through many places, passing where Harare is today and on into the Mazowe valley. When they reached a certain place, Zvimba said he had to stop as his legs were hurting him. ('Kuzvimba' means to swell up painfully). Zvimba remained there and that's how the place called Zvimba got its name. Chingoo and Mutota continued. They found a tree with bees in it. They were unable to reach the honey, so Chingoo bent his spear into the shape of a curved stick (called 'ngoo') used to fetch down honey from trees and that's why he was called Chingoo. Some of the honey was wet and fell on Mutota and that's why he was called Mutota. ('Kutota' means

Chisvingo zimbabwe on the edge of the Mutapa state, close to where Harare is now.

to become wet, especially with rain.) When they reached the country of Guruve, Chingoo stopped and made his home there while Mutota continued towards Dande.

As they travelled, Mutota told Nyakatonje to warn him before they reached the edge of the escarpment and saw the Zambezi river in the valley. Mutota needed time to perform certain magic (mapipi). But Nyakatonje failed to warn him and Mutota saw into the valley before he was ready. Now he was unable to continue his journey. He turned back and made his home on the escarpment. When he died, the earth opened for him and he was placed inside a rock. Around his grave were placed eight small baobab trees (tuuyu tusere) brought from Dande by his followers.

Before Mutota died he told his sons that, if they wished to enter the valley, one of them would have to marry their sister Nehanda. All the brothers refused to perform this forbidden act. Only Nebedza, the youngest, agreed. When this was accomplished, Nebedza inherited his father's position as head of the lineage and all the sons climbed down the escarpment and made their homes in Mbire, now called Dande.*

In this tradition, who was the head of the lineage?
What does 'Mutota' mean?
Why is Mutota connected with rain?
Why is this connection important?
How many people of Mutota's lineage are named in this tradition?
In the story, what supernatural things happen?

Understanding traditions

Traditions may have many hidden meanings. When we study the tradition about Mutota, we can see its hidden meanings. The tradition is about two different worlds — the world of spirits and the real world of living people.

Guruuswa is not a real place. It is part of a spirit world, where all the ancestors live. It is the source of all life. Dande is a real place. In the tradition, it is the home of all living people.

Mutota is the greatest ancestor. He lives in the spirit world. He gives rain to the living world. Nyakatonje is a messenger from the living to the great ancestor. It was believed that only people, not spirits, ate salt. In this tradition salt is used to *tempt* Mutota from the spirit world to the land of the living.

The escarpment is the hills on the edge of Dande and the Zambezi valley. It is the place where rain always falls today. In the legend, it is the *boundary* between life and death. Mutota remains there. As a spirit, he cannot enter the living world.

Nebedza is the first living man. He is also the first chief. He can live in the valley, among the living. Nehanda is the first real woman. Her spirit and her spirit medium remain today. They are among the great leaders of the people of Zimbabwe. The earliest Mutapas are also part of this legend. They are Nebedza Matope, Nyahuma, Chikuyo and Chivere.

We can see that the story of Mutota is not real history. It is not about the real start of the Mutapa state. Instead, it is a great and beautiful story about the creation of the whole world. Christians have a similar story about Adam and Eve and the Garden of Eden. This too is not real history. We saw this when we studied the evolution of humankind in chapter 3.

Environment

The territory of Mutapa reached from the highveld north of Harare across the mountains of the Zambezi escarpment. Mutapa territory

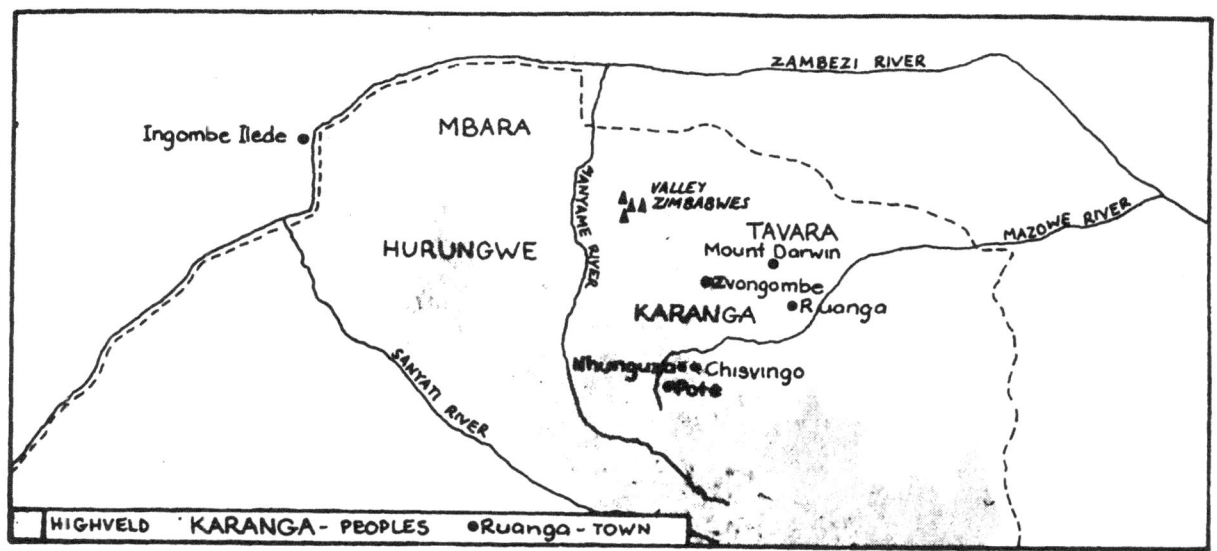

The Mutapa state.

This is the way people wove cloth in the Mutapa state.

stretched down into the Zambezi valley and along the river. It went west beyond the Manyame river and east as far as the Mazowe river.

The highveld is the best farming land in Zimbabwe. Most of the people living there were farmers. They remained farmers.

In the valley, farming was very difficult. The valley has
- a hot climate,
- very little rain,
- sandy, infertile soil,
- tsetse flies, which carry a disease that kills cattle.

There were many resources in the Mutapa state. People
- washed gold from many of the rivers,
- mined copper in Hurungwe,
- grew cotton and wove it into cloth to wear, and thick cloaks and blankets called 'machira',
- made salt in the valley and traded it on the highveld,
- hunted elephants for their ivory,
- made canoes to carry goods quickly and easily down the Zambezi river.

People

The Mutapa state included people of many different cultures.

On the highveld there were many separate Karanga groups. The ruling class came mainly from the Karanga.

The Tavara lived in the valley. They had lived there longer than any other people. Other groups respected the Tavara because they were the original owners of the land. The early Tavara people made the Musengezi pottery which we learned about in chapter 11.

The farmers and copper workers of Hurungwe lived west of the Manyame river. Their state was called Mbara. Their trade in copper made them very wealthy. We know about

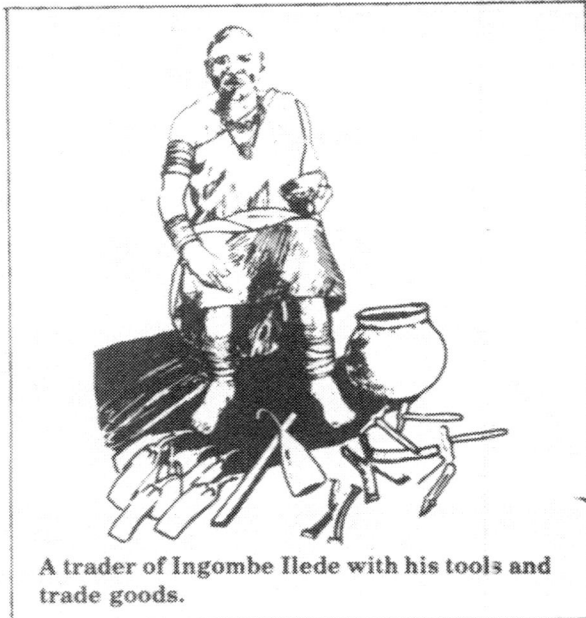

A trader of Ingombe Ilede with his tools and trade goods.

At Ingombe Ilede, archaeologists found the graves of copperworkers like this one, who was buried with copper trade goods.

them from their graves at Ingombe Ilede on the Zambezi river. At Ingombe Ilede they were buried with
- all their tools for making copper jewellery,
- heavy cross-shaped *ingots* of copper for trading,
- bars and rolls of copper wire from which they made jewellery.

They wore necklaces of golden beads and sea shells. They received large iron hoes in exchange for their copper.

The Mutapas controlled the wealth of Mbara and its people.

Exercise. Can you remember the features of a state?
It will help you to look at chapter 14.

Organization

The Mutapa state had to keep control of many different peoples. It developed a complicated system of government.

There was a danger of rebellion whenever members of the ruling class argued about who should be the Mutapa or ruler. Such disputes arose often. Many times, wars and *rebellions* resulted. These wars weakened the state and encouraged foreign interference. We will learn more about this in chapter 20.

The Mutapa state needed many officials to look after all the different activities of the state. There were officials to
- *supervise* trade with foreigners,
- lead the army,
- collect taxes and tribute,
- be *ambassadors*, messengers, law enforcers and *spies*.

The spies watched all that went on in every part of the state and in the traders' towns.

Officials were members of the ruling class. They had great power and wealth of their own. Whether they were men or women, they were called 'wives of the Mutapa'. This name showed how important they were. It showed that they were close to the Mutapa.

Tribute

The people of the Mutapa state produced a wide variety of valuable goods. These goods were traded. Trade made the Mutapa ruling class wealthy. Wealth from trade made the state strong.

The people paid tribute to the state from all they produced.
- Villagers who washed for gold gave some of each day's washings to the Mutapa's tax collectors. The collectors supervised the washings.
- Elephant hunters gave one of the tusks from each elephant they killed to the Mutapa.
- The Mutapa gave cattle to the gold miners to *encourage* them to do their hard and dangerous work. In return, the miners had to sell all the gold they mined to the Mutapa.

The Mutapa encouraged foreign traders to come to his capital to trade for gold. The Mutapa kept the profit from this trade.

The Mutapa taxed all trade goods that entered or left his territory. Every trader paid tribute to the Mutapa. Every visitor to the Mutapa brought him gifts. People brought disputes and complaints to the Mutapa. They paid fees for his judgement.

Ruling class life

The Mutapa, his wives, officials and the whole ruling class lived in great luxury. They covered the insides of their houses in *imported* cloth of many different colours. Some of this cloth was dyed. Some was embroidered in gold and silver. The floors were covered with mats and carpets.

Members of the ruling class wore long wrappings of the same rich cloth. They also wore bangles of copper and gold. They wore so many that it was difficult for them to move their arms. Officials carried spears, bows or ceremonial wooden staffs. These were decorated with gold wire and sheets of gold. They were the signs of the *rank* that the officials held.

The Mutapa's own home stood amongst the houses of the ruling class. It was much larger than the others. Chiefs from the Mutapa's territory sent their sons and daughters to live at the Mutapa's court. They worked for him as '*pages*' and '*wives*'. They lived round the Mutapa's home.

Many thousands of people lived in the capital. It was surrounded and defended by a wall thousands of metres long. The wall was built of thick wooden posts.

Documentary sources

Portuguese travellers and traders visited the Mutapa state. Some wrote descriptions of what they saw. These descriptions are sources for historians.

Here is a description of the Mutapa's court. It was written by a Portuguese called Antonio Bocarro, who died in 1649. Read the description carefully and then answer the questions that follow.

The Mutapa ruling class wore clothes like these.

❥ Besides all these there is also a larger and principal kingdom, which is that of Mokaranga, where the monomotapa resides with his court, and most of these lords or their sons, of whom the monomotapa makes use. There is also another kingdom adjoining this Mokaranga, which is the kingdom of Beza, where there is a palace of the ancient monomotapas which the people hold to be a supreme piece of work. All the monomotapas are buried there, and it serves them for a cemetery.

The dwelling in which the monomotapa resides is very large, and is composed of many houses surrounded by a great wooden fence, within which there are three dwellings, one for his own person, one for the queen and another for his servants who wait upon him within doors. There are three doors opening upon a great courtyard, one for the service of the queen, beyond which no man may pass, but only women; another for his kitchen, only entered by his cooks, who are two young men from among the principal lords of his kingdom, his relations in whom he has the most confidence, and the boys who serve in the kitchen, who are also nobles between 15 and 20 years of age. These are also employed to lay the food when the king wishes to eat, which they spread upon the ground, upon a carpet or mat.

The officers of the king's household are as follows: Ningomoxa, who is the governor of the kingdoms; Mocomoaxa, captain general; Ambuya, chief of the royal household, whose charge it is, when Mazarira, the king's great wife, dies, to name another Mazarira to inherit her house and state, and she must be from among the king's sisters; Inhantouo, the chief musician, to whom all the king's other musicians, who are very numerous, are subject, and he is a very great lord; Nurucao, who is chief captain of the vanguard in time of war; Bucurume, which signifies the king's right hand; Maguende, the chief wizard, Netambe, the king's nanga, who keeps his spells and unguents; and Nehonho, the chief door-keeper. All these are great lords, and have lands and vassals. There are many other officers of lower rank, whom it would be unending and tedious to enumerate.'

What did Bocarro call the Mutapa state?
What did he call the ruler?
How many officials are named in this description?
Which do you think were the three most important officials? Why?
What did the young sons of chiefs do?
Why did they stay at the court?
What is another name for 'a palace of the ancient monomotapa'?
What does Bocarro mean by 'a supreme piece of work'?

Discussion. The Mutapa state included peoples of various origins and cultures. In what ways did this strengthen the state? In what ways did it weaken the state? What did the Mutapas do to try and prevent rebellions? Can you think of other ways to prevent rebellions and encourage unity in such a situation?

Essay. Describe the economy of the Mutapa state, under the following subheadings:
a) Mode of production,
b) Different forms of tribute,
c) Products,
d) Trade,
e) Classes.

20. Mutapa politics

In this chapter:
We will see how the Mutapa state changed in the course of its history.
We will look at
- disputes within the Mutapa ruling class,
- *civil wars*,
- relations with the Portuguese,
- neighbouring states.

You will need to know the meanings of these words:

civil war — war between people of the same country.
prejudice — opinion formed without reason or knowledge.
rumour — unproved story or report that people pass on in conversation.
exaggerate — describe something beyond its true limits, value or size.
suspect — consider guilty without proof.
aggression — act that starts war, or unprovoked attack.
expel — force or drive out.
treaty — formal agreement between states.
hostage — a person given to or held by another to ensure that a promise is kept.
rival — a person who competes with another.
ancestral — belonging to or inherited from the ancestors.
refuge — shelter or protection from danger.
betray — give someone or something to the enemy, or act disloyally.

Early rebellions

The Mutapa state began sometime in the 15th century. Its early years were difficult ones. There were many rebellions against the new state.

One rebel was called Changamire. He fought to be the Mutapa against Mukombero Chisamarengu. Changamire became Mutapa for four years, after 1490. He continued to fight against Mukombero Chisamurengu until he was defeated in 1512.

Early trade

When the Mutapa state was finally peaceful and secure, trade with east Africa grew rapidly. Swahili traders settled near the Zambezi river. They probably started the towns of Sena and Tete.

Some Swahili came to the Mutapa capital. They set up markets at the capital and in many other places in Zimbabwe. These traders were called mwenyi or torwa. These names mean 'strangers'.

The Portuguese at Sofala soon heard about the Mutapa state. They sent spies to see if they too could trade there. The best known of the spies was a degredado called Antonio Fernandes. He made several long journeys through Mutapa lands. He wrote about these journeys. We can still read his reports.

Portuguese sources

From this time on, we know most about the Mutapa state from Portuguese reports. The Portuguese came to Zimbabwe knowing only their own society. They could not see how different Mutapa society was. Many Portuguese reports show that they knew very little about Zimbabwean society. The reports are full of *prejudices*. Many are just about *rumours*. Others are just copied from earlier reports.

Many reports were biased because of the writer's own interests.
- Missionaries wanted to show that the people of Mutapa were uncivilized and needed the Christian god.
- Portuguese officials wanted to show that the Mutapa had very large lands. They hoped he would give them some of these lands. They knew that all the lands did not really belong to him.
- Traders *exaggerated* the wealth of Mutapa. They wanted to get support for their trade.

Historians have to be very careful when they study these reports.

Trade with the Portuguese

When the Portuguese found out about the wealth of Mutapa, many sertanejos moved into Mutapa. The Mutapa controlled their trade very carefully.

By 1541, the sertanejos at the Mutapa capital had chosen a sertanejo to settle all their trade disputes. This man was called the Captain of the Gates. The Mutapa made him an important official of his own court. He was considered one of the Mutapa's wives. He was a servant of the Mutapa state. Through him, the Mutapa controlled all the trade.

The Captain of the Gates made sure that
- the Portuguese obeyed the laws and customs of Mutapa,
- the Portuguese paid a regular tribute (called the 'curva') to the Mutapa for allowing trade,
- traders paid taxes to the Mutapa on all goods that passed in and out of Mutapa.

If the rules of trade were broken, the Mutapa declared a mupeto. This meant that, until the Portuguese paid the taxes and tribute, the Mutapa
- closed the mines,
- confiscated Portuguese property,
- did not allow any trade.

What did the Portuguese traders gain?

The traders made great profits. Trade was peaceful and well organized. The diagram shows what goods were exchanged.

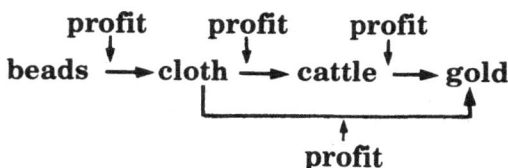

The traders made profits from each of these exchanges. They ended with gold worth 30 times as much as the beads they started with.

What did the Mutapa state gain?

The Mutapa state benefited from tribute and taxes. The ruling class helped to make trade easier. In return, the traders gave the ruling class many presents.

The ordinary people benefited least. They got some cloth, beads and cattle for their gold, ivory and cloth. The Portuguese rewarded men who worked for them as a porters and guides.

Portuguese invasion

For nearly 50 years, trade between Mutapa and the Portuguese continued peacefully. But the Portuguese became more and more greedy. They decided that they needed to gain complete control of the Mutapa state.

A Portuguese missionary, Goncalo Silveira, had been killed in Mutapa in 1561. Mwenyi traders at the Mutapa capital were *suspected* of causing his death. The Portuguese used this as an excuse for their *aggression* against Mutapa.

The Portuguese decided that all Swahili merchants or mwenyi must be *expelled* from Mutapa. To do this, they raised an army of 1 000 soldiers in Portugal in 1569. The commander was Francisco Barreto. The army sailed from Portugal to invade the Mutapa state.

Barreto's army never reached Mutapa. Hunger and disease made the army turn away

A colonial drawing of Barreto's expedition. It makes the expedition look peaceful, organized messengers of Christianity. Why is this drawing inaccurate?

from Mutapa. They realized that the Mutapa army would be too strong for them. The only battles that Barreto's army fought were against the Tonga on the lower Zambezi.

Barreto died. A man called Vasco Homem took command. He took the army back to the coast and down to Sofala. He then invaded Manyika, the rich gold-producing state between Mutapa and Sofala. Homem's army tried to take over the Manyika mines. The Portuguese planned to control gold production themselves. They tried to force people to work as slaves in the mines. This plan failed.

The Portuguese did not understand that the only way to produce gold profitably in the Mutapa and Manyika goldfields was for the work to be done by farmers. Farmers supported themselves through their farming. They only mined for a short time each year when their lands were empty of crops. Mining was extra work done by people who wanted extra wealth. It was not done to provide essentials of life. The goldfields were not rich enough to support full-time working by anyone, even slaves. The slave labour system of ancient Europe was not suitable for gold mining in Africa. Slaves also had to be fed, housed, guarded and forced to work. This would have used up all the profits from the mines.

Homem left Manyika in 1575. Only 200 men of his army remained alive. The Portuguese had learnt a lesson. They did not try to invade any state in eastern Africa for the next 200 years.

From 1575, the old pattern of trade continued for another 20 years. The Mutapa controlled the trade as he had done before the invasion.

Civil wars

In the 1590s, there were new threats to the Mutapa state. The Mutapa was Gatsi Rusere. Armies from Marave crossed the Zambezi

This picture shows what European historians of the 18th century thought the Mutapa looked like.

river and invaded the Mutapa state. Marave was a state on the north side of the Zambezi river. It was just as powerful as Mutapa. The struggle between Marave and Mutapa went on for years. Marave armies reached the gold mines of Mutapa. They came very near the Mutapa capital.

Disputes began about who was the rightful Mutapa. The ruling class was split. The people on the highveld rebelled. The state lost control over the lands outside the Zambezi valley. Civil wars broke out.

In these struggles, Gatsi Rusere had one of his uncles killed. He was the Nengomasha, the man who had led the Mutapa armies against the Marave invaders. The Nengomasha's relatives, first Chiraramuro and then Matuzianye, rebelled against Gatsi Rusere.

Gatsi Rusere asked the Portuguese to help him. This gave the Portuguese a chance to get power for themselves. A trader, Diogo Simoes Madeira, defeated Matuzvianye. Madeira then forced Gatsi Rusere to sign a *treaty*. The treaty said that the Mutapa had to

- give the mines of Mutapa to the Portuguese,
- give some of his own children to the Portuguese as *hostages*.

The Portuguese took his children to make sure that Gatsi Rusere would never harm the Portuguese. They wanted to make Gatsi Rusere's son think and act like a Portuguese. They thought that he would help them when he became the Mutapa. This son became a Roman Catholic priest in Goa in India. He never returned to Africa.

Sources

Here is Antonio Bocarro's description of the treaty between the Portuguese and the Mutapa Gatsi Rusere in 1607.

❛ 'I, the emperor Monomotapa, think fit and am pleased to give to his Majesty all the mines of gold, copper, iron, lead and pewter which may be in my empire, so long as the king of Portugal, to whom I give the said mines, shall maintain me in my position, that I may have power to order and dispose therein in the same manner as my predecessors have done up to the present time, and shall give me forces with which to go and take possession of my court and destroy a rebellious robber named Matuzianhe, who has pillaged some of the lands in which there is gold, and prevents merchants trading with their goods.'

The said emperor Monomotapa also said in the presence of the said Diogo Simoes Madeira and other Portuguese who were present, that he gave his son, the prince, to be conducted to India with the ambassador Samangana, in confirmation of all he had agreed upon with the said captain Diogo Simoes Madeira, and which is contained in this document.

The said emperor further said, in presence of all, that he had given him two of his sons to teach and to keep in his house, and had also promised him two daughters, and he said in presence of all, that he, the said Diogo Simoes Madeira, might make them all Christians, with which he, the said emperor, would be well content.

And the captain Diogo Simoes Madeira dealing with the said emperor concerning the silver mines, he answered him in the presence of all: 'The silver mines are yours, I have given them to you for the many services you have rendered me in my wars, you may give them to his Majesty if you please, since they are yours, and I have given them to you.' Then the said Diogo Simoes Madeira answered the said emperor in presence of all, that since he had given him the silver mines, he, Diogo Simoes, gave them to his Majesty, as he had asked for and acquired them as his subject. ❜

Who was Diogo Simoes Madeira?
Who was Matuzianhe?
What was the real dispute between Matuzianhe and Mutapa Gatsi Rusere?
Why did the Portuguese demand Gatsi Rusere's son?
What happened to his son later?
Where were the mines that the Portuguese were given?
Were the Portuguese successful in exploiting these mines? Give reasons.

The skeletons of two Portuguese soldiers found underneath the church at Dambarare.

Portuguese religious medals found at Dambarare.

Rebuilding the state

Nearly 40 years of trouble ended when the Mutapa was murdered by the Portuguese or by rebels. Then, in 1663, the first ruler to be known as Mukombwe became Mutapa. He started to rebuild the state. He rejected the agreements that had made the Mutapa a Portuguese vassal. He regained control of the territories of Mutapa on the highveld. He moved his capital from the valley back to the highveld. He made allies of other states and united with them against the Portuguese. Together they were strong enough to threaten the town of Sena and the prazos around it.

A new state was growing powerful in southwest Zimbabwe. It was the Rozvi state. Its rulers were called Changamire. (We will learn about the Rozvi state in chapter 23.)

Mukombwe was able to make an ally of the Rozvi. Rozvi armies attacked the Portuguese throughout Mutapa and Manyika. In 1693, they destroyed the Portuguese feiras at Dambarare and Masapa. They killed all the Portuguese soldiers, traders and missionaries living inside these feiras. From all over Zimbabwe, the rest of the Portuguese fled in fear. This victory gave the Mutapa the opportunity to strengthen his state further.

The Portuguese took *refuge* in their towns of Tete and Sena. They never regained any power in Zimbabwe. Few were ever allowed to enter the country again.

Portuguese exploitation

After the Portuguese forced Gatsi Rusere to sign the treaty, they exploited Mutapa with a new harshness. More and more sertanejos came into Mutapa. The Captain of the Gates was no longer a servant of the Mutapa. The Portuguese seldom paid the curva to the Mutapa. They never paid in full. The Mutapa could no longer punish the Portuguese for this. He was not strong enough to enforce a mupeto.

Gatsi Rusere died in 1624. Civil wars then split the state again. Kaparidze was a son of Gatsi Rusere who had not been taken hostage by the Portuguese. He now fought his uncle, Mavura, to be the Mutapa. Each of them became Mutapa for a time. Each was defeated by his *rival*. Civil war continued for nearly 40 years, even after Mavura died in 1652.

The Portuguese again took sides. This time, they supported Mavura. When he won, they forced him to sign a treaty with them. In 1629, he agreed to give up the independence of Mutapa. He agreed to pay tribute to the king of Portugal. He became a vassal of the king of Portugal.

The Captain of the Gates was now master over the Mutapa, instead of being the Mutapa's official and servant. Portuguese missionaries were allowed to turn people away from their traditional religion and customs. They tried to make them Christian.

The Portuguese could now do exactly as they wished. Prazeros raided the country with their large armies of chikunda slaves. They took *ancestral* lands and called them their own. They built new markets, called feiras, at many places:

- at Dambarare, at the top of the Mazowe river, among the Mazowe goldfields,
- at Masapa, near Mount Darwin and the Mutapa capital,
- beside the Angwa river,
- at Bocuto, beside the Mazowe river,
- at Ruhanje, near Mutoko,
- at Maramuca, in the Kadoma goldfields.

The feiras were small towns. They were surrounded by ditches, earth banks and wooden walls for defence. There was space inside the walls for houses, and for the prazero armies and trading expeditions to camp. Some feiras, like Dambarare, had churches inside them.

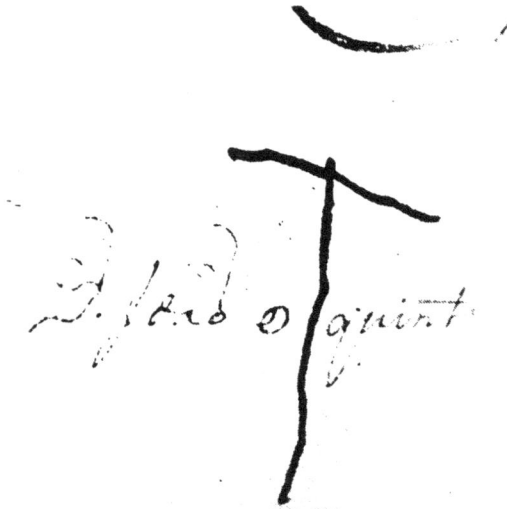

A Mutapa's signature on a Portuguese treaty.

A 19th century drawing of one of the Mutapa's soldiers.

The end of the Mutapa state

When the last Mukombwe died, in 1693, wars over the leadership began again. The Mutapas were never able to regain their former power. Despite this, Mutapas continued to rule some of their former lands until the 20th century.

The history of Mutapa is the story of a state with many great advantages. It had great resources, industries, skills, trade and wealth. It also had great weaknesses. The worst of these was the disunity of the ruling class. This led many members of the ruling class to *betray* the state to the Portuguese. As a result, they allowed the Portuguese to almost destroy the state.

Neighbouring states

The Mutapa was only one of several states in south-east Africa during the 15th to 17th centuries.

The **Manyika** state was governed by a ruler called the Chikanga. The territory was small and hilly, but rich in gold.

Because of its gold, the Portuguese wanted to control Manyika. Homem and his Portuguese army invaded it in 1575. He tried to take over the gold mining. He wanted to force slaves to work full-time in the mines. As we have seen, such a system of production could not work. Mining was only successful as the part-time work of farmers.

The Portuguese opened a feira called Masekesa on the borders of Manyika. They also tried to interfere in the government of Manyika. The Chikangas prevented this. They stopped the Portuguese from entering the state. They forced the Portuguese to use African agents to do their trading.

Teve was the state that ruled the land between Manyika and the sea at Sofala. In

Excavations of the Gambe capital at Manekweni

the 15th and 16th centuries, a great deal of the trade of Zimbabwe passed through Teve. The ruler of Teve taxed all the trade. If he thought that traders did not pay him enough taxes, he did not allow them to pass. He never allowed Portuguese traders to enter his lands.

The **Barwe** state was east of Manyika. The **Danda** and **Gambe** states were south of Teve. One of the capitals of Gambe was the stone zimbabwe of Manekweni. Archaeologists have excavated Manekweni. They show that it was the capital between about 1200 and 1700. This is a very long time for a capital city to remain in one place.

All these states were independent. Their rulers all shared the culture of the ruling class of Mutapa. They all had the same forms of government and organization. They all depended on a mixed cattle and grain economy.

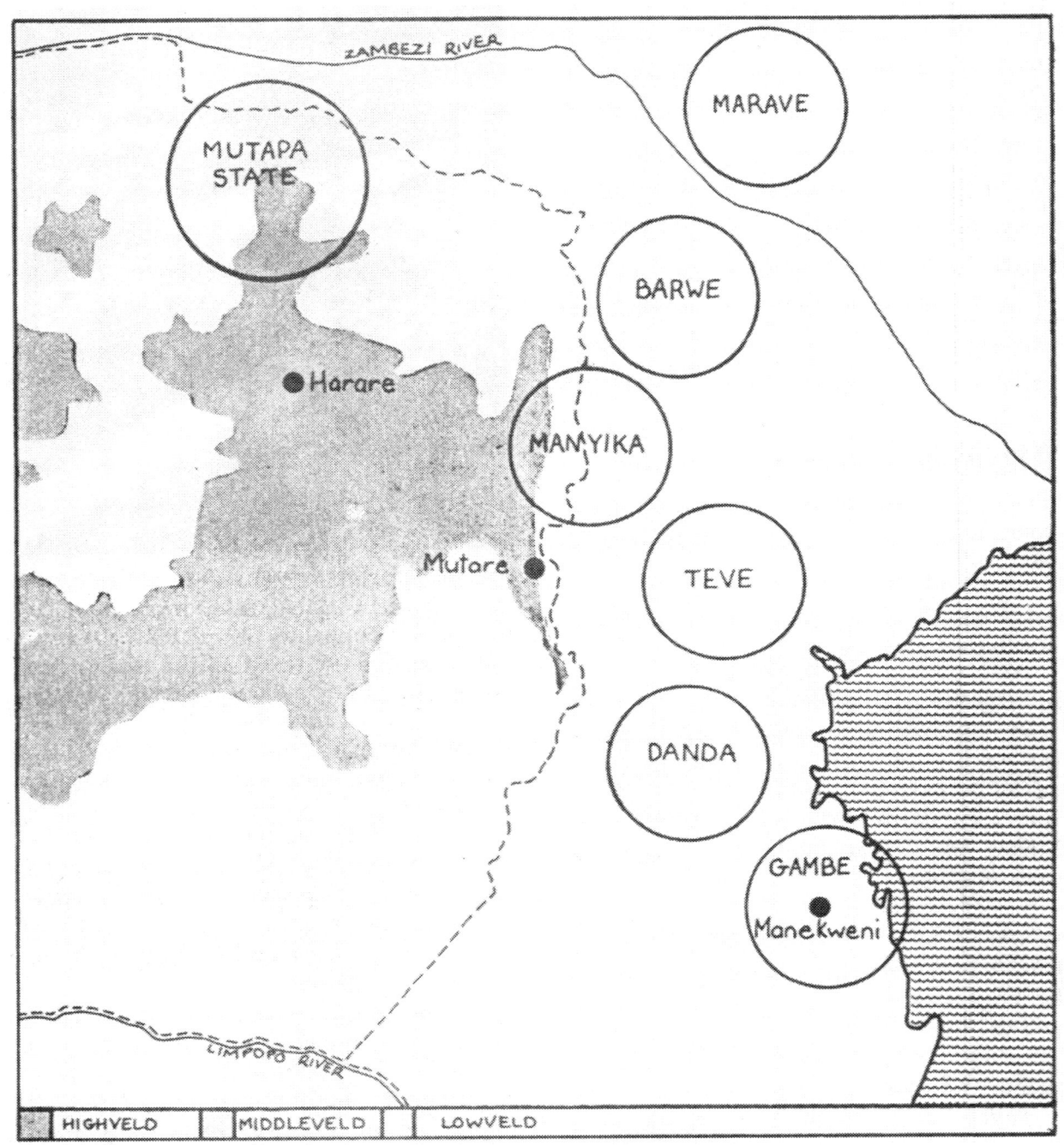

Mutapa and other states

Was the Mutapa state an empire?

The Mutapa state had some power over some other states for short periods.

Sometimes other states paid tribute to the Mutapa for a few years. Sometimes they were raided by Mutapa armies when they stopped paying. Sometimes the rulers became partners with the Mutapa against the Portuguese, Marave or Tonga. Sometimes they made these partnerships stronger by exchanging wives. This brought the ruling lineages closer together.

The Mutapa state never had a system of exploiting other states. Mutapa never became rich simply by taking a lot of products from other states as tribute. It never forced them to produce goods that the Mutapa state needed. The Mutapa state did not have enough power to do this. It did not want to or need to.

So it is wrong to think of the Mutapa state as an empire, except perhaps for a short time. An empire rules over and systematically exploits other states. The Mutapa state did not do this.

Essay. Write a brief history of relations between the Mutapa state and the Portuguese. Include a short paragraph on each of these periods:
a) early trade,
b) 1541 — 1569,
c) 1569 — 1575,
d) 1575 — 1607,
e) 1607 — 1629,
f) 1629 — 1663.

The effects of trade

We have talked a lot about foreign trade in this chapter. Remember that the foreign trade was always in luxury goods, such as gold, ivory, cloth and beads. Trade did not change ordinary people's lives very much. They continued to support themselves by farming and herding.

Foreign traders were mainly interested in gold. To meet this demand, people were forced to work in the gold mines. So the demand for gold weakened food production, local industries, and local trade in cloth, copper, salt and cattle.

Because the traders brought cloth into Zimbabwe to exchange for gold, the local weaving industry could not develop.

The Portuguese state fought hard to get the trade from this region. But it did not benefit very much. The trade did not help to develop agriculture or industry in Mozambique. The prazeros wasted their wealth in easy living. Portugal remained a poor and backward country.

21. South-western Zimbabwe

In this chapter
We will discuss five states that developed in this area.
First we will look at features that all these states had in common.
Then we will study the history of two of the states.
We will study the other three states in the next chapters.

You will need to know the meanings of these words:
found — establish, or begin building.
conquer — overcome by force, or defeat.
hierarchy — an organization with grades of people one above another.
staff — a stick or pole used for walking or fighting.
flourish — grow, or prosper, or be successful.

Five state systems developed in this area, one after the other. They all had a tributary mode of production. They were:
1. The Leopard's Kopje states. 1000–1250. There were capital towns at Mapela and Mapungubwe.
2. The Great Zimbabwe states. 1100–1450. These states had capitals in the area, at zimbabwes like Chomunanga, Mitole and Mtelegwa. Their ruling class shared the culture developed at Great Zimbabwe.
3. The Torwa state. 1450–1700. Its first capital was on the Kame River.
4. The Rozvi state. 1700–1830. The Rozvi people had their capital at Danangombe. Their rulers were called Changamire or Mambo.
5. The Ndebele state. The Ndebele state was quite different from the others. It was *founded* in 1838 when Mzilikazi invaded Zimbabwe. He *conquered* the weakened Rozvi state.

Names
Some of these names have been invented by modern historians. 'Leopard's Kopje' is the translation of the Ndebele name, 'Ntaba zingwe'. It is a hill near the Kame zimbabwe. 'Kame', 'Mapela' and 'Mapungubwe' are modern place names. 'Torwa' is a Mutapa word meaning 'stranger'.

Often, several different names for the same state have been used in old traditions and documents. For example, other names for Torwa are Togwa, Butua and Burrom.

Historians have given the first four states different names. This does not mean that the people living in them changed. All we know is that the ruling lineages changed. Perhaps they were not really different states. Changes in the ruling lineages affected the ordinary people of the south-west very little.

Sources

Because there were few foreign visitors, we have very few descriptions of the south-west states in Swahili or Portuguese documents. The descriptions that exist are mostly based on rumours. The Portuguese told of what they had heard, not what they actually saw.

Archaeology gives us almost all our knowledge of the Leopard's Kopje and Great Zimbabwe states and Torwa. Traditions tell us most of what we know about the Rozvi state.

Environment

The states of south-west Zimbabwe lasted for nearly a thousand years. Few other parts of Africa had
- such a long and continuous story,
- such long-lived and powerful centres of organized government.

We must try to understand why this was. Geography and environment give us some of the reasons.

South-west Zimbabwe is far from the sea. There are no large rivers, like the Zambezi, which traders could use to reach the area. Swahili merchants seldom came to the south-west. The Portuguese never intruded or interfered. So they did not harm these states in the same way that they harmed the Mutapa state.

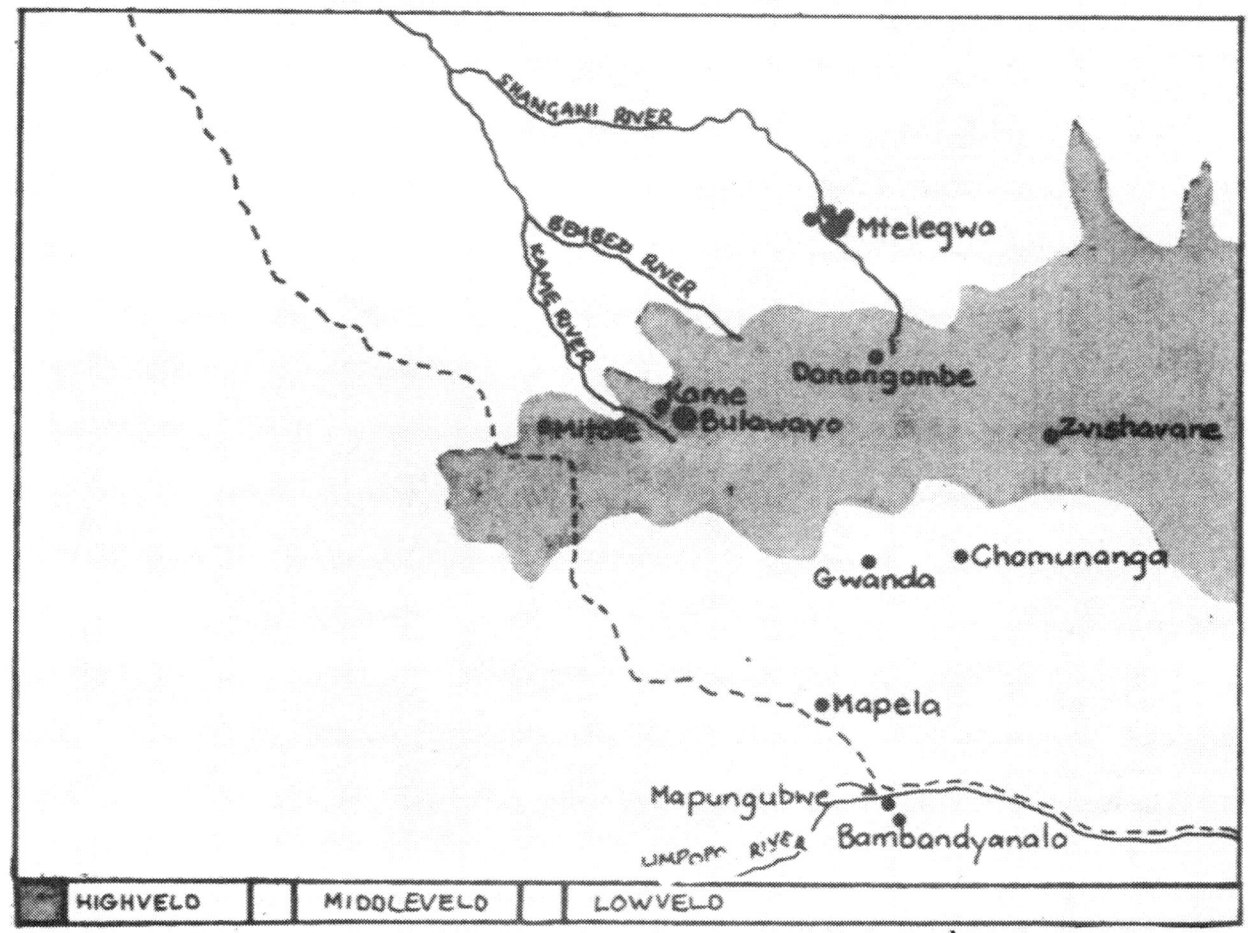

This map shows south-western Zimbabwe, the area of central and southern Matebeleland today.

In the south-west, local rulers always kept control of foreign trade. Foreign trade was much less important in the development of these states than it was at Great Zimbabwe or Mutapa.

Farming

The south-west is hard land to farm because:
- there is very little highveld. Most of the land is hilly middleveld, between 900 and 1200 metres above sea level.
- it is very dry. There are often droughts. Even in normal years, less than 600 millimetres of rain falls. A lot of this rain is wasted. Heavy storm water runs straight off the lands and into the streams.
- only a few types of crops can be grown.

People have to try and grow enough food in the good years to last them through the drought years. This is difficult, even for people with big lands and large storage bins. People cannot survive by growing crops only.

Cattle

To survive, the villagers of the south-west had to have cattle. It is a very good area for cattle. The thorn veld, with scattered acacia trees, has many bushes, plants and sweet grasses. Cattle can feed on these all the year round. In the lower and drier areas, cattle eat the leaves of mopane trees, especially in winter when the grass is finished. Tsetse fly cannot survive in this area, so they do not spread disease among the cattle.

This photograph was taken from Mapela Hill. It shows the veld and scattered trees of south-western Zimbabwe. It is a good area for cattle.

Cattle are wealth. They are a form of wealth that
- is easy to look after,
- increases as calves are born,
- can easily be exchanged for other things,
- can be used by rulers to reward soldiers, miners, metalworkers and traders.

We have seen how states like Great Zimbabwe got their power from their cattle herds.

In the south-west of Zimbabwe, people relied on their rulers and their rulers' cattle herds for their security. Rulers lent cattle to people whose own had died or been exchanged. Rulers also gave people cattle to pay bridewealth. Rulers and villagers were linked together through this system of loans and gifts of cattle.

Poor people with no cattle became the clients of rich patrons with many cattle. Clients looked after their patron's cattle. In return, clients were given some of their patron's calves and all the milk.

Cattle were more than food, security and wealth. Relationships between rich and poor, and men and women were seen in terms of cattle. From its cattle, a homestead could survive and grow. The size of cattle herds decided who were members of the ruling class.

South-west Zimbabwe had other resources. There were goldfields round what are now Bulawayo, Gwanda, Zvishavane and Shangani. These goldfields were mined by all the states we have named. But it was the cattle of the south-west that were famous. Even the Portuguese heard about them. They wrote of big herds of the finest beasts, to be found far beyond Portuguese reach.

Early towns

The first towns in southern Africa grew up on the edge of the Kgalagadi desert in eastern Bostwana. They were started in the 10th century. There were only about three of them. One is called Toutswe. They were about 100 kilometres apart. Around each town were several large villages. There were also very many small homesteads within reach of each town.

Most of the homesteads were along rivers where there was water for livestock. Each settlement had a cattlepen in the centre. The pens in the towns were very large. There were smaller pens in the homesteads.

In the Botswana towns there was already inequality. Society was organized in a *hierarchy*. People had ranks, from strong authorities in charge of the towns, to ordinary herders in the homesteads. Trade started. It spread far from the towns. Cattle from the towns were probably exchanged for grain with farmers further north.

Leopard's Kopje

In the 10th century, the Leopard's Kopje people lived the same kind of life as the people in Botswana. They also protected their cattle herds in pens in the middle of their settlements. They too built towns.

One town, called Bambandyanalo, was near the southern bank of the Limpopo river. People lived there during the 11th and 12th centuries. It was not just a society of cattle herders. People hunted elephants in the river valley. They carved the ivory. Gold reached Bambandyanalo from the goldfields of the north. The people of Bambandyanalo traded gold and ivory for foreign glass beads.

In the late 12th century, a ruling class developed. The ruling class settled on the flat top of Mapungubwe Hill near Bambandyanalo. They used a new type of pottery. They had beautiful, shallow, serving dishes. These were polished to a shiny black colour.

The ruling class at Mapungubwe buried their dead with many objects covered in sheets of beaten gold. There were bowls, carvings and *staffs* of office. These objects show how different the ruling class had become from ordinary villagers.

Mapela was another Leopard's Kopje town. It was 85 kilometres north-west of Mapungubwe, on the Shashi river. It was also on a flat hilltop, surrounded by high cliffs. The cliffs could only be climbed in one or two places.

In the 12th and 13th centuries, the ruling class of Mapela lived on the highest point of the hill. The walls and furniture of their houses were made of clay, polished and moulded in beautiful patterns. The houses were just like the houses of the ruling class at Great Zimbabwe. They were quite unlike the thin-walled houses of the ordinary people who lived on the lower hillside at Mapela.

People were organized to work together to build stone platforms on the slopes of the hill. These made Mapela very difficult to attack. Ordinary people built their houses on the platforms.

The people of Mapela received many foreign beads and other goods. The ruling class had control of the gold, ivory and other goods that the foreign traders wanted. Mapela was too remote and difficult for foreign traders to reach themselves. Local people exchanged goods from village to village. In this way, the goods reached foreign traders at the coast.

Mapela looked like this in the 12th and 13th century. What can you see in the drawing that made Mapela safe from attack?

Wood carvings covered in gold sheets, beads and a serving bowl from Mapungubwe.

Discussion. From what source have historians learned about the Leopard's Kopje state? Give reasons for your answer.

Zimbabwes

While the Leopard's Kopje towns of the south-west *flourished*, Great Zimbabwe was also developing. Its first stone walls were built in the early 13th century. After some time, there were several independent states. Each state had zimbabwes at their capitals. They had the same ruling class culture as Great Zimbabwe. We can see this in the designs of their houses, jewellery and pottery. It is most obvious in the skill and beauty of the stone walls of the rulers' courts.

There were important zimbabwes in the south-west. One was at Chomunanga, at the head of the Bubi river. Treasure hunters found more than 2 kilograms of golden jewellery and wooden carvings covered in beaten gold sheets at Chomunanga. Other zimbabwes were at Mitole on the Botswana border, and at Mtelegwa on the upper Shangani river. These were all the capitals of rulers. They were independent of Great Zimbabwe, although they copied many features of Great Zimbabwe's culture.

The cultures of the ruling classes who lived in zimbabwes and the cultures of the ruling class of Mapela and Mapungubwe were different. We do not know how these differences affected the organization or economy of the societies. They probably affected them very little.

Essay. Explain the ways in which the environment of south-western Zimbabwe affected the states that developed there between 1000 and 1450. In your explanation, answer these questions:
a) What are the main features of the environment in south-western Zimbabwe?
b) What states developed there between 1000 and 1450?
c) How did these states take advantage of the environment?
d) What kind of social organization resulted?

22. Torwa or Kame

In this chapter:
- We will learn more about the Torwa state of south-west Zimbabwe.
- We will discuss Torwa's architecture, craft, trade, and politics.

You will need to know the meanings of these words:
regalia — decorations and objects to show importance, especially of a ruler or monarch.
divine — learn, or predict, or discover.

The beginning of the Torwa state

The Great Zimbabwe state lost its importance in the middle of the 15th century. This did not affect the ruling classes of the south-west. They were not weakened.

One state grew even stronger. It was wealthy enough to build many zimbabwes all over the south-west. It improved the traditions of Great Zimbabwe in its pottery, houses and stone architecture. The south-west became united into a single state. Historians call it the Torwa state. 'Torwa' was one of the early Portuguese names for the south-west. The Portuguese wrote about rulers of lands beyond Mutapa that they knew little about. We do not know any of the actual names of the rulers of this time.

Architecture

This new state began sometime in the 15th century. A new capital was built beside the Kame river, just outside present Bulawayo. We can see how Torwa developed by studying this capital.

The builders at Kame used the masonry skills developed at Great Zimbabwe. But

Naletale was one of the Torwa zimbabwes. Notice the lower wall to hold the platform in place. How many patterns can you see in the wall above? Draw the different patterns in your exercise book.

they did not build high, bare, stone walls like the walls at Great Zimbabwe and Chomunanga. The new builders kept the Leopard's Kopje tradition of building houses on stone platforms, as at Mapela.

The houses of the ruling class were built on small hills. The builders enlarged these hills with stones and earth, to make wide platforms. Very skilfully made walls held these platforms in place. The masons made all sorts of patterns in the walls, such as chevrons, herring bones, checkerwork and lines of coloured stones. This was a new sort of architecture.

Houses were built on top of the platforms. The houses were surrounded by courtyards. The courtyards were separated by walls made of pole and daga (not stone like at Great Zimbabwe). These walls spread out from the main house like the spokes of a wheel. There were deep stone-lined latrines in the rulers' houses.

Exercise. In chapter 21, we learned about the features that states in the south-west had in common. We saw that the lives of ordinary villagers did not change very much when the rulers changed.

How did villagers in the Torwa state support themselves?

What was their most important form of wealth?

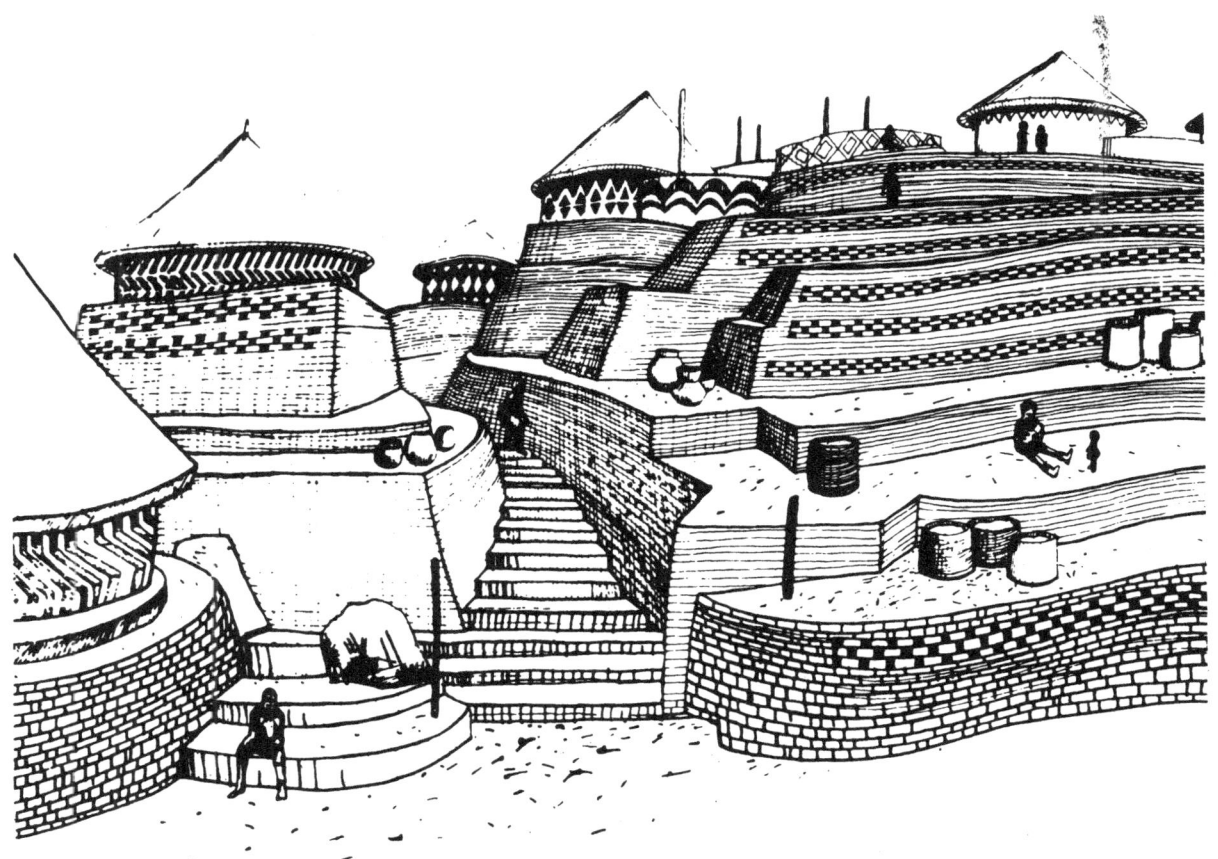

Part of the Kame zimbabwe. Study the drawing carefully. How was the architecture of Kame different from the architecture of Great Zimbabwe?

This is a modern photograph of the Kame passage. When the rulers of Torwa lived here, there was a daga roof over the passage.

The royal court at Kame

The ruler lived in great privacy, above the town. The ruler's court was surrounded by nine smaller zimbabwes. These were the homes of other members of the ruling class. The town was by far the biggest in the state. It was only a quarter of the size that Great Zimbabwe had been.

The Torwa ruling class built at least 80 other zimbabwes at the same time as Kame. They existed throughout the territory of the Kame state. Many of these zimbabwes were very small. Often there was just a round, stone-faced platform on which the main house stood. One small zimbabwe was even built next to Mapela in the 15th century. Here the new ruling class could control the people of the old Leopard's Kopje town.

The ruler's wealth

At Kame, the ruler lived on the hilltop. To reach his house there was a secret passage under the platforms. The passage was covered by a flat daga roof supported on thick poles. The top of the roof was part of the pavement of the courtyard. Elephant tusks stood along the passage. At the top of the passage was a secret room.

In 1947, an archaeologist found part of the royal *regalia* in the ruler's secret room. Someone had wrapped it in cloth and hidden it in a basket. There were
- seven copper spears, each of a different design,
- iron spears,
- iron axes, one with a wooden handle covered in beaten copper sheets,
- small ivory carvings of lions and leopards from the tops of ceremonial staffs,
- a set of carved ivory *divining* dice,
- drinking pots decorated with the Kame ruler's traditional red and black patterns.

Trade

We do not yet know much about the society or economy of the Torwa state. Archaeologists have found pieces of Chinese, Persian and Portuguese pottery. These were all made in the early 17th century. They show that there was some trade with the Portuguese. This does not mean that the Portuguese themselves travelled to Torwa. Mwenyi from the east African cost brought foreign goods to trade with the Torwa rulers.

As we learned in chapter 20, the Portuguese had driven the mwenyi from the Mutapa markets. The mwenyi came to Torwa because they wanted
- new areas to trade in,
- new sources of gold to buy and export,
- to avoid places where the Portuguese were powerful.

Torwa politics

From its earliest years, Torwa was a powerful state. At the end of the 15th century, it was strong and *ambitious* enough to try and interfere in the Mutapa state. As we learned in chapter 20, the Mutapas were struggling to unite their state at this time. A Changamire, possibly from Torwa, even took control of the Mutapa state in about 1490. The Torwa invaders were defeated in 1512. But they were only driven out of the Mutapa land finally in about 1547.

A hundred years later, Torwa was suffering from its own disputes. The ruling class disagreed about who should be ruler. Torwa was also trying to stop mwenyi traders within the state from becoming too powerful.

A defeated Torwa ruler fled to the Portuguese feira at Manyika in 1644. He asked a Portuguese prazero, Sismundo Dias Bayao, to help him regain his power. Bayao agreed. He invaded Torwa with his army. He was the first and only Portuguese to do so. He was soon driven out.

During these troubles, the capital at Kame was probably set on fire and destroyed. The royal regalia was lost. The Torwa capital was moved. A new zimbabwe was built at Danangombe. It was smaller than Kame. The stonework was even more richly decorated. It is possible that when the capital moved, the Torwa state lost control over the lands west of the Bembesi river.

Essay. Compare the Mutapa and Torwa states. Discuss:
a) sources (how have historians collected information about these states?),
b) dates,
c) territory,
d) environment,
e) trade,
f) relations with the Portuguese,
g) success and failure.

23. The Rozvi state

In this chapter:
We will study the Rozvi state, which developed in the south-west after the Torwa state. We will learn about the Rozvi state's relations with other states and with traders, and its army, economy, growth and *decline*.

You will need to know the meanings of these words:
decline — weaken or decrease.
argument — reasons for a point of view.
victorious — conquering.
mobilize — prepare large numbers of people for action, especially war.

The beginning of the Rozvi state

By 1680, the rulers of south-west Zimbabwe were called Changamire. Another name for the ruler was Mambo. The people also had a new name — Rozvi. It means 'warriors', or 'destroyers'.

Historians do not agree about the Rozvi. Some historians say that the Rozvi were outsiders who invaded the south-west. Other historians say that the Rozvi were the people of Torwa, with a new name. Let us look at the *arguments* of the different historians.

Who were the Rozvi?
1. Some historians believe that the Rozvi had been subjects of the Mutapa. They believe that the Rozvi came from the area between Mutapa and Torwa. These historians believe that the Rozvi invaded Torwa and conquered it.

    Two Portuguese documents, written in 1684 and 1696, support this explanation. Some Rozvi traditions seem to say the same thing. But the documents and traditions are not clear or certain.

2. Other historians have a simpler explanation. They say that the Rozvi and Torwa were the same people. Rozvi was just a new name for Torwa. There was no invasion or conquest. The old Torwa state continued. Only the name changed.

We can certainly agree that the Rozvi ruled Torwa after 1680.

Rozvi and Mutapa

The Changamire's army was strong enough to make war far beyond Rozvi territory. The army attacked Mutapa Mukombwe in the 1680s. The Changamire then agreed to help Mukombwe to stop Portuguese interference in the Mutapa state.

By 1684, the Changamire was making war on the Portuguese, as we learned in chapter 20. In 1693, his army killed all the Portuguese soldiers, traders and missionaries at Dambarare and Masapa. The Rozvi army also drove the Portuguese from the feira of Masekesa, in Manyika. The Portuguese fled from Zimbabwe. Very few ever returned.

Traditions about Dombo
Rozvi traditions say that the Changamire who defeated the Portuguese was called Dombo or Chikurawadyembewu. The traditions say that
- Dombo's father was Mwari (god),
- his mother was a virgin,
- Dombo was called by Mwari to lead the Rozvi.

Traditions describe a court built by Dombo's people on the top of a hill, with a stairway built of ivory. This is a reasonable description of the Kame and Rozvi zimbabwes.

Perhaps there was a real historical figure called Dombo. Perhaps these traditions bring together stories of several early rulers into a single person. This *victorious* leader might be a figure of legend, like Mutota, the father of the Mutapa state. These are things that we do not yet know for certain. This does not matter. In history, we try to study the story of all the people, more than the lives of particular individuals. Every ruler got power from the ordinary people and the way that they were *mobilized* and organized.

Exercise. In chapter 21, we learned about the geography of the south-west of Zimbabwe. Describe the environment.
What work did ordinary people do?

The rulers of the Rozvi state lived in the old Torwa zimbabwes, such as Naletale.

A wall with herring bone and check patterns at Danangombe.

The Rozvi army

We still know very little about the organization of the Rozvi state. All we can see is the result of its power. We can see that its armies were especially strong.

Rozvi armies defeated the Portuguese in 1693 and drove them from Zimbabwe. The Portuguese were allowed to start new settlements at Zumbo on the Zambezi river, and in Manyika. In the 100 years after the victory of 1693, the Rozvi armies often marched on these settlements. When the Portuguese were being rebellious, the Rozvi armies attacked them. When the Portuguese were being helpful, the Rozvi armies defended them against others.

Rozvi armies could travel and make war wherever they wished in Zimbabwe. No other state could successfully oppose them.

We do not know
- what made young men join the Rozvi armies,
- how they were organized and trained,
- for how long armies could make war,
- how the armies were supplied.

Traditions say that the Rozvi armies used magic, medicines, tricks and spies to win their battles. These are not helpful historical explanations. Probably, the Changamire used his royal cattle herds and cattle captured in war to reward young men for their army service. This would encourage young men to join the army.

Tribute

Rozvi territory was quite small. It only reached for about 100 kilometres around the capital zimbabwe at Danangombe. There were other

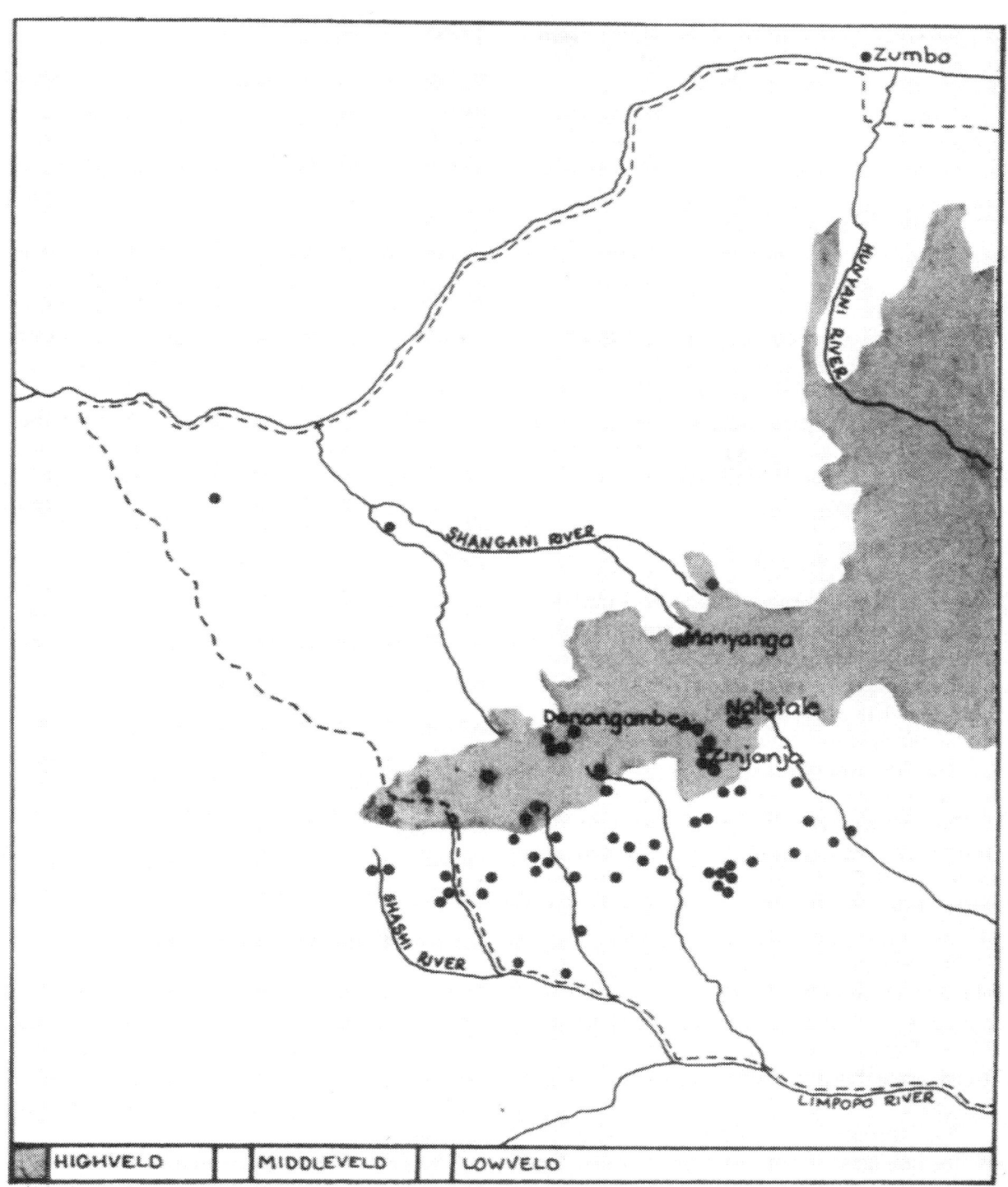

The Rozve state and tributary area.

zimbabwes. Three were at Naletale, Zinjanja and Manyanga (NtabazikaMambo). There were also many smaller ones.

Many small states outside Rozvi territory paid tribute to the Changamire. The Portuguese at Zumbo also paid tribute to the Changamire. This meant that they accepted the Changamire's rule. The area where the Rozvi collected tribute stretched right across Zimbabwe, and as far as the Shoshong Hills in Botswana.

The Rozvi army often collected tribute for the Changamire directly. The tribute was not passed from junior to senior chiefs.

It was through tribute, not through trade, that the state got a lot of gold from the miners. Tribute from the Portuguese was paid in foreign trade goods.

The Tumbare

Traditions tell us that the Rozvi army was always led by a person called the Tumbare. He always came from one of the senior families of the ruling class. He was the army commander and the chief tax collector. He also took over the authority of the Changamire

- if there were disputes about who would be the next ruler, or
- if the real ruler was too young to rule.

This arrangement helped to prevent disputes over who should rule. Such disputes were one of the biggest weaknesses in many other states. Outsiders often took advantage of civil wars that took place between rivals. They placed their own allies in power. Rulers who got their power in this way served the interests of the outsiders who had helped them. These things did not happen in the Rozvi state because of the authority of the Tumbare.

The Tumbare's family may have been one of the lineages of the old Torwa state. The Changamire allowed the old ruling class of Torwa to keep a lot of its former power. In this way, the Rozvi state remained united.

Trade

The Rozvi state became an important trading partner of the mwenyi. Later it became the trading partner of the Portuguese at Zumbo. The rulers at Danangombe received many pieces of Chinese porcelain and bottles of Dutch alcohol in trade. The Changamire received Portuguese cannon and Portuguese jewellery, including a huge gold ring. All of these were made in the late 17th century. Treasure hunters found nearly 20 kilograms of gold jewellery in the ruins of Danangombe in 1893.

The Rozvi continued to take gold from the mines that had been started many centuries before. But some historians believe that gold was becoming more and more difficult to get. Miners had to dig very deep mines to find any gold.

Gold was traded with the vashambadzi. They were the agents of the Portuguese prazeros. The Changamire did not allow any Portuguese to enter the Rozvi state.

The Rozvi rulers may not have been very interested in trade. They traded because they were strong. They did not become strong through trade. Trade did not create and support the ruling class's power. Trade did not make the ruling class different from the rest of the people. In these ways, the Rozvi state was different from Mutapa.

The end of the Rozvi state

The Rozvi state was the greatest power in south-west Zimbabwe for nearly 150 years, as the Torwa state had been for 250 years before that. Early in the 19th century, Rozvi power declined. Many people stopped paying tribute to the state.

The end of the state came between 1830 and 1840. This was the result of the invasion by several Nguni groups. The Rozvi defeated early attacks by Sotho and Nguni armies.

Then Zwangendaba's Nguni army invaded. One of his followers attacked Danangombe. He drove the Changamire, Chirisamhuru, to his death at Manyanga. Nxaba's Nguni caused further disasters.

When Mzilikazi's Ndebele invaded in 1838, they found the Rozvi state broken and defeated. But the Rozvi continued to raid the Ndebele for the next 15 years, until 1853. Then all resistance stopped.

Essay. Write an account of the Tumbare in the Rozvi state.

Include the answers to these questions:
a) Who was the Tumbare?
b) What were his duties?
c) Why was he important for the unity of the Rozvi state?
d) From what sources do historians know about the Tumbare?

A Portuguese cannon belonging to the Changamire at Danangombe.

24. Nguni societies in the 19th century

In this chapter:
> We will see how a *crisis* caused great changes in Nguni society.
> We will study the new states that developed in southern Africa as a result of these changes.

You will need to know the meanings of these words

crisis — a turning point, or time of change or danger.
famine — serious shortage of food, leading to widespread hunger and starvation.
abolish — put an end to.
disband — break up or separate a group.
tactic — plan or way of fighting.
confederacy — alliance of people or chiefdoms.
exile — force someone to leave their home or country for a long time.
Boers — descendants of early Dutch settlers in South Africa.
aggressive — warlike, or often attacking others.

At the end of the 1700s, people in South Africa could be divided into two main groups, by the languages that they spoke. They were the Sotho and Nguni.

There were three separate Sotho language groups:
- the northern Sotho or Pedi,
- the southern Sotho,
- the western Sotho or Tswana.

There were two groups of Nguni:
- the southern Nguni or Xhosa,
- the northern Nguni.

In this chapter, we will study only the northern Nguni.

The northern Nguni

At the end of the 18th century, the northern Nguni were farmers. They grew millet and sorghum, and many different vegetables and root crops. They were also great cattle breeders. Cattle were very important to them. There were probably more cattle than people in the Nguni lands.

Organization of society

The Nguni needed a lot of land to graze their cattle. So they did not live in villages or towns. They lived in separate homesteads. The homesteads were scattered across the country.

Each homestead had between five and 40 houses. To make a house, people fixed poles in the ground. They bent the poles and joined them together to make a dome shape. They laid grass or mats over the poles.

Each homestead was laid out in the same way. The head of the homestead lived in the middle of a line of houses. The houses of each of his wives were placed in order of their rank, on either side of his house. The houses curved round in a ring. The cattle were penned in the middle of the ring of houses.

The people of a homestead included the head of the homestead, his wives, all the unmarried young men and women of his family, and his children. Friends or strangers were allowed to join a homestead if they wished. Parents often joined a new homestead when their own children had left the original homestead.

Each homestead was self sufficient. Each homestead
- grew all its own food,
- made most of the things that it needed.

Homesteads all belonged to a chiefdom. All the homesteads of a chiefdom belonged to the same lineage. So people of the same chiefdom could not marry each other.

As chiefdoms grew in size, they divided. Often one of the senior sons of a chief started a new chiefdom, when his older brother became chief of the old chiefdom. The chiefdoms were all very small. Each had only a few thousand people. Their territories were never more than 40 or 50 kilometres across.

Chiefs lived better than other people, but they were not separated from them. They did not form a separate class. Chiefs
- settled disputes between their people,
- made sure that wrong-doers were punished,
- organized the protection of the herds and grazing lands,
- worked in their own fields with their families.

People helped the chiefs in several ways. They helped to build the chiefs' houses and to clear their lands.

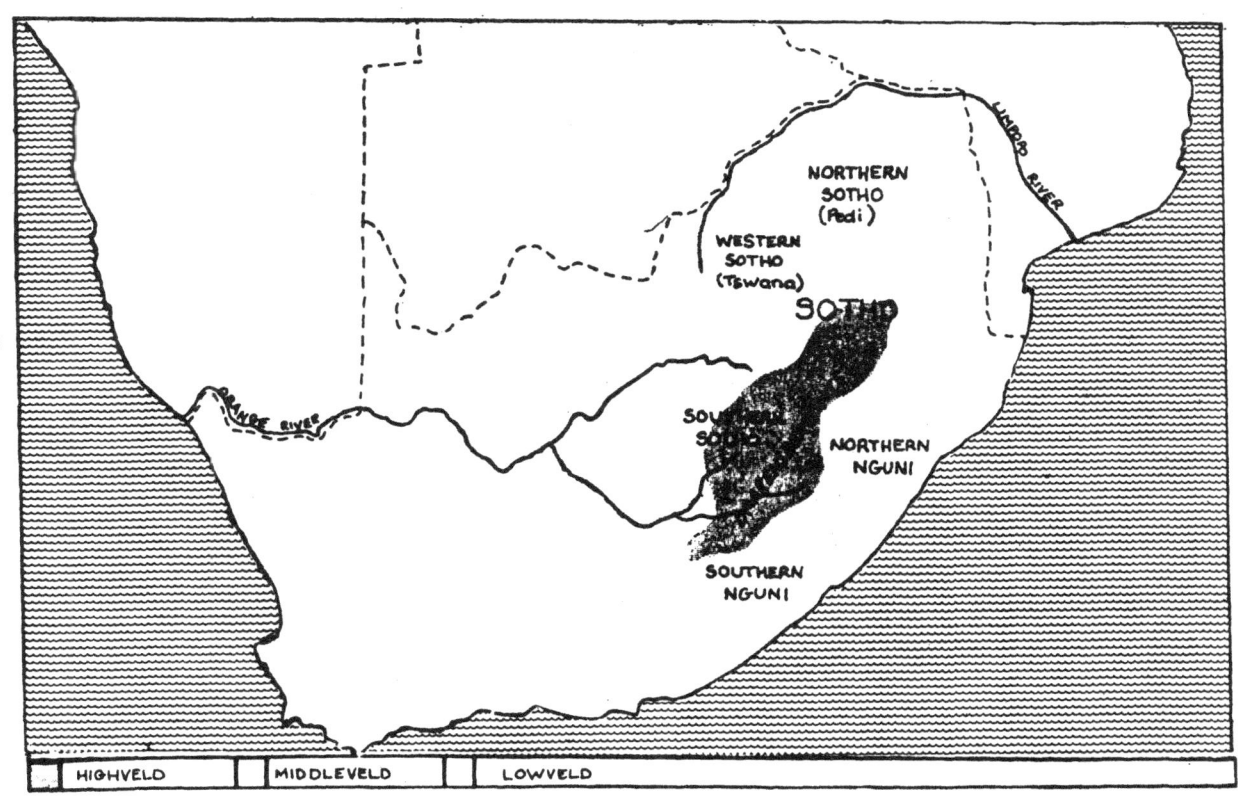

This map shows where different language groups lived in South Africa at the end of the 1700's.

Environment

The lands of the northern Nguni stretched from the foot of the Drakensburg mountains to the sea. The land was broken by many rivers, flowing from the mountains. The bigger rivers had deep valleys. Most homesteads were on the ridges between rivers.

There were many different sorts of soil and vegetation. The high ground got most of the rain. It had good grazing after the rainy season. But the grass, called sourveld, soon became tough and dry, and gave little food for cattle. The valleys were drier and covered in bush and scrub. The grass and bushes here are called sweetveld. They provided food for cattle throughout the year, especially in the dry winter months. The bigger rivers had water throughout the year. Their valleys had fertile soils, so they were very good farmlands. The land near the sea was a mixture of sweet and sour veld.

It was good land for farmers, and especially for cattle. But it could be damaged very easily. Too many cattle, or cattle kept for too long in one place, destroyed the grass. The cattle could turn the veld into useless thorn bush or bare earth. Undergrazing did as much harm. Cattle ate only the best grass. This allowed the poor grass to spread and spoil the lands. So each community needed to move its cattle from pasture to pasture. Everyone had to manage the grazing of their herds carefully.

Discussion. What is overgrazing? How can farmers prevent it? What is undergrazing? How can farmers prevent it?

An Nguni homstead. Notice the cattle pen in the middle and the dome-shaped houses.

The crisis

For a long time, the numbers of people and cattle increased steadily in the Nguni lands. At the end of the 18th century, rainfall decreased throughout the area. Many years of poor rain caused a crisis:
- land became infertile,
- grazing became poor,
- crops started to fail,
- cattle started to die.

There were few new farmlands that people could move to. The people faced hardship and *famine*. This led the chiefdoms to guard their lands more fiercely. Stronger chiefdoms tried to take land from weaker chiefdoms. There was more and more conflict between Nguni chiefdoms.

Reorganization of society

To save itself, society had to organize itself in new ways. Some chiefdoms decided to come together to form bigger chiefdoms. They could control land more efficiently in this way. Some of the stronger chiefdoms conquered the smaller ones and included them in new and bigger chiefdoms.

Nguni society changed completely. The way work was divided between people changed. The new chiefdoms had much more control over the people. As a result, many new and powerful Nguni states developed in different places.

Dingiswayo was one leader of change. He was the chief of a northern Nguni group, the Mthethwa. He looked at some of the traditional customs of the Nguni, especially the initiation schools. At these schools, young men were taught the traditions and customs of their elders. They were then circumcised and accepted as adults, able to marry. Dingiswayo also examined the tradition of hunting parties. Many young men of about the same age joined together in collective hunts.

Age regiments

Dingiswayo ordered that circumcision be *abolished*. This meant that young men could not become adults or marry. Dingiswayo changed the hunting parties into age regiments called amabutho.

All young men of the same age joined an ibutho. They
- lived together in their own large settlements,
- worked for the ruler, on his lands,
- grew crops for the ruler and for themselves,
- herded and protected the ruler's cattle.

Older women from the homesteads or from the ruler's own family cooked for the young men in their regimental towns. Younger women often joined the young men for a while. But the young men could not marry, because they were not considered adults. They could not start their own families or homesteads.

The ruler decided when a regiment had served for long enough. Some regiments served until the men were 40 years old. When the regiment was *disbanded*, the ruler chose an area for them to settle in and provided them with cattle. He gave them bridewealth. They could marry and start their own homesteads.

Results

This new organization caused all sorts of very important changes. The young men and their regiments were a new and separate class in society. There was a new relationship between the ruler and the young men.

Young men's work was no longer used in the homesteads, but for the ruler and the state. The new system gave the state a great deal of new power. The ruler could decide the age at which people could marry. He could make sure that people married later in life than they did before. This meant that families had fewer children and so the population stopped increasing as fast.

The ruler decided where new homesteads would be. He made sure that people made the best use of the land. He also controlled where people grazed their cattle. He made sure that cattle were grazed away from places with cattle disease or where the grazing was unsuitable.

A new fighting force

The age regiments developed into a very powerful army. In their raids and wars, they captured cattle, women and children. These increased the wealth of the state. There were more cattle and more people to work for the state.

Many history books praise the Nguni as great warriors. These books describe:
- the Nguni's new weapon, the short stabbing spear or assegai. This weapon forced men to fight their enemy hand-to-hand. Before, armies had thrown spears at their enemy from a long distance away. Thrown spears had much less chance of killing the enemy than stabbing assegais.
- new *tactics* in warfare. Several regiments worked together. Some fought the enemy from the front. Others went round and encircled the enemy so that they could not run away. With such tactics, many of the enemy were killed.
- the hard training of the regiments. Men were not allowed to wear sandals. Their feet became hardened, and so they could cover long distances quickly and attack at great speed.

It is true that the new regiments used all these improvements in warfare. But they were not new inventions. All Nguni groups had used these weapons and tactics for many years. The regiment system changed much more than just the ways of fighting.

Joining a regiment was not a hardship for young men. They were proud to be such good

Young Zulu men who belong to an age regiment.

warriors. Through the regiments, young men of any lineage had a chance to have important positions in their regiments and then in the state. The men of the regiments were admired by those left behind in the villages.

Discussion. How did the regiment system change the Nguni ways of
- working?
- marrying?
- forming settlements?

Life in the homesteads did not change very much when so many young men left. Women already did most of the farming. The women did have to work harder. They had to do some of the work usually done by men, like building and clearing land. But the young men all went home to help sometimes. Life became harder for the women, and the men got all the honour.

Nguni soldiers show their loyalty to their king.

The Mthethwa and Zulu

We saw that small Nguni chiefdoms began to form alliances with each other at the end of the 18th century. They joined together to form large *confederacies*. The three largest were the Mthethwa, Ndwandwe and Ngwane confederacies.

Exercise. Why did small chiefdoms join together at the end of the 1700s?
How did they benefit from forming confederacies?

The Mthethwa confederacy was ruled by Dingiswayo. This confederacy did not last long.

Dingiswayo made a man called Shaka the commander of one of his regiments. Shaka was the illegitimate son of the chief of the Zulu. The Zulu chiefdom was not very important at that time. In 1816, Dingiswayo helped Shaka to become chief of the Zulu. Dingiswayo was killed fighting the Ndwandwe in 1818. After that, the whole Mthethwa confederacy was made part of the new Zulu state. Shaka perfected Dingiswayo's social changes. He turned the regiments into an expert army.

Shaka was an absolute ruler. He did not allow anyone to argue with him. His chiefs and councils had no influence over him. Those who disagreed with him were *exiled*.

Shaka's ruthless leadership made the Zulu regiments the most powerful force in all the Nguni territories and far beyond. Zulu armies raided every community within their reach. They took cattle and grain and killed soldiers. They took women and children back to become part of the Zulu state and to work in Zulu fields.

Zulu attacks and wars weakened many societies. Communities were forced to move out of reach of Zulu armies. These communities tried to settle in new lands. They fought each other for the new lands. This period has been called the Mfecane, which means the 'forced migration'.

The Zulu defeated the Ndwandwe in 1819. After 1819, there were many more wars between the Ndwandwe and the Zulu. But the Ndwandwe were never strong enough to conquer the Zulu.

Between 1826 and 1828, Shaka sent his armies to fight the Ngwane. He also attacked the people south of the Zulu, and the Gaza Nguni in the far north. The attack on the Gazi Nguni was unsuccessful. The army returned dissatisfied. Before it arrived home, Shaka was murdered by his half-brother, Dingane.

Dingane was not as good a leader as Shaka had been. His army and many of the Zulu chiefs became dissatisfied with Dingane. Dingane also fought with the first *Boers* who tried to settle in Nguni lands. The Zulu army was finally defeated by the Boers. The defeat of the Zulu is still celebrated by the Boers. They call it the Battle of Blood River.

After this defeat, the Zulu nation split into two. Half the Zulu followed Dingane's brother, Mpande. Mpande allied himself with the Boers. He became head of the whole nation when Dingane died in 1840. Mpande ruled until 1872. He continued to raid neighbouring states.

King Mpande of the Zulu state.

Discussion. In chapter 10, we saw that migrations are usually harmful to societies. We saw that people very rarely choose to migrate in order to solve their problems. What forced Nguni people to migrate in the 19th century?

Why do you think migration was a good choice for the Nguni, but an unlikely choice for the first farmers? Tto help you answer this question, make a list comparing the first farmers and the Nguni under these headings:
a) environment,
b) technology,
c) population size and growth,
d) mode of production,
e) social organization.

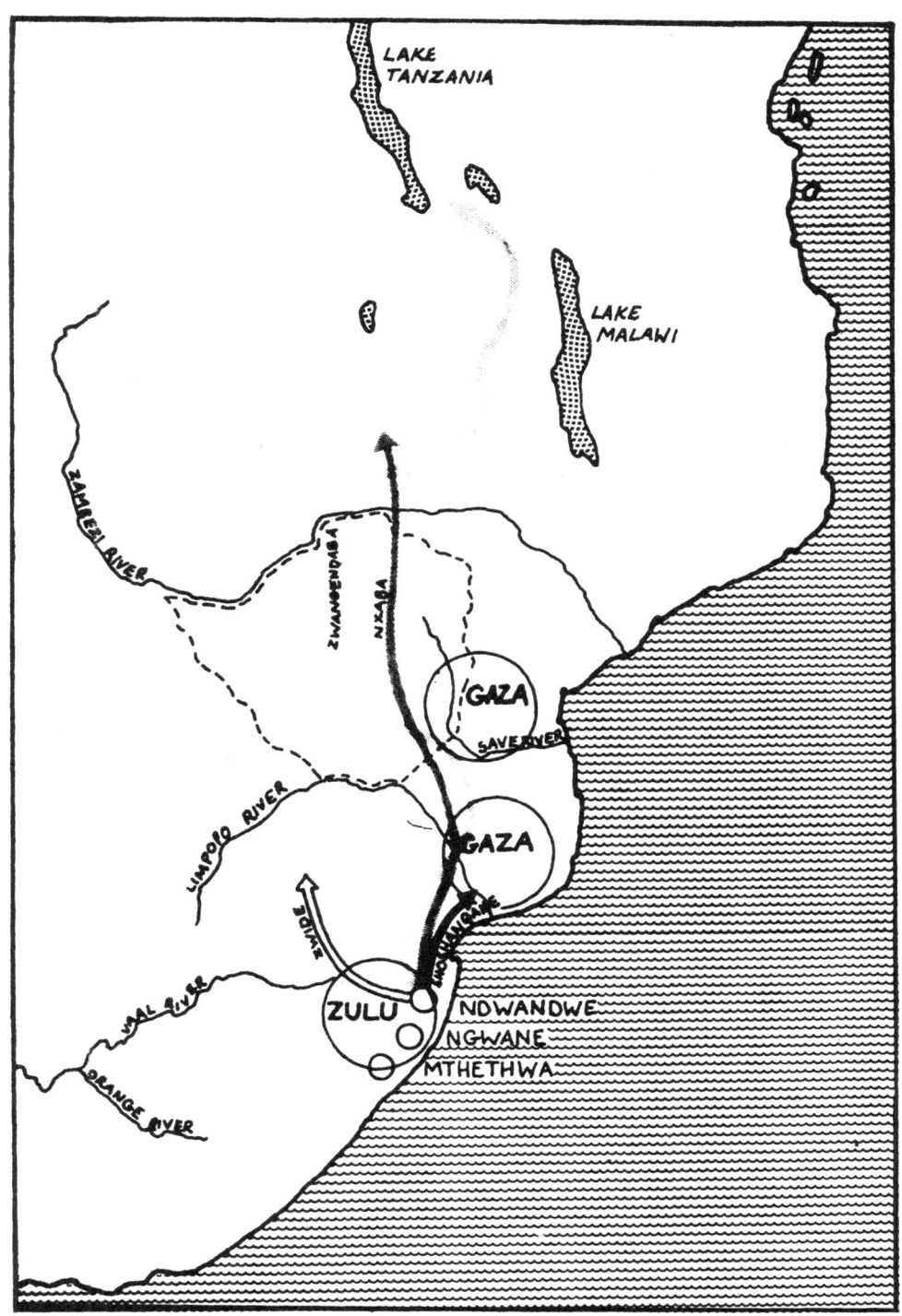

The forced migration of Nguni groups in the early 1800's is called the Mfecane. Zwide, Soshangane, Nxaba and Zwangendaba led groups of their people along the routes shown here.

The Ndwandwe

The Ndwandwe were a very *aggressive* society. They fought the Mthethwa. They caused the death of Dingiswayo. They attacked the Ngwane and drove them out of the Ngwane lands.

When they were defeated by Shaka in 1819, the Ndwandwe split into four groups. The leader of the largest group was called Zwide. His group moved into the eastern Transvaal.

The other three groups were very small. Their leaders were Soshangane, Zwangendaba and Nxaba. All three moved northwards into the coastal plains of what is now Mozambique. There, the three leaders quarrelled.

In 1825, Soshangane's army drove Zwangendaba away. Zwangendaba led his people up the Save river and into Zimbabwe. For several years, his army fought and raided in Zimbabwe. In the early 1830s, it attacked the Rozvi state. Many people believe that Zwangendaba's army killed the last Changamire.

In 1833, Zwangendaba was living on the middle Mazowe river. His army raided the remains of the Mutapa state. In 1835, Zwangendaba crossed the Zambezi river and moved north. By this time, his people were called the Ngoni.

After Zwangendaba's death, the Ngoni were split by a leadership dispute. Some moved to Zambia. Some moved still further north. Finally, they settled around lakes Malawi and Tanganyika.

The fourth Ndwandwe group was led by Nxaba. After the Zulu defeated them, they also moved northwards into what is now Mozambique. Nxaba also quarrelled with Soshangane. He was forced to move into Zimbabwe.

Nxaba tried to form a state in the southeastern highlands of Zimbabwe. His army attacked the Manyika many times in the early 1830s. Eventually, they moved across Zimbabwe and crossed the Zambezi river into Zambia.

In chapter 26 we will learn how Soshangane founded the Gaza state.

The Ngwane

The Ngwane ruler was also called Ngwane. The Ngwane suffered badly from continual Ndwandwe raids. After the Ndwandwe were defeated by the Zulu, the Zulu armies attacked the Ngwane many times. Often it seemed that the Zulu would completely destroy Ngwane society. The Ngwane had to move their home many times.

They settled among Pedi and Tsonga communities. After Ngwane, Sobhuza became the leader. He brought Pedi and Tsonga communities into the Ngwane state. The Pedi were mainly crop farmers. They did not compete with the Nguni, who were mainly cattle breeders and herders. The two together gave the new state a single strong economy.

When Sobhuza died in 1839, his son Mswati became the ruler. Mswati ruled until 1856. He continued to strengthen the new state. He formed it into the nation that has been named after him, the Swazi.

The Swazi were invaded by the armies of Soshangane, Zwangendaba, Nxaba and Mzilikazi, the Ndebele ruler. Each army was trying to escape from the Zulu. The Swazi rulers tried to form alliances with each invader. They gave daughters to the invading rulers as wives. They took daughters from the invaders as wives. Mzilikazi married one of Sobhuza's daughters. She was the mother of Lobengula, who became the ruler of the Ndebele after Mzilikazi.

Mswati and the elders of his court.

Essay. Imagine that you are a Swazi in 1850. Write a brief account of your people's history over the last 60 years (from the end of the 1700s). Divide your account into paragraphs as follows:

a) Where did your people live the end of the 18th century? What language did they speak? How did they produce the things they needed?

b) How did the environment change at the end of the 18th century? How did this affect your people? How did the organization of society change?

c) Which Nguni chiefdom became a very strong state after 1816? Who was the first ruler of this state? How did this state affect your people? What did it force your people to do?

d) Where did your people start a new state? What were the names of the rulers of your people since 1800?

e) Which people have invaded your state since 1820? Why did they do this? What has happened to them?

25. The Ndebele state

In this chapter:
We will learn about a group which left the Zulu state and started the Ndebele state.
We will see how the Ndebele
- united people from many different groups into one state,
- used the regiment system to develop the state,
- collected tribute from other chiefs and states.

You will need to know the meanings of these words:

induna — commander of a regiment, or, later, chief.

caste — a hereditary social group, whose members do not marry people of other castes.

policy — plan or course of action.

Origins of the Ndebele

In 1822, a group of two to three hundred men left the Zulu state. They were all from the Khumalo lineage. A man called Mzilikazi led them across the Drakensberg mountains into the Transvaal.

Shaka sent Zulu armies to follow and attack them. Mzilikazi's group was unable to settle in one place and grow their own crops because of these attacks. So they got food and cattle by raiding the Sotho people who lived in the Transvaal. They destroyed many villages.

The Sotho called Mzilikazi's group the Ndebele. 'Ndebele' means 'soldiers with long shields'. This was a Sotho way of saying 'foreigners'.

The Ndebele and the Sotho

In 1825, the Ndebele settled near where Pretoria is now. They continued to raid the Sotho people of the area. To find peace, many Sotho joined the Ndebele community.

The Sotho were mainly grain farmers. The Ndebele were mainly herders of cattle. When the two groups united, they could exchange their produce. They created a strong and balanced economy.

The Ndebele army

Dingane's regiments continued to attack the Ndebele. So in 1832, Mzilikazi moved even further west. He built a new capital at Mosega near present-day Gaborone.

A great many more Sotho now joined the Ndebele. The Ndebele army grew to three or four thousand soldiers. It was the most powerful army north of the Vaal river. With their army, the Ndebele controlled a territory of 30 000 square kilometres. The army raided all over this territory, and beyond, to Tswana, Venda and Shona lands.

Conflict with the Boers

Some Boers wanted to escape from the Cape, which was ruled by the British. In 1834, these

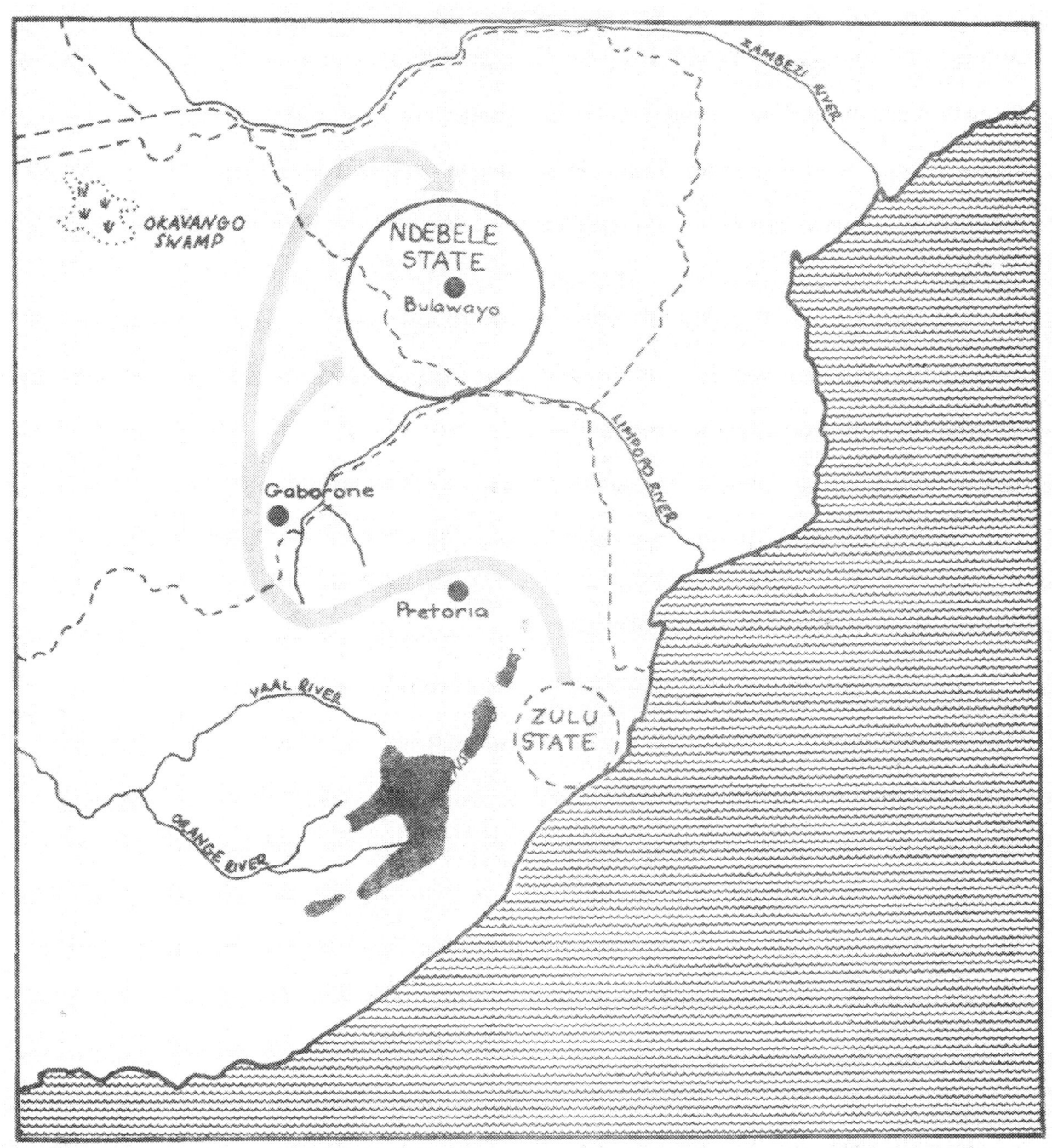

The movements of the Ndebele, from the Zulu state until they settled in south-western Zimbabwe.

Boers began to move northwards. They wanted farmlands on the highveld. They were a new threat to the Ndebele.

The first groups of Boers crossed the Vaal river in 1836. They entered Ndebele territory. Mzilikazi tried to drive them away. The Ndebele army's first attacks were successful. They killed many Boers and took their cattle. But more Boers kept coming.

In 1837, both the Boers and the Zulu attacked Mzilikazi's capital at Mosega. Mzilikazi then decided to move even further north. He wanted to get out of reach of invasion and attack. He led one group of the Ndebele through eastern Botswana to the edges of the Okavango swamp. One of his *indunas* led another group to south-west Zimbabwe. Mzilikazi's group joined them in Zimbabwe in 1840. Mzilikazi started to rule the united Ndebele nation again, in their final homeland.

Different groups in Ndebele society

Mzilikazi united people of different origins and cultures into a single nation. This was one of his greatest achievements.

The enlarged Ndebele state included people who had been Nguni, Sotho, Tswana and Shona. More than half of the people in the new Ndebele state were originally Shona. They came from Rozvi and Kalanga communities.

Ndebele people were described by the regions from which their ancestors had come. They were called
- the zansi if their ancestors were Nguni,
- the enhla if their ancestors were Sotho or Tswana,
- the hole if their ancestors were Shona.

These were not separate classes, or separate *castes*. People from different groups were allowed to marry. But the three groups did have different positions in society. The zansi were given more respect than the others. The hole were given less respect than the others.

Children with one Sotho parent and one Nguni parent were brought up as Ndebele. The women and children captured in war were sent to live with Ndebele families, in Ndebele homesteads. They were brought up to be Ndebele. They had the same rights and duties as any other Ndebele. When the boys grew up, the Ndebele king provided them with cattle for bridewealth. They could become indunas and chiefs.

Discussion. Which state was powerful in south-west Zimbabwe before the Ndebele arrived? In what ways did people from the different groups become part of the Ndebele state?

Culture and religion

Rozvi religion and culture remained strong in the Ndebele state. The Rozvi and Kalanga name for god was Mwari. Mwari spoke to people through priests from cave-shrines. Mwari and his priests became an important part of Ndebele religion.

The Ndebele king accepted the traditional Rozvi position of the king as a rainmaker. People believed that he could make the land fertile. The ceremony of Inxwala, or 'first fruits', was held at the king's capital. Every Ndebele was meant to attend, as a sign of loyalty to the king. Inxwala gave the king some control over production. No one could eat any of the harvest until after the ceremony.

The king took wives from the families of important chiefs and subjects. This helped to make alliances and loyalties stronger.

Mwari

Shona traditions tell of a supreme god who created the world. They say that this god is responsible for everyone's welfare, and for the land's fertility and rain. People cannot speak directly to this god. They must approach him through the ancestors and their spirit mediums.

This god had many different names. Mwari is one. Christian missionaries have taken 'Mwari' as the name of the Christian god also. Some see Mwari and the Christian god as the same person.

Traditions say that
- the Rozvi people had a special relationship with Mwari,
- Mwari was the father of the first Changamire, Dombo,
- Mwari caused the downfall of the Rozvi when they offended him.

Another special relationship with Mwari exists at shrines in the Matopo hills. People believe that there Mwari still speaks through men and women chosen by him. They have representatives throughout Zimbabwe. Many people pay tribute to the shrines and their priests and servants. Many visit the shrines to consult with Mwari.

Historians do not agree about the relationship between the Ndebele state and the Mwari priests and shrines. Some historians say that the Mwari priests
- had great influence with the Ndebele king,
- played a part in the ceremonies of Inxwala and rainmaking,
- received tribute from the kings.

Other historians say that the Ndebele state
- did not recognise the Mwari priests,

One of the shrines of Mwari in the Matopo Hills.

- sometimes threatened the Mwari priests and shrines.

There is no doubt that Mwari beliefs and traditions were strong before the Ndebele entered Zimbabwe and remained so in the new state. Mwari was important in hole traditions, and some enhla and zansi came to share these beliefs.

Inxwala ceremony.

The ruling class

As in any state, the Ndebele ruling class remained small. Members of the ruling class married people of other ruling lineages. In this way, they kept their property and power within a small circle of people. Indunas hoped that the king or someone from a senior lineage would marry one of their daughters. They also hoped to marry one of the daughters of a ruling family themselves. In this way, their sons or grandsons would become part of the king's councils. Marriage alliances are planned like this in any ruling class in every part of the world.

Membership of the ruling class was not decided by the group from which people's ancestors came. Mzilikazi respected the Rozvi ruling lineages. He allowed Rozvi chiefs to keep their power in the Ndebele state.

Mzilikazi listened to the advice of his chiefs and councils a great deal. In this, he was different from the rulers of other Nguni states. He chose the members of his main council himself. Like any such council, the members wanted to keep the king's favour. So they usually agreed with Mzilikazi's ideas and *policies*.

This was painted in 1835. Hunters are presenting a lion skin as tribute to Mzilikazi who is sitting in a wagon.

The king united many chiefdoms into a single nation. The king's amabutho protected the chiefs. In return, the chiefs were willing for their young men to serve in the nation's amabutho. Because the king and chiefs were united, the king and his council could make plans for the whole territory. The state could carry out policies that would not be possible for any single chief to carry out.

Discussion. In the last chapter, we learned about the system of age regiments (amabutho) in Nguni societies.
Who joined the regiments?
What work did they do for the ruler and the state?
In what ways did the regiments change society?

Regiments

Mzilikazi used the age regiments to put his policies into action. He made some changes in the Nguni regiment system. Fighting became less important. The duty of regiments was to defend the state, not to attack others. The king only formed new regiments when there was a threat of war or attack. This did not happen very often during Mzilikazi's time. It happened even more seldom when his son, Lobengula, was king.

Young men served in the amabutho for only five to ten years. The regimental towns were a very small proportion of the total number of Ndebele towns. Many regimental towns were temporary homes for the young men. Young men visitied their own homes regularly. They worked in their local areas for the local chief and indunas.

Indunas were in charge of the regiments. They were state officials, chosen by the king. The position of induna became hereditary. An induna's son took over his father's position. Gradually, indunas became hereditary chiefs.

In the same way, the regimental settlements changed gradually into ordinary farming villages. The regiment was a way of starting new villages in a planned and organized way. Regimental towns were started in areas where there were few people. The state grew in a planned way around the former regimental homes.

Discussion. We learned about homesteads in earlier chapters. How were people organized in homesteads? How was work divided?

Farmers

Most Ndebele lived in homesteads, often as large as small villages, called imizi. About 100 people lived in each umuzi. Imizi were very close together, especially along streams and rivers. A group of imizi, under the control of a local chief, was called an isigaba.

The people of the imizi were mainly farmers. The heart of the Ndebele state was on the highveld. Here grain farming had most chance of success.

Amabutho and imizi were organized in different ways. They farmed differently. So we can say that they were different classes. Together they made the Ndebele economy strong.

Discussion. People had different positions in Ndebele society. In what ways were their positions decided by
- their origins?
- the work they did?

In what ways were all the different people united into a single nation?

What were the advantages of such unity?

Tribute

Many small states and chiefdoms paid tribute to the Ndebele. Almost all of them were in the middleveld. There was a good reason for this.

The middleveld was an area of sweet grass, so it was good for cattle to graze. It was the main winter grazing for the Ndebele cattle. The middleveld was not part of the heart of the Ndebele state. The chiefs of this area ruled fairly independently. They paid tribute to the Ndebele state in return for protection by the regiments and freedom from raiding. The tribute they paid was small. It was a sign of loyalty to the Ndebele state, not a form of exploitation. Tribute was not at all harsh. It did not take all surplus food and cattle from the people.

An Ndebele village or umuzi.

It was in the interests of the Ndebele state that the tributary states of the middleveld remained strong and peaceful. In this way, their lands remained safe for Ndebele cattle. The cattle were either put in the charge of young men of an ibutho, or lent out to local people. In return for looking after the cattle, they were allowed to take the milk and keep some of the calves.

Discussion. What is tribute? Why is it important? Who pays it? How is it collected? What does the ruling class do with it? Is the tribute itself important or is it a sign of something else? What is the difference between tribute and tax? Use the Ndebele state as an example when you discuss these questions.

Tribute was important in other states that we have learned about. Which ones? How did tribute differ in the different states?

Lobengula

Mzilikazi ruled the Ndebele for 50 years, from 1818. He died in 1868. His court and lineage disagreed about who should be the new king. Eventually, one of his sons, Lobengula, became king in 1870.

During the 24 years that he ruled, Lobengula suffered more and more from **interference** by British missionaries, traders, hunters and miners. While there was no king, from 1868 to 1870, many of the royal cattle herds were taken by local chiefs. The local chiefs used the state's cattle to trade directly with the invaders. The traders brought so many trade goods into the country that the king could no longer control trade.

In Book 2, we will learn about the colonial invasion of the Ndebele state in the 1890s.

Essay. Mzilikazi continued the Nguni system of organizing young men into age regiments. But the amabutho in the Ndebele state were different from the Nguni amabutho. Write a short account describing
a) the Nguni ibutho system,
b) the ways the ibutho system changed in the Ndebele state,
c) the reasons for these changes.

Ndebele soldiers guarding people who carry tribute to Mzilikazi.

26. Gaza

In this chapter:
We will learn about the Ndwandwe group, led by Soshangane, which formed the Gaza state.
We will study Gaza's problems, classes, and relations with other peoples and states.

You will need to know the meanings of these words:
infested — overrun with large numbers.
preserve — keep whole or safe or alive.

Discussion.
In chapter 24, we learned about the wars and movements of different Nguni groups in the 19th century.
What was the Mfecane?
Who was Shaka?
Who were the Ngwane?
Who were the Ndwandwe?
Who was Soshangane?

Origins of the Gaza state

Shaka's armies fought and defeated the Ndwandwe many times. In 1821, **Soshangane** led a small group of the Ndwandwe to the north. This group were all from the Gaza lineage.

They travelled past the lands of the Ngwane, into the lands of the Tsonga in what is now southern Mozambique. In a few years, the Gaza defeated people from south of the lower Limpopo river as far north as the lower Zambezi and into south-east Zimbabwe.

Many **Tsonga, Chopi, Shona** and **Tonga** people were forced to accept Gaza authority. They had to pay tribute to the Gaza state.

The Shona who paid tribute to Gaza became known as the Ndau.

Environment

Most of Gaza was *infested* with tsetse fly. No cattle could be kept in such areas. The dry grassland, inland of the Limpopo river mouth, was healthy for cattle. This area became the heart of the Gaza state. Most of Gaza was farmland, not grazing land. Raising crops in the fields was very hard work.

The territory of the Gaza state was very large. Many different people lived there. So Gaza never had the same unity as the Ndebele state.

Classes

There were deep divisions between classes in Gaza society:
- the true Nguni formed the ruling class;
- conquered people who accepted Nguni culture were exploited;
- captured Chopi and Tsonga people were almost a slave class.

At first only the Nguni had cattle. Some Nguni men used their cattle to buy wives from the Nguni peoples to the south. These wives did not work in the fields. They spent their time bringing up their children as pure Nguni. They *preserved* Nguni culture and language.

Some of the conquered people accepted

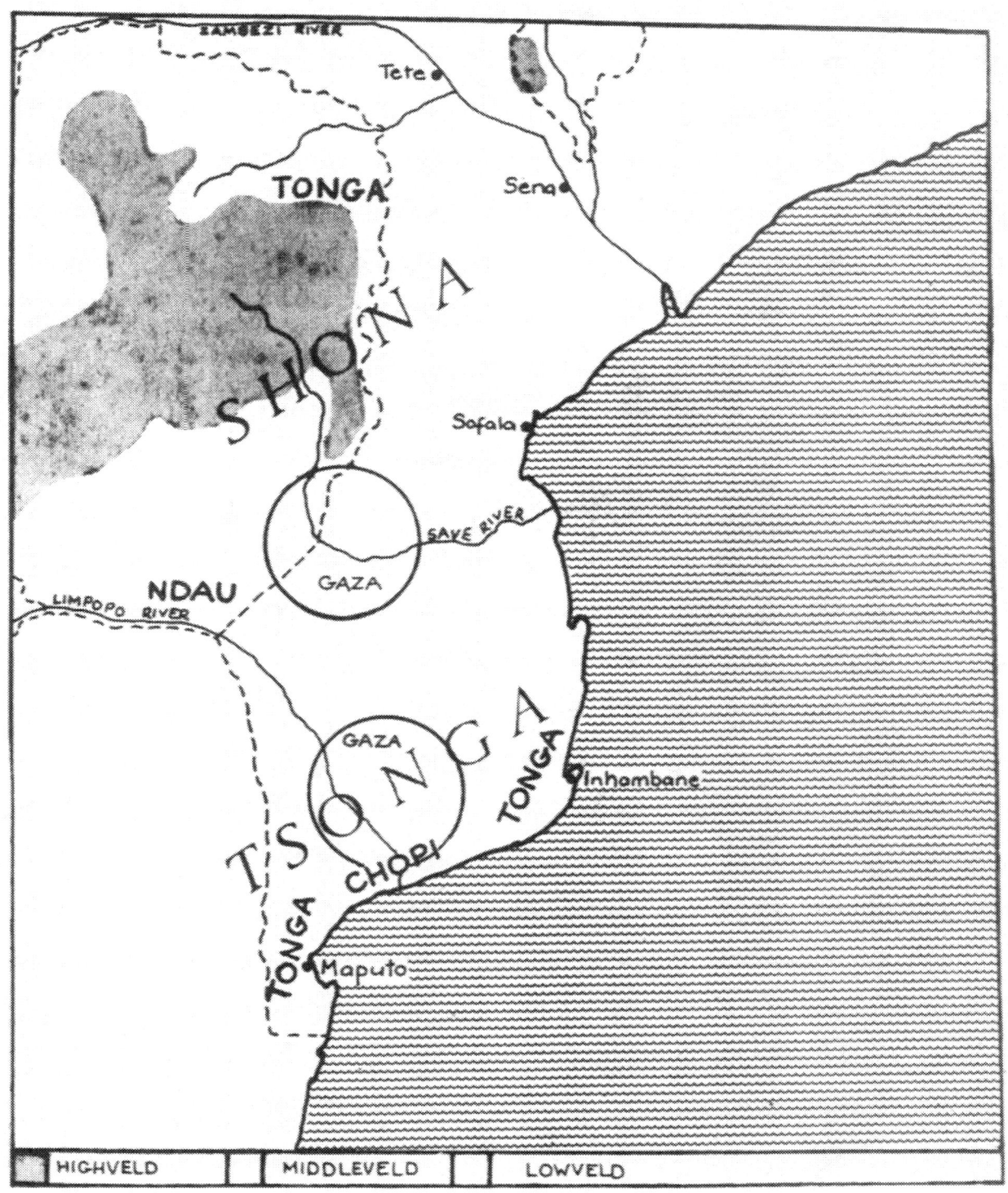

The northern and southern locations of the Gaza state.

Nguni culture and customs. They accepted Nguni indunas to govern them. They paid tribute to the Gaza state. The Nguni bought wives from these people. These wives worked in the lands for their Nguni husbands. Their children were considered true Nguni. These children increased the small Nguni population.

The Tsonga and Chopi people refused to accept Nguni rule. The Gaza army raided them and captured many people as slaves. The Tsonga and Chopi were even more oppressed than the other conquered people.

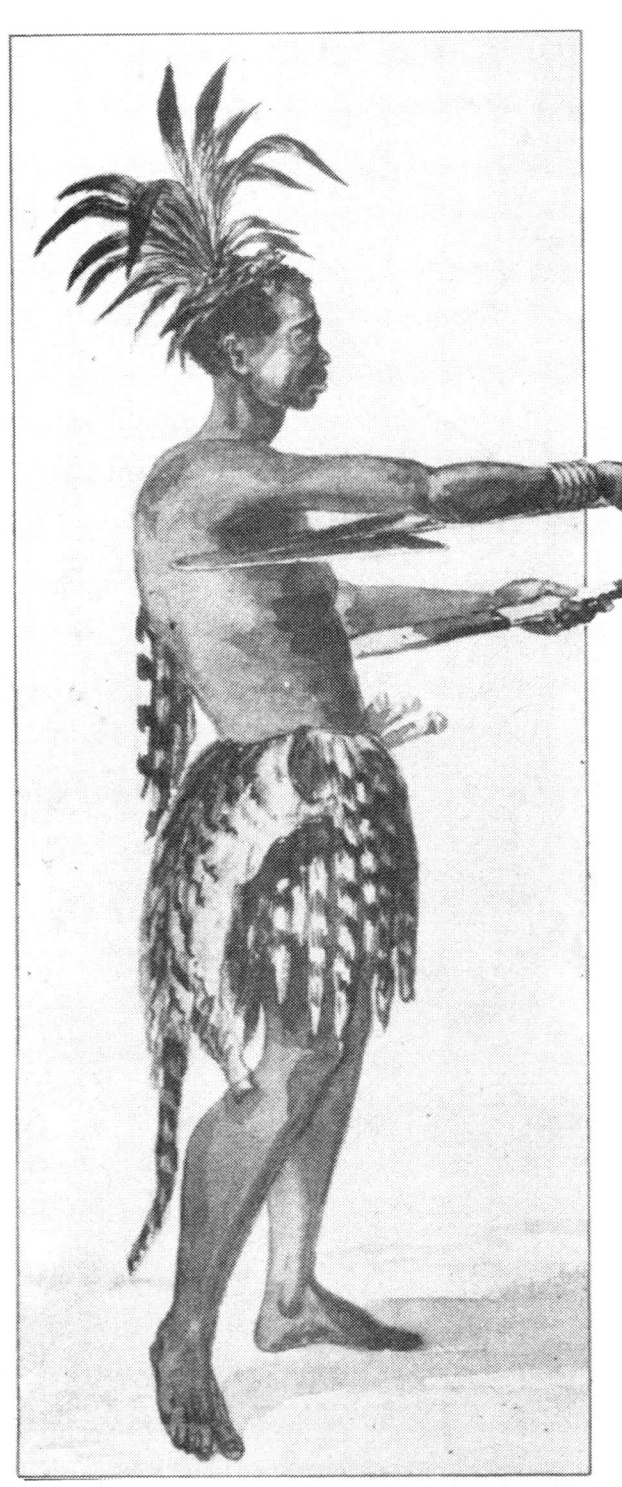

A Gaza Nguni chief.

Some were sold to Portuguese traders at Maputo and Inhambane. They were taken in ships to work on sugar plantations in Mauritius. Some of the captured men were made soldiers in the Gaza armies.

The women were made to work in Nguni fields as slaves. Some married Nguni husbands. Because no bridewealth was paid for them, they had no rights in Gaza society. Their female children were sold for bridewealth in cattle. But their male children could become Nguni. For this reason, we cannot say that they were a real slave class.

Army

The Nguni army remained small. The regiments spent most of their time in raids and wars. Their duty was to show Nguni power and collect tribute.

The regiments could not settle down in regimental towns. They did not work in the lands or with the cattle herds. The soldiers were not released to become farmers like the Ndebele regiments were. The Gaza army was always an oppressive, exploiting force.

Discussion. The Gaza state had problems that no other Nguni state had.
What were these problems?
What difficulties arose because of
- the environment?
- the size of the territory?
- the different groups of people in the territory?

Why was it necessary for the regiments to remain as soldiers, instead of becoming farmers?

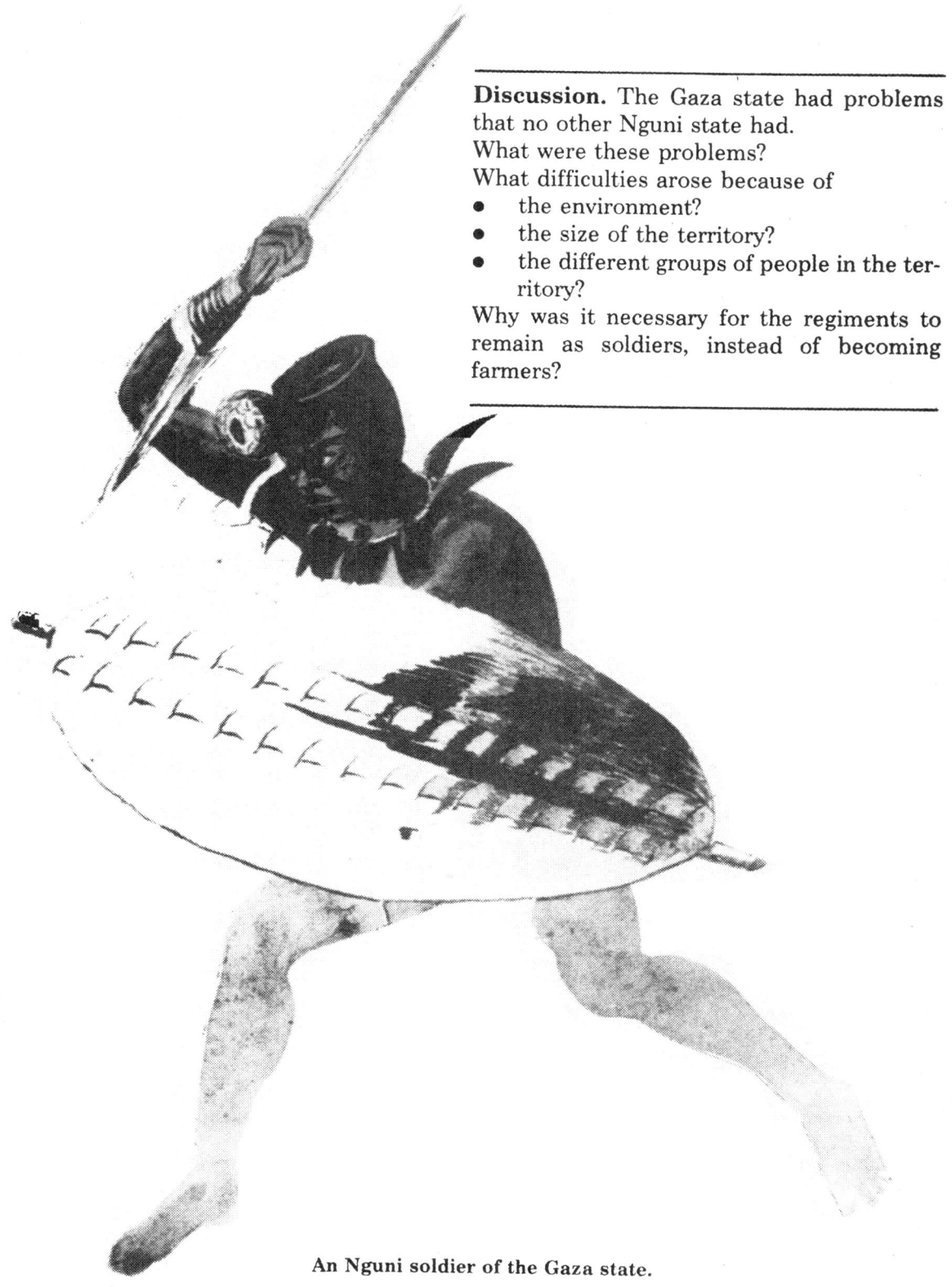

An Nguni soldier of the Gaza state.

Gaza politics

Gaza was closely tied to the Portuguese traders of southern Mozambique especially the towns of Maputo and Inhambane. Gaza sold slaves and ivory to the Portuguese.

For many years, there was no peace in Gaza. Soshangane fought against both Nxaba and Zwangendaba, until they left the coastal plains.

The Zulu continually attacked Gaza, up until 1833. The Zulu never succeeded in defeating Gaza. To avoid Zulu attacks, Soshangane moved his capital northwards, from the lower Limpopo river, into Zimbabwe near the Save river. He returned to the Limpopo in 1839, when the Zulu state was weak at the end of Dingane's rule.

When Soshangane died in 1858, there were four years of civil war. His two sons, Mawewe and Mzila, fought to be king.

Mawewe had married one of Mswati's daughters and was supported by the Swazi. Mzila became king in 1862 and moved his court away from the Swazi raids to the southeast highlands of Zimbabwe. He asked for help from the Portuguese. They made him sign a treaty making himself a vassal of the Portuguese state. Mawewe and the Swazi did not give up their struggle to rule Gaza until 1865.

Mzila was as strong and oppressive a ruler as Soshangane. Mzila made an alliance with the Ndebele king, Lobengula. Each married a daughter of the other. Mzila died in 1884. His son, Ngungunyane, was the next Gaza ruler. He moved the capital of Gaza back to the Limpopo once again in 1889.

Under Ngungunyane, Gaza fought bravely against the whole Portuguese colonial army for many years. Finally, in 1895, Gaza was defeated. It became part of the Portuguese colony of Mozambique.

Discussion. Who were Nxaba and Zwangendaba?
In what year did Soshangane's army defeat them?
Where did Nxaba go after that defeat?
Where did Zwangendaba go after that defeat?

Essay. Compare the Ndebele and Gaza states. Make two columns on the chalkboard or in your exercise book. One column is for the Ndebele state, and the other is for the Gaza state. In each column, make notes about
a) the size of the state's territory,
b) the environment,
c) the army,
d) relations with other peoples,
e) exploitation — who was exploited and how?
Use your notes as a plan for your essay.

27. Ancient Egypt

In this chapter:

> We will see that the ancient Egyptian state was very different from the other states we have studied.
> We will learn that, at first, ancient Egypt had an Asiatic mode of production. Later in Egypt's history, a ruling class developed and the mode of production became more feudal.

You will need to know the meanings of these words:

monument — structure built in memory of a person or event.
communicate — pass on or share information.
conservative — opposed to any great or sudden change.
reign — period during which one ruler or dynasty rules.
dyke — a ridge or wall built along a river to stop the water from rising onto the land.
insecure — unsafe or uncertain.
tomb — building round a grave.
mummify — use chemicals to preserve a dead body.
after-life — life after death.

Contrast

In this book, we have looked mainly at the history of societies in eastern and southern Africa. We have seen that these societies had similar environments, technologies, economies and cultures. Now we will compare these societies with one that was completely different in almost every way.

These are some of the differences that you will notice:

- The environment of Egypt was very unusual. It was a single river valley of great fertility, surrounded by desert.
- Egyptian technology was similar to that of the societies we have studied, but farming practices were completely different.
- Unlike any other society we have studied, government and power were completely controlled by one person, called the pharaoh.
- The Egyptian state did not depend on tribute.
- Trade was not very important in Egypt. The state was the only trader. Those who traded were all officials of the state. They did not make any profits themselves.
- Everything and everyone belonged to the state. This gave the Egyptian state greater strength than any other state we have studied.
- Much of the wealth of Egypt was spent on creating *monuments*, palaces, temples and art. No other society has ever created state culture on such a scale.
- The Egyptian nation-state began earlier, lasted longer and changed less than any other state in world history. It lasted 3 000 years. Only a few of the states we have studied lasted as long as 300 years. The Egyptian state began 5 000 years ago. None of the states we have studied began more than 1 000 years ago.

The Nile Valley

Many people believe that the Egyptian state and culture were simply the result of the special environment of the Nile river and its valley. This is not so, although the river had a great influence on everyone who lived in the valley.

Egypt has a very harsh climate. It has almost no rain at all. For many months it is extremely hot.

The river flows through a valley eight to 25 kilometres wide. On either side is the dry, rainless rock and sand of the desert. There are no grass or trees, and almost no plants. There is no shelter for people or animals. No one could live there.

The valley is quite different. It is covered with very rich and fertile soil. Every year, at exactly the same time of year, the river floods. It gently overflows its banks and settles on the low-lying fields. Here the flood water gradually deposits its mud. The water sinks into the soil and provides moisture. This natural irrigation and deposit of new fertile soil enables farmers to grow two or even three crops in the same fields every year. They can do this year after year, even when there is no rain at all.

Hunter-gatherers settled in villages in the Nile valley 15 000 years ago. They started cultivating crops (wheat and barley) at least 7 000 years ago. This was among the earliest farming in the world. The villagers knew when the floods would come and how to manage the waters with dams and channels that they built together. This was not difficult because the valley was already divided into natural basins by the banks of old channels of the river.

The beginning of the state

By 3000 BC, the villages all along the Nile valley were united into a single nation-state. Many independent states already existed in south-west Asia at this time. These were city-states. They were based on the temples and markets of single cities. Each city had its own traders, craftspeople and many other specialists. They traded for themselves in local

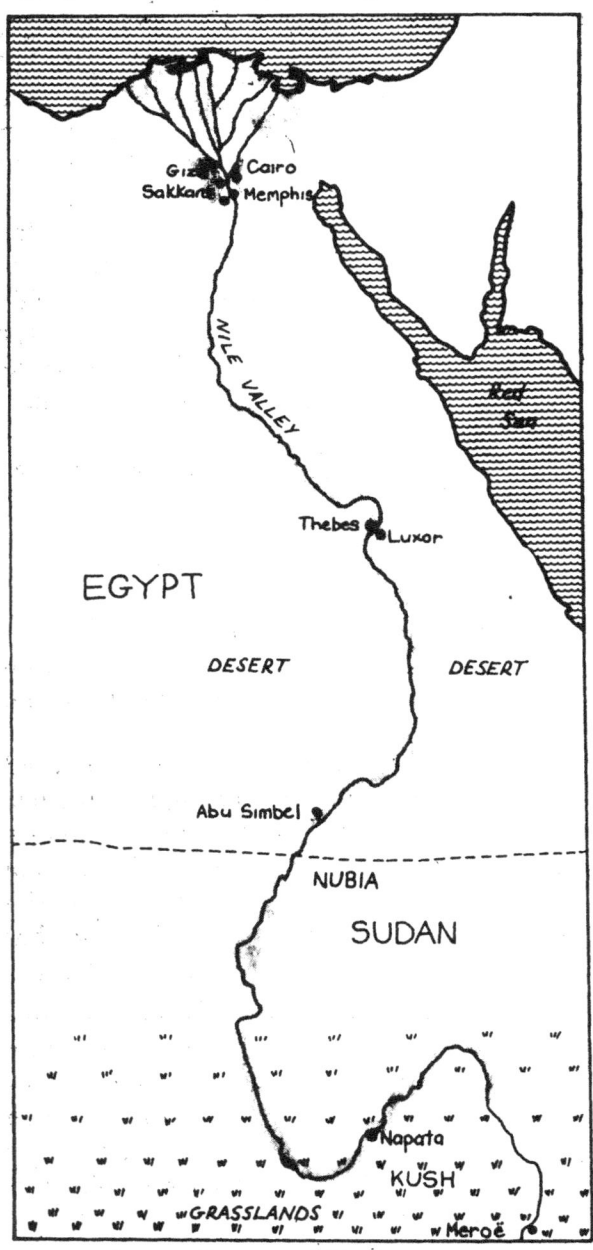

Egypt and Kush.

markets in the surrounding villages and countryside. Cities, markets and craftspeople were never very important in Egypt.

We do not know exactly how or why the Egyptian state was formed. We do know that inequalities developed within village society in much the same ways as we we have already studied. Chiefs increased their power. Small states developed along the valley. Then almost suddenly, one small group was able to unite the whole Nile valley and take control of it.

Why did this happen? The villagers did not need a state to help organize their farming or irrigation. They were not conquered in war. They were not forced to become subjects of a ruler.

But some factors made a state possible and necessary in the Nile valley. The population of the valley was large. People could not leave the valley, because no one could live in the desert. Travel by boat up and down the river was very easy. All the villages could *communicate* with each other. Also, in the desert there were rich deposits of gold, copper and stone for building. The only way to get them was to take large, well organized and well equipped expeditions into the desert. These expeditions needed central organization. Expeditions to trade with the cities of Asia needed similar organization. Only a state could provide this organization.

The Egyptian state was very *conservative*. Once religion, culture, arts and crafts were established, they changed little for almost 3 000 years, through the *reign* of 31 different lineages or dynasties.

The pharaoh and his government

The ruler of Egypt, the pharaoh, was the only power in the land. People believed that
- the pharaoh was god,
- all things came from him,
- his health affected the fertility of the land and the welfare of the whole state,
- the state was the pharaoh's family and he was its father.

There were no councils or assemblies of the the people. The pharaoh ruled the country through a huge number of officials — priests, clerks, tax collectors, army commanders, and traders. There were governors (called 'nomarchs') who looked after each province (called a 'nome'). All their power came from the pharaoh and they were completely dependent on him.

The pharaoh's palace was not just his home. It was also a temple and army barracks. In the palace were the offices of the pharaoh's clerks and accountants, the storehouses for all the grain collected in taxes, and the workshops of many artists, architects and craftspeople.

The pharaoh had absolute power over every sort of activity. He controlled
- land,
- trade and mining expeditions,
- irrigation,
- the temples and the priests.

Trade was a state monopoly. People saw no difference between trade and tribute to the pharaoh.

Central organization like this benefited Egypt in many ways. One example is the use of land. In earlier times, the Nile delta was a swamp of mud and bush so thick that no one could travel, live or work there. Under the pharaoh, *dykes* and canals were built so that people could clear and cultivate the delta.

Discussion. The pharaoh was an absolute ruler. What does this mean? Few southern African states had absolute rulers. Which state came nearest? Discuss the reasons why rulers of different societies have such different powers.

The ruling class

At first, Egypt was a state without classes. As we have seen, no classes came between the pharaoh and the villages. Marx called such a system the Asiatic mode of production.

Gradually a ruling class developed. The pharaoh gave land to temples and their priests. Later he gave land to favoured officials and governors. After about 1 000 years, many officials owned big estates. They became rich landowners. Official positions were handed down from father to son. At times, under weak pharaohs, nomarchs took over the power of the pharaoh in their provinces. They became almost independent feudal rulers. Governors, senior officials and landowners were made nobles by the pharaoh. They formed the ruling class. Egypt was becoming feudal.

Discussion. What is feudalism?

Villagers

The land belonged to the pharaoh or, later, to the temples and the ruling class. Most villagers were tenants on large estates. They had to pay rent for their land. They had to farm the land for the nobles. Most of the food that the villagers grew was taken by the nobles. The rents were so high that villagers led miserable, *insecure* lives.

In the hot summer months, from May to October, the fields were empty and flooded by the Nile. During these months, food was short and villagers were forced to work for the state. In return, the state fed them from the huge state granaries filled with the grain collected in rents and taxes.

So the village farmers provided all the labour needed to build the great temples, *tombs* and monuments to the pharaoh. They were not slaves. They were free to farm the

The golden mask placed on the mummified body of Tutankhamen.

land they owned or rented during the rest of the year.

A small number of craftspeople, masons and builders worked throughout the year for the state. They were rewarded well, with pleasant houses and plenty of food. They were also allowed to organize themselves into co-operatives and work some of their time for nobles. The nobles paid them for this extra work.

Culture

Ancient Egypt has provided the world with some of its oldest and greatest monuments. The pyramids of Giza, built in the desert outside Cairo, are the biggest stone monuments in the world. They were built as tombs in about 2500 BC. They contained the *mummified* bodies of Egyptian pharaohs. The mummified bodies were enclosed in many, beautiful coffins, the inner ones of gold and the outer ones of carved stone. Carvings, jewellery, furniture, food, pottery, clothes and models of houses were all buried in the tombs for the pharaohs to use in their life after death.

The pyramids are not the only tombs in Egypt. Many tombs of pharoahs, nobles,

One of the pyramids at Giza.

This wall mural shows palace servants carrying Queen Hatshepshut's possessions to her tomb. Why were the Egyptian pharaohs' possessions buried with them?

priests and officials were hidden in the desert or cut into rock. The insides of many of these tombs were covered in carved and painted pictures. The pictures show the life and work of the dead person, and the gods and the *afterlife*. Egyptian temples were filled with carved columns. Outside the temples were long avenues lined with statues. Enormous stone statues of the gods, the kings and their servants stood at the entrances of tombs and temples.

This art was made for the pharaoh, his priests, officials and ruling class. Most of the art was made to be enjoyed by the dead. No one was meant to see it after the tombs were sealed. It is among the best known and most admired art in the world. It is also the oldest state art. The style did not change.

The ancient Egyptians invented one of the earliest sorts of writing in the world, using pictures called hieroglyphics. By observing and measuring the sun, moon and stars, they developed a calendar. They used their calendars and measurements of time to tell exactly when the river Nile would flood each year. They developed systems of mathematics.

They needed these to
- keep account of how much food was produced,
- keep account of how much tax was collected, stored and distributed,
- measure and plan plots of land and buildings.

The Egyptians invented the shaduf, to raise water from the river onto the lands. The shaduf is a long pole, supported in the middle. It has a bucket at one end and a heavy stone at the other end to balance the bucket. The bucket is swung down into the river, filled with water and then raised, swung round and emptied onto the lands. It needed many hours of hard work with a shaduf to raise enough water to irrigate even a small area. Later, about 100 BC, a water-wheel was invented. It was called a saqia. It was driven by oxen walking round and round in a circle.

The origins of the Egyptians.

The ancient Egyptians were a mixture of the races of western Asia, north Africa and the Sudanic grasslands. The Egyptians accepted anyone as Egyptian who adopted their culture. It is impossible to describe the ancient Egyptians as a single race. A few historians say that Egypt was the first 'civilization' of 'black' Africa, of the negroid people or race. There is much argument among some historians about this.

This argument does not matter. History shows that states or civilizations are not made only by some races. Race has nothing to do with human abilities. Like all great states, the Egyptian state was the result of society adapting itself in a particular way to the environment and technology that it had. Egypt developed its social system, its political system, its art and culture because of its special history and surroundings, not because a particular race lived there.

Carved columns in a great Egyptian temple. You can see many examples of hieroglyphics.

Important events in Egyptian history

Dates (BC)	Dynasty		Pharaoh	Events
c 3100	1	↑	Menes	Unites Egypt into one state with capital at Memphis.
c 2700	3	Old Kingdom	Zozer	Builds first pyramid at Sakkara.
2600 — 2500	4	↓	Cheops Chephren Menkaure	Build pyramids at Giza outside Cairo
2200 — 2000	7 — 11			Time of unrest. No more pyramids built. Local governors take power.
1600	12 — 13	Middle Kingdom		Capital at Thebes
1500	14 — 17			Invaders from Palestine take power. Nomads settle in Nile Valley.
c 1400	18	↑	Queen Hatshepshut	Capital at Luxor. Sends ships down Red Sea to trade with Punt (Somalia).
c 1300	18	New Kingdom	Tutankhamen	Tomb and treasure discovered by archaeologists in AD 1923 at Thebes
c 1250	19		Rameses II	Builds seven temples in Nubia, including one at Abu Simbel. Trade and expansion into Asia. Jews,led by Moses flee from Egypt to Israel.
c 1150	20	↓	Rameses III	Conquered lands in Asia lost.
			Invaders from Libya take power. Kush becomes independent.	
751 — 668	25		Plankhu	Pharaohs from Kush. Small pyramid tombs built.
650			Invaders from Asia (Assyria, Persia).	
c 600	26		Necho II	Sends ships to explore African coast.
330			Ptolemy	Egypt conquered by Greece.
30			Queen Cleopatra	Egypt conquered by Rome

Egyptian politics

Study the table of important events in Egyptian history. Then answer these questions.
a) Where were the capitals of the Egyptian state?
b) How many pharaohs were women? What were their names?
c) Which pharaoh's tomb was found by archaeologists in 1923?
d) From which pharaoh did the Jews, led by Moses, flee?
e) Which pharaoh organized the building of the temple at Abu Simbel? Who did the building? How were they rewarded?
f) For about how many years did
   i. the Old Kingdom last?
   ii. the Middle Kingdom last?
   iii. the New Kingdom last?
g) Where did Pianky come from?
h) How many times and by whom was Egypt invaded or conquered?

Project. Look in your class, school or local library. Make a list of books about ancient Egypt. Are they primary or secondary sources?

Draw pictures of the pyramids, tombs, treasures and inventions of ancient Egypt. Make a display of Egyptian art and culture for your classroom wall.

Essay. Describe the life of an Egyptian farmer. Consider
a) where he or she lived,
b) what he or she needed for farming,
c) work at different times of the year,
d) relations with the ruling class and the state,
e) the advantages and disadvantages of these relations.

28. Kush

In this chapter:
We will see how Kush society became independent of its Egyptian rulers.
We will learn how and why the culture and economy of the Kush state were different from those of Egypt.

You will need to know the meanings of these words.
nomads — people who move from place to place.
pastoralist — sheep or cattle farmer.
cemetery — place for burial of the dead.
regent — a person who rules when the real ruler is too young or weak or away.
alphabet — set of letters representing the sounds in a language.
script — writing in which the letters are joined together.

Origins of Kush

The area of the Sudanic grasslands was called Nubia. Along the Upper Nile (in what is now the Republic of Sudan), the cultures of ancient Egypt and of Nubia mixed. Together they produced a new culture and society. This became the state of Kush. Some historians of ancient Greece and Rome called it 'Ethiopia' which means 'the land of the blacks'. (This name had nothing to do with the area which is now the Republic of Ethiopia.)

The land of Kush was ruled by the pharaohs of Egypt for 500 years, from 1500 to 1000 BC. During this time, Egyptian culture, ways of government, art, architecture, language and hieroglyphics were established in Kush. They remained a powerful influence on Kush.

About 800 BC, Kush began to show its independence from Egypt. For 80 years, between 751 and 671 BC, rulers from Kush became pharaohs of Egypt. They were Egypt's 25th dynasty. When they were driven out of Egypt by invaders from Asia in 671 BC, Kush began to develop its own, separate culture and society.

Capitals

Kush had two capitals — Napata and Meroe. Napata was the first. It was lower down the Nile than Meroe and surrounded by desert. The flood plain was very narrow and difficult to irrigate and cultivate. Even with a shaduf or a saqia, only a small area of land could be watered.

So Napata could not depend on agriculture alone. It became a centre of trade. It exported the products of tropical Africa, such as ivory, leopard skins, ostrich feathers and gold. These were all carried down the Nile river to Egypt. The gold was mined south of Napata and in the hills near the Red Sea.

Meroe was in a much more fertile area than Napata. It lay in the grasslands of the Sudan, which received small but regular summer rains. The valleys eroded by river floods (called 'wadis') around Meroe were particularly fertile. Their soils held enough flood water to give good crops. Farmers grew sorghum and

A frieze from a mural in Meroe, showing elephants.

millet. There was good grazing for large herds of cattle. Many of the people around Meroe were *nomadic pastoralists*, moving their cattle with the seasons. There are still many nomadic pastoralists in the area today.

Meroe grew more important from about 600 BC. Eventually, it was the only capital of Kush. The rulers of Kush were buried in small pyramids in royal *cemeteries* in Napata until 300 BC. After that, they were all buried in similar cemeteries in Meroe.

Culture

We have seen that Egyptian culture was very important in Kush's early history. As Meroe developed, tropical Africa began to have a stronger influence on the culture of Kush. Here are some of the changes that resulted.

- The succession of rulers no longer passed from father to son as it did with the pharaohs. Instead, a ruler's brother often succeeded him. The one best able to rule was chosen by many members of the ruling class, such as army commanders, senior officials and lineage elders. The ruler's mother was a very important influence on the ruler. She was called the 'Candace'. Many Candaces actually controlled the state as *regents* or queens.
- The first official language of Kush was Egyptian. Egyptian hieroglyphics were not an *alphabet* or a *script* because each word or part of a word had a picture to represent it. Egyptian was gradually replaced in Kush by a local language which used an alphabet written in script. Historians have not yet worked out how to read the Meroitic script.
- The religion of Kush introduced gods that were unknown in Egypt. One was the lion god, Apedemek. Many temples were dedicated to him.
- The style of the art and architecture of Kush was Egyptian. But Kush's artists began to show tropical African subjects more and more. Pictures of elephants and cattle were carved on the walls of temples. The rulers were shown with African features, and jewellery from tropical Africa. The queens were often shown as fat, an appearance that suggested wealth and power in many African cultures.

A temple at Meroe. We can see that Kush's artists used the Egyptian style, but showed tropical African subjects.

Meroe's economy

The industries of Meroe included iron-smelting. There was very little iron in ancient Egypt. One reason was that there was not enough timber in Egypt to provide the firewood and charcoal needed for smelting. But Meroe was surrounded by trees which provided fuel.

People in Meroe may have begun to smelt iron very early in the city's history. Many historians think that Meroe was the source of African iron-smelting technology, and that knowledge of smelting spread from Meroe to eastern and southern Africa.

Meroe also developed painted pottery. It was mass-produced for the ruling class by full-time specialists. In the villages, women continued to make much plainer pottery by hand, in the traditional African way.

Trade was important in Napata. It continued to be important when Meroe became the capital. Meroe traded down the Nile and across to the Red Sea. Through the ports of the Red Sea, and the Mediterranean coast, Meroe traded with Egypt, Arabia, Greece and Rome. Traders from Meroe also travelled up the Atbara river to trade in the kingdom of Axum in what is now Ethiopia.

After a long decline, Meroe was finally conquered by Axum in AD 300.

Essay. Describe the economy of Kush. Consider
a) agriculture,
b) trade,
c) crafts.

29. Stages of history

In this chapter:
- We will look back at what we have learned in this book.
- We will discuss the main features of the modes of production that we have studied.
- We will compare them with the modes of production that Marx and Engels described.
- We will see how historical materialism helps us to understand African history.

Modes of production

In this book we have learned about pre-colonial societies in Zimbabwe and other parts of Africa. We have studied these modes of production:
- primitive communal,
- lineage,
- tributary,
- Asiatic.

Activity. Your class gets into four groups. Each group discusses one of the four modes of production above, listing what you know about its
- way of owning resources,
- divisions of labour,
- relations of production.

Use societies you have studied in this book as examples.

The lineage mode of production was organized around homesteads.

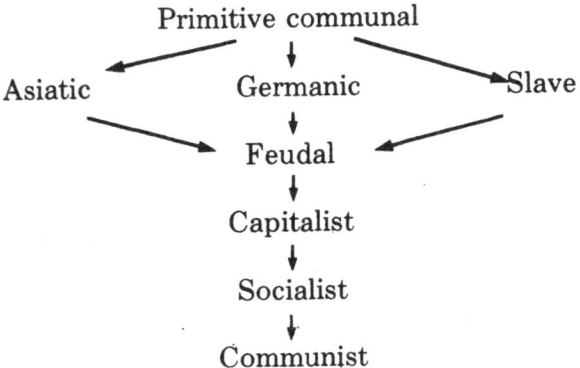

In the Asiatic mode of production, a leader organised villages to work together.

Marx and Engels' theory

In chapter 2, we learned about Marx and Engels' theory of history. They said that the most important change from one stage of history to another is the change in the mode of production. These are the modes of production that Marx and Engels described, based on the societies that they were able to study:

```
           Primitive communal
          ↙        ↓        ↘
   Asiatic    Germanic      Slave
                 ↓
              Feudal
                 ↓
             Capitalist
                 ↓
              Socialist
                 ↓
              Communist
```

Marx and Engels said that societies changed from primitive communalism to an Asiatic or a Germanic or a Slave mode of production.

Exercise. We have learned about primitive communal societies in Africa. Why were they called 'primitive'? Why were they called 'communal'?

The Asiatic mode of production

Marx and Engels described the features of the Asiatic systems that they studied. The village was the most important part of society. The villagers together owned the land they farmed. Everything the villagers needed was grown or made by themselves.

After some time, many villagers united to make a single society. They chose one leader

182

In the Germanic system, each homestead produced everything it needed.

who organized several villages to do things that one village could not do alone. The leader organized things like building dams, digging irrigation channels, and terracing fields.

The leader and his or her helpers were the villagers' servants. They were not the villagers' masters. They did not form a separate class from the other villagers.

Exercise We learned about a state with an Asiatic mode of production. Which state was it?

The Germanic mode of production

Marx and Engels studied societies on the plains and in the forests of northern Europe. About 3 000 years ago, these societies changed from a primitive communal to a Germanic mode of production.

In the Germanic system, the homestead was the most important part of society. A single, large family formed a homestead. The family produced everything it needed. Farmland belonged to the homestead. The rest of the land was used for grazing animals and for hunting. Anyone could use this land.

There were no classes. There was no central organization, government or state. No one organized or ruled over the different homesteads.

Discussion. Which of the modes of production that we have learned about in earlier chapters is most like the Germanic system?

This drawing shows slaves, landowners and a soldier in a slave system.

The Slave mode of production

Slavery followed primitive communalism in ancient Greece and Rome. It developed between 2 500 and 1 500 years ago. Classes and states first developed in Europe with this mode of production.

A class developed which owned very large, private farms. Cities also grew up. The private farms produced all the food to feed the people in the cities. The landowners were the ruling class. Only landowners could be part of the government that ruled the society.

The land-owning class forced huge numbers of other people to work for them as slaves. Slaves had no rights in the society. They did the hardest work on the farms and in the cities. They did farm work, mining, road-making and building. They were given nothing except food and shelter. They were treated in the same way as animals.

Feudalism

In Europe, feudalism grew out of the Germanic and Slave modes of production.

Exercise. We learned about the feudal mode of production in chapter 17. Who owned the land? Who worked on the land? How were they exploited?

We will discuss capitalism, socialism, and communism in *People Making History* Book 2.

Marx's theory and African history

We can see that the modes of production that Marx described are not found everywhere in the world in exactly the way that Marx described them. But his ideas are important for studying

A feudal lord leading his serfs to fight in war.

African history. Marx's theory teaches us
- the sort of questions to ask about history,
- how to analyse history.

His theory does not give us all the answers to the questions we should ask.

Many people use Marx's theory to analyse and describe societies outside Europe. When we use historical materialism to analyse African history, it helps us
- to understand our past better,
- to understand historical materialism better.

Multiple choice questions

1. Fossils are
A. oral sources.
B. documentary sources.
C. physical evidence.
D. dried mud.

2. Charles Darwin was the first scientist
A. to use microscopes.
B. to describe the theory of evolution.
C. to study apes.
D. to develop the theory of historical materialism.

3. The first stone tools were made by *Homo habilis*. These tools are called
A. hand-axes.
B. flakes.
C. Oldowan pebble tools.
D. Neandertals.

4. The first hominid to use language was
A. *Australopithecus.*
B. *Homo habilis.*
C. *Homo erectus.*
D. *Homo sapiens sapiens.*

5. Human beings can live in many different environments because
A. they are unspecialized.
B. they are specialized.
C. they are isolated.
D. they are selfish.

6. Human teeth are used for
A. defence against enemies.
B. eating a variety of foods.
C. making tools.
D. a variety of climates.

7. The most important Late Stone Age tools were
A. iron spears.
B. handaxes.
C. microliths.
D. cleavers.

8. People in primitive communal societies
A. worked together, with complex tools.
B. worked alone, with simple tools.
C. worked alone, with complex tools.
D. worked together, with simple tools.

9. Hunter-gatherers of long ago had few possessions because
A. they were poor.
B. they moved a lot.
C. they were self-sufficient.
D. they lived in the desert.

10. Which of the following was most important for the survival of hunter-gatherers?
A. A warm, wet climate.
B. Knowledge of the environment.
C. A rich environment.
D. Hunting skills.

11. Rock paintings are
A. oral traditions.
B. interviews.
C. secondary sources of history.
D. primary sources of history.

12. Farmers get a delayed return for their work. This means
A. that they give their families the wrong food.
B. that they need a thorough knowledge of their environment.
C. that they have many possessions.
D. that they do not benefit immediately from their labour.

13. We say that people practise extensive farming when they
A. move to a new piece of land every few years.
B. build walls to prevent soil erosion.
C. continue to grow crops on the same piece of land.
D. settle down and build permanent villages.

14. Early farmers made and used many pots. They were able to do this because
A. they made different sorts of pottery in different areas.
B. they lived in settled villages instead of moving often.
C. they grew a variety of crops.
D. they used iron instead of stone tools.

15. The first farmers in southern Africa developed several new crafts. One of these new crafts was
A. making snares to catch animals.
B. rock painting.
C. hieroglyphics.
D. iron smelting.

16. A group is self-sufficient when its members
A. are not exploited.
B. trade with their neighbours.
C. live far apart.
D. produce everything they need.

17. Later Iron Age societies had specialists to
A. make all the pottery.
B. smelt iron and copper.
C. build shelters.
D. wash for gold in rivers.

18. People in lineage societies were
A. equal.
B. unequal.
C. divided into classes.
D. slaves.

19. Cattle belonging to a lineage were herded by the
A. young women.
B. old women.
C. young men.
D. old men.

20. Chiefs and senior lineages became the ruling class in southern African farming societies because
A. the controlled resources and trade.
B. the owned the land.
C. they had slaves to work for them.
D. they were wealthy.

21. In the tributary mode of production, the ruling class
A. live next to rivers.
B. pay tribute to traders.
C. get tribute from villagers.
D. wash for gold in rivers.

22. The strength of pre-colonial African states was based on
A. gold mining.
B. owning the land.
C. people's labour.
D. warfare.

23. A society with organizations and officials to help the ruling class control the rest of the people is called
A. a territory.
B. an empire.
C. a colony.
D. a state.

24. The main purpose of the huge stone walls at Great Zimbabwe was to
A. give the rulers more privacy.
B. protect the people against attack.
C. show the power of the state.
D. shelter the people from wind and rain.

25. Great Zimbabwe's economy was **not** based on
A. trade.
B. spirit mediums.
C. cattle management.
D. tribute.

26. The economies of the east African city-states were based on
A. cattle.
B. tribute.
C. trade.
D. craft production.

27. The shenzi of the east African city-states were
A. members of the ruling class.
B. farmers.
C. heads of councils.
D. fields.

28. Serfs in Europe could not leave their feudal lord's lands because
A. of kinship ties.
B. they were slaves.
C. they owned the land.
D. they were bound to that lord.

29. The last stage of feudalism was absolute monarchy. This means that the state was almost completely controlled by
A. the king.
B. the aristocracy.
C. the new bourgeois class.
D. the serfs.

30. When a person or group has total control over trade, we say they have a
A. monopoly.
B. treaty.
C. viceroy.
D. prazero.

31. The wealth of the Mbara state came from
A. gold washing.
B. trade in cloth.
C. making salt.
D. trade in copper.

32. The Mutapa who formed an alliance with the Rozvi to defeat the Portuguese was
A. Gatsi Rusere.
B. Mukombero Chisamarengu.
C. Kapararidze.
D. the first Mukombwe.

33. The most important form of wealth in the states of south-western Zimbabwe was
A. grain.
B. pottery.
C. cattle.
D. gold.

34. After their capital at Kame was destroyed, the Torwa ruling class moved their capital to
A. Danangombe.
B. Mapela.
C. Mitole.
D. Bambandyanalo.

35. Rozvi armies drove the Portuguese from Zimbabwe in
A. 1684.
B. 1693.
C. 1742.
D. 1893.

36. Until 1818, the Mthethwa confederacy was ruled by
A. Dingiswayo.
B. Shaka.
C. Dingane.
D. Soshangane.

37. Mzilikazi died in
A. 1818.
B. 1868.
C. 1870.
D. 1894.

38. The Gaza state was formed by a group of the
A. Ndwandwe
B. Ngwane.
C. Mthethwa.
D. Swazi.

39. Villages along the Nile river united to form the nation-state of ancient Egypt. One reason was that
A. farmers needed help to organize irrigation.
B. pyramids had to be built.
C. organization was necessary for mining in the desert.
D. people were forced to become subjects of a ruler.

40. Kush was an independent state for about
A. 300 years.
B. 800 years.
C. 1 100 years.
D. 3 000 years.

www.ingramcontent.com/pod-product-compliance
Lightning Source LLC
Chambersburg PA
CBHW081353230426
43667CB00017B/2818